MANAGING
THE
MERGER

MANAGING
THE
MERGER

Making It Work

Philip H. Mirvis

Mitchell Lee Marks

PRENTICE HALL
Englewood Cliffs, New Jersey 07632

Prentice-Hall International (UK) Limited, *London*
Prentice-Hall of Australia Pty. Limited, *Sydney*
Prentice-Hall Canada, Inc., *Toronto*
Prentice-Hall Hispanoamericana, S.A., *Mexico*
Prentice-Hall of India Private Limited, *New Delhi*
Prentice-Hall of Japan, Inc., *Tokyo*
Prentice-Hall of Southeast Asia Pte. Ltd., *Singapore*
Editora Prentice-Hall do Brasil, Ltda., *Rio de Janeiro*

© 1992 by

Philip H. Mirvis

Mitchell Lee Marks

10   9   8   7   6   5   4   3   2   1

Library of Congress Cataloging-in-Publication Data

Mirvis, Philip H.
   Managing the merger : making it work / by Philip H. Mirvis and
Mitchell Lee Marks.

     p.   cm.
   Includes index.
   ISBN 0-13-544636-8
   1. Consolidation and merger of corporations—Management.
I. Marks, Mitchell Lee.   II. Title
HD58.8.M56   1992   91-30043
658.1'6—dc20   CIP

ISBN 0-13-544636-8

PRENTICE HALL
Business Information & Publishing Division
Englewood Cliffs, NJ 07632

Simon & Schuster, A Paramount Communications Company

PRINTED IN THE UNITED STATES OF AMERICA

To our parents,
Peg and Harold Mirvis,
and Elaine and Albert Marks

ACKNOWLEDGMENTS

The ideas in this book come from many people trying out new approaches to managing a merger and from many minds sifting through experiences—good and bad—to distill lessons. We want to, first, acknowledge and thank Will Clarkson and Mike Blumenthal for their confidence in us, for their sharing of themselves and their organizations, and for their willingness to have us present their stories to others who manage or might manage a merger.

We would also like to thank the following people for offering their experience and insights, for working with us to learn more about M&A, and for their kindness, criticism, and comradery:

From Graphic Controls, Lyman Randall, Don Quinlan, Bill Gates, Wally Greenholt, Bob Evans, Clark Carnes, Larry Drake, Jan Reicis, and Jim Grady, offered generously, both intellectually and emotionally. At Unisys, Jim Unruh, Dick Bierly, Mike Losey, Curt Girod, Paul Stern, Reto Braun, Jack Baline, Al Robbins, Jeanette Lerman, and Scott Harvey shared considerably and graciously with us. We thank also Pete Peterson, Brian Moore, John Eaton, Dave Perozek, Glen Tines, Solomon Atkins, Susan Bowick, Hartmut Scholz, and Andre Breukels from Hewlett-Packard/Apollo; Steve Clifford, Joe Duffy, and Christina Moris from KING Broadcasting; Donne Moen from Union Bank; Mike Pickett from Merisel Computer Products; Rhea Serpan and Priscilla Silvey from AT&T; and Joe Henson, Alex Mandl, Kathy Cote, Andy Spohn, Mel Friedman, Priscilla Bijur, Larry Bornstein, Rob Moore, Harry Hutson, Chris Newell, and the many other individual executives who gave so much to us during their times of merger madness.

Dan White and everyone at William M. Mercer, Incorporated provided important support and encouragement, while colleagues including Peter Lawton, Bob Dods, Jaques Chaurest and Harry Gudenberg offered great insight into the merger process. Joe Cutcliffe, Srinivasvan Umpathy, Barry Cohen and Chris Hickey are among the fellow consultants from whom we have learned. Thom Zimerle made a special contribution.

We would also like to acknowledge the work of many scholars whom we have learned from: Bob Kahn, Gerry Ledford, Dave Schweiger, Jim Walsh, Todd Jick, Ken DeMeuse, David Bastien, Tony Buono, Jim Bowditch, Philippe Haspeslagh, Sim Sitkin, Dave Jemison, David Nadler, and Gordon Walter.

Finally, warmest thanks to Katherine Farquhar, and to Alexa, Lucy, and Suzanne.

INTRODUCTION

Why Mergers Fail

When you ask for reasons, do you mean "business school" reasons or "real" reasons?
   —Managing director, electronics company, in *Acquisitions—The Human Factor*[1]

Buying is fun. Merging is hell.
   —Group vice president, parent company[2]

Between two-thirds and three-fourths of all corporate mergers and acquisitions fail.[3] Study after study comes to the conclusion that, whether the yardstick is combined earnings, sales, growth rates, and even shareholder value, the M&A track record is dismal. Why?

Price. Companies paid higher premiums versus book value to merge and acquire in the 1980s than ever before. Bidding wars, junk bonds, and merger mania in the decade past all served to jack up prices. But the trend continues into the 1990s with cash still burning a hole in the pockets of many American companies and the urge to merge overtaking Europe and Japan.

As a result, buyers have had to contend with staggering debt loads. Divestitures and downsizing, the practices of selling off parts of the business and getting rid of excess people, have proved to be short-term palliatives. Studies confirm that while profits can rise up to 40% in the first year after such cost cutting, the gains are offset by debt service and losses in the years thereafter.

Many of the high flying acquirers of the 1980s—Robert Campeau, the Bass brothers, and Asher Edelman among others—have been grounded by debt and had to sell off their holdings. On a more everyday basis, paying too much has forced many buyers to focus exclusively on short-term costs to the detriment of longer-term strategy. This has meant cutting out muscle, not just fat, from the work force and sacrificing investments in new ventures.

Purpose. Despite in-depth analyses by corporate planners and consultants and the highly paid assistance of investment bankers and lawyers, many companies make acquisitions for shortsighted or wrongheaded reasons. As an example, a Federal Trade Commission study of merger motives identified 12 general business reasons companies make buys but cited the 13th, the chief executive officer's ego, as most critical to the transaction itself.[4]

The comments of the chief executive of a British consumer products company illustrate the point:

> Why did we go after them? There's the obvious business reason: to get an increased share of the market. But we could have got that from someone else, maybe for less effort. The defensive reason: to prevent a competitor from getting them? True, but not quite. If I'm honest, the real reason is that there is something tremendously satisfying about taking a company from a rival and being seen to have turned it around in a very short time. The chairman wanted to put one over on the other side, and our production people wanted to prove they could do it.[5]

Ego always plays a part in mergers and acquisitions. But an inflated ego can get in the way of sound business decisions.

Bank of New England began to hemorrhage in the late 1980s after its chairman masterminded a series of regional acquisitions aimed at surpassing Bank of Boston. Although hailed as a "Deal King," the chairman never developed a clear and coherent strategy for dealing with subsidiaries. Initially, his bank adopted a "hands-off" policy toward acquired management but then later ran roughshod over them. New products and promotions proposed by the "home office" were resisted. In turn, corporate staffers sniped at acquired bankers in the "boondocks." Customer service plummeted and so did profits.

Partner. In our six years of seminars on M&A with the American Management Association, we've heard countless executives say that they wouldn't have bought the same company if they had to do it over again. An analyst for the Hay Group estimates that over 90% of merger partners don't live up to expectations. Statistics show, moreover, that one in every three acquisitions is sold off within five years.[6,7]

A. D. Little Consultant Richard Davis finds that when a buyer's attitudes toward risk taking, return on investment, and the disposition of profits don't match the acquired company's, it can undermine an otherwise sensible deal.[8] Take the case of Pain Webber's merger with Blyth Eastman Dillon. Paine thought it was acquiring the research capability to compete with Merrill Lynch. It did not, however, anticipate the compensation requirements of Blyth analysts who left in droves when more lucrative offers came from competitors. The only consolation was that Merrill Lynch made the same mistake with its acquirees.

Timing. Finally, even when the price is good, motives are sound, and the partnership has promise, timing can kill you. Xerox, for example, purchased Shugart to diversify its product line. However Shugart dominated the 8-inch disk drive market, and its business collapsed when 5 1/4-inch drives became the industry standard. People Express purchased Frontier Airlines and was thereupon rocked with intense price competition. People faced a cash crisis and was bought by Texas Air to avoid bankruptcy. Mergers in the computer industry in the 1980s were aimed at preserving market share. With the domestic market flat, U.S. computer makers who merged got a larger share of a shrinking pie. As one high-tech manager described the new math: 1 + 1 = 1.

Price, purpose, partner, and timing: These are the "business school" reasons mergers fail. When you dig deeper into the human side of buying and selling, into the mind sets and motivations of people, and into the dynamics of the combination itself, another crucial factor emerges: *how the merger is managed*.

Management. Merger mismanagement often starts at the front end of a deal when the buyer never develops a credible strategy, focuses on finance to the neglect of the organizational and cultural "fit" between companies, and then lets its turf-grabbing executives impose themselves on a resentful subsidiary. Next comes a flawed integration where planning is one sided or perfunctory, and power politics determine what gets merged and who runs the show. Finally, there is reorganization, some layoffs, and clarion calls to cut costs and increase sales. People, who have been mismanaged before, during, and after the sale, tune out the message and look out for themselves.

"We were up, up, up!" recalled one executive right after his company acquired a competitor. "Now we're down, down, down..." he confided when a politically motivated restructuring and unplanned downsizing turned the combination into a conquest. Functions didn't fit together, and 1,000 employees were canned without warning. His experience is not unusual. Most mergers are marked by politics, and every deal today seems to produce a casualty list. But costs escalate when the best and most marketable performers leave on their own accord. And mistrust and trauma linger when executives look out for number 1 and fail to reach out to their people.

Some of this is inevitable: It's the price of doing business today. But some is not: It's the price paid because of bad decisions on whom to buy, of poor planning on how to put companies together and when, and of the failure to convince people what's right about a combination and to respond effectively to all the things that go wrong. Managers can do better. That's what this book is about.

We began our work in this area in the late 1970s when a company we had been studying was suddenly his by a hostile takeover attempt and subsequently purchased by a conglomerate in what is termed a "white knight" acquisition. To that point, we had been assessing work life in Graphic Controls (GC), a Buffalo recording charts manufacturer, documenting its steady improvement in spreading participative management to the shop floor. Then all hell broke loose.

From Times Mirror, the new owner 30 times GC's size, came "herds of accountants" and countless corporate "henchmen." William Clarkson, GC's longtime family head, was seen as a "wounded leader." His top team was in rebellion. Initially, our work was to document the impact of the merger on GC's work force—disastrous was the way people described it. We found, however, that many at GC were more distressed with their own management than with Times Mirror. GC's top executives had become secretive, clannish, and, to many eyes, political.

We spent the next several months helping GC management to digest these findings and sort through the implications. Ultimately, managers recognized that they had been their own worst enemies and began to work with their new owners in a more genuine, less conspiratorial fashion. We continued to work with GC for ten more years, conducting regular surveys, meeting with employees and managers, and developing programs to keep the "old" GC culture breathing. Throughout, our intent was to blend research and action—an aspiration we have tried to maintain ever since.

This study of GC helped us to identify symptoms of the "merger syndrome"—people's predicable reactions to the uncertainty and threat of an acquisition. It also made us especially empathetic to the plight of an acquired company. Then the tables were turned and our minds opened when we began to work with the *other side*. W. Michael Blumental, the chairman of computer manufacturer Burroughs Corporation, called us in the mid-1980s to help him manage his firm's merger with Sperry, another multibillion-dollar computer maker. This was an unfriendly takeover, at the time the third largest in history, and the first big deal in the computer industry. The prospects looked dim when we first met Sperry management, and one executive remarked, "Burroughs has knocked down our door, is ready to rape us, and you're here to tell us how to lie back and enjoy it?"

Mergers and acquisitions bring out primal feelings. In some cases, warm images of marriage and gallantry are evoked. Here companies metaphorically court, marry, and go through a honeymoon period. And there are "white knights" who save "damsels in distress" and sometimes the two live happily ever after. But mergers can also entail warfare and plunder—however much this may be disguised by strategic rhetoric and corporate niceties. The page turner, *Barbarians at the Gate*, shows this drama writ large.[9] On a human scale, however, the story can be chilling. Sperry managers recognized their vulnerability: "Let's face it," said one, "we are the fuckee." Many on the Burroughs side, in turn, relished the prospects of conquest.

Blumenthal's hope was to fashion a true partnership between Burroughs and Sperry. This meant helping people on both sides, individually and collectively, to come to grips with their emotional reactions to the deal and get into a merger mind-set. In addition, we worked with several transition teams, staffed by top managers from both sides, who were charged with understanding the strengths and weaknesses of each company and planning the integration of business units. This involved sensitizing managers to cultural differences between the two companies and helping them to build a new and unifying company culture.

For a time, this combination sizzled and *Fortune* dubbed it a "surprisingly sexy computer marriage." Since then it has been rocky, with competitors' moves and downturns in the industry eating into profit margins. We've continued to work with the combined company, called Unisys, and find that, despite the downturn, most agree that the merger gave the two companies a fighting chance where so many others have gone belly up.[10]

We'll be referring to these two cases—the merger of Burroughs and Sperry and GC's acquisition by Times Mirror—throughout this book. In addition, we'll cite some of our more recent M&A experiences (individually and together) in high tech (Hewlett-Packard's acquisition of Apollo, and the creation of Merisel Computer Products), in banking (how deals are planned by Citicorp and Chemical Bank), in health care (Milwaukee Mt. Sinai's merger with Samaritan hospital and California's UniHealth America corporation), in transportation (CSX and SeaLand), in brewing (Molson and Carling O'Keefe), and in several international deals. We'll also discuss our work in the oil industry (Marathon/USX and Imperial Oil of Canada), in the media (with KING Broadcasting and human resource groups at Time/Warner), and with regional managers at AT&T.

To conclude, let us address some questions you may have on you mind:

1. Is this book still relevant? The merger madness of the 1980s is over. With the death of junk bond financing, changes in tax laws affecting merger write-offs, and glamor gone from arbitrageurs who made their money from asset stripping, the number of domestic deals is in decline. However, megamergers, involving more assets and greater numbers of people, are booming. The recent mergers of GTE and Contel, of Georgia Pacific and Great Northern Neekoosa, and of AT&T and NCR illustrate continuing turmoil in telecommunications, natural resources, and high tech. An accelerated merger wave is forecast in banking and insurance, and a large number of biotech deals loom. And international acquisitions, ranging form Japanese purchases of American entertainment "software" to U.S. buys in Europe in anticipation of 1992, suggest that many managers will be involved in M&A in the 1990s. Indeed, as *Business Week* notes:

> Mergers and acquisitions have become an ingrained way of doing business, an important method of dislodging lackadaisical management, an easy opportunity to make money, and a prime means of staying competitive.[11]

There are two good reasons why companies will continue to merge and acquire well into the 1990s: to further *strategic* purposes and to achieve a *global* presence. Still, these kinds of deals are tricky. Success in a strategic merger, for example, depends on mutual synergy—the buyer and seller have to transfer technology and know-how across company lines.[12] This means carefully knitting operations together and keeping talented people loyal and motivated. Furthermore, global mergers are complex and introduce the vagaries of joining businesses across national cultures. All of this puts more rather than less emphasis on joint planning, effective leadership, cultural sensitivity, and people mindedness—central messages of this book.

2. Is this a "human resources" book? Mergers and acquisitions involve people. And there are special human problems in combining companies and their cultures. But many human resources (HR) books and consultants focus their attention exclusively on handling the rank and file with counsel on easing anxieties and winning them over to the cause. The advice is sound and well intentioned. But is assumes that seniors managers are "in charge" and ready to "take command."[13]

Instead, we find many of them in a panic. Some are giddy in anticipation of gaining more power, resources, and pull. Others are fearful and suffer from insomnia, infections, impotence, or other psychosomatic symptoms of distress. Get two groups of competing executives together and you find that their thinking is one-sided and simplistic. Even the most seasoned managers are overwhelmed by all the work that they face. And they are surrounded by various self-interested schemers and nervous nellies, all of whom are hepped up by events and urge that "something" be decided and done— fast!

Company leaders are not omniscient nor are they immune from all the stresses and strains of courtship and conquest. Like everybody else in a company, top executives and their teams go through personal and organizational crises during a merger. And, like everybody else, they misjudge and misfire and can be shortsighted and self-serving. However, unlike everybody else, when they screw up, the costs reverberate through an organization, and no amount of "damage control" by human resource specialists can turn things around.

This is a book about managers for managers and for anyone else interested in managerial work during what many say are the most challenging (and trying) times of their career. It offers a behind-the-scenes look at the problems top executives encounter during a merger and how they deal with them—for better and worse.

3. Well, isn't it about "soft" stuff? This is _not_ a book about corporate finance or strategy. It won't show you how to run the numbers or formulate a comprehensive strategic plan. Nor does it address legal matters, the ins and outs of due diligence, or other technical considerations in doing deals. We're not experts on these subjects.

On the technical end, we recognize that different kinds of deals produce different dynamics. For example, size differences between the two companies matter as does the friendliness of the transaction. The pace of the combination differs when the two companies are healthy versus a turnaround situation. And there is bound to be more conflict in combinations where integration is full and complete versus cases where the two companies choose to more or less coexist. As appropriate, we'll make these distinctions. But, regardless of the combination type, managers must contend with some common challenges.[14]

This book diagnoses what's behind these challenges—before a merger, as companies combine, and in the aftermath. The chapters concretize the process, step by step, for managing mergers in an organizational- and people-minded way. Blumenthal captured our point of view when speaking about the challenges facing the merger manager:

> [It] is not so much a question of numbers as of people. The issues here relate less to stock market quotes, discounted cash flow, and accretion-dilution calculations in earnings per share. Rather they involve human motivation and emotion, team building and group psychology, ideology, and corporate culture.... Faced with the challenge of making a merger work, what emerges is a picture of a corporate executive as a leader, team builder, and motivator...and possibly a corporate "shrink."

Make no mistake: Addressing these challenges and filling these roles is "hard" work. One study of a modest-sized acquisition found that managers had to contend with 10,000 independent integration decisions.[15] When you consider interdependencies between decisions, the demands on time and talent increase exponentially. Making mergers work requires logical thinking and tough choices; tangible things have to happen and the bottom-line matters. As one acquired engineer lamented when dealing with his counterparts, "They're nice people, really nice. They just don't know ****　about how to win in this business."

4. Does good management really make a difference? We're not pushing a panacea. If you miss on price, purpose, and partner, that's three strikes and you're out. And bad timing can put you on the bench, too, as Burroughs and Sperry have learned. But how people are handled is also crucial to success. As one chief financial officer we worked with put it,

> What will make or break this merger's financial success will be how people are treated, not the business decisions. Business losses can be recouped, but if you treat someone poorly early in the game, you never can change the feelings that result.

However, genuine and caring people management is only one factor in merger success, albeit a crucial one. A *Wall Street Journal* survey of top executives involved in M&A found that the effective integration of business units (cited by 87%) and compatibility of management styles and cultures (67%) were key success factors.[16] In turn, the absence of a good management process for handling people, integrating units, and implementing the multitude of changes required was cited as the prime factor in failure.

Here we will see how top executives put these management processes into motion and how middle managers and staff specialists implement them. We will also draw on our own experiences and that of many other managers, consultants, and academicians, to highlight what can work and why and what doesn't work and why not.

However, there's more at stake here than success or failure in any one deal. How a company handles a merger or acquisition sends a message to all employees about management's competence and their own value to their company. Read the new corporate credo posted on the bulletin board by employees in a company undergoing a massive reduction following a merger:

We can't promise you how long we'll be in business.

We can't promise you that we won't be bought by another company.

We can't promise that there'll be room for a promotion.

We can't promise that your job will exist until you reach retirement or that money will be available for your pension.

We can't expect your undying loyalty, and we aren't sure we want it.

One consequence of the way mergers were handled in the 1980s is lost loyalty. A recent Harris Poll shows that 65% of middle managers sampled in *Business Week*'s 1000 top companies believe salaried employees are less loyal to their companies today than they were ten years ago.[17] Professor Paul Hirsch contends that we have entered an era of "free-agent" management where savvy businesspeople, like baseball players, peddle their services to top bidders and even lesser lights keep their résumés current and stay in regular touch with corporate headhunters. The message today is: "Be your own best friend."

Every business deal today, whether friendly or unfriendly, large or small, and however benign, carefully orchestrated, and strategically sound is being shaped by this new ethos. Merger horror stories are the stock in trade of newspapers and magazines. People have come to expect the worst and know of neighbors, friends, and family who have been done in or "done dirty" by a deal. Or they may have been done over once or twice themselves. It's no wonder that advertisements in the financial pages announcing tender offers, stock underwritings, mergers, and divestments are glumly referred to as "tombstones."

Cynicism is in—even chic—among savvy corporate climbers and job hoppers.[18] Still, national surveys of the U.S. work force show that the great majority of people want to believe in their companies but are lacking trust and confidence in their own management. They know that industries are undergoing massive change and, according to polls, are willing to accept some sacrifices and learn new skills, so long as they perceive that everyone is "in this together." Companies can't count on loyalty anymore. They can, however, counter the mistrustful mind-set with credible leadership and face-to-face dialogue until Doubting Thomases can be won over by more tangible and meritorious deeds. However, good public relations and a dose of human relations are not enough.

Mergers and acquisitions can turn otherwise rational executives into emotional wrecks and transform well-meaning managers into seeming monsters. Read on if you want to know how this happens—and what can be done about it for the sake of people *and* the success of the business.

CONTENTS

Introduction: Why Mergers Fail vii

PART I. MERGERS AND ACQUISITIONS

Chapter 1: What It Takes to Succeed 1

Retaining GC's Identity • The CEO as Hero • A Vision of
Partnership • Managing Merger Madness • What Has to
Be Managed? • Process Is the Prescription • Theory and
Practice

Chapter 2: Contested Terrain 29

Merger Mania • Merger Activity in American Business •
The New Rules of Engagement • Restructuring and
Downsizing • Love and Warfare • Writing a New Script •
The Human Costs of M&A

PART II. THE PRECOMBINATION PERIOD

Chapter 3: Organizing to Buy and Sell 57

"Textbook" Steps in Making a Deal • The Politics of
Buying a Company • Hewlett-Packard Buys Apollo/Apollo
Buys Hewlett-Packard • Lessons on Search and Selection •
Understanding Organizational Fit • Cultural Compatibility
• The Rush to Close • "KING Broadcasting for Sale—
Everything Must Go!"

**Chapter 4: Strategic and Psychological
            Preparation 83**

*Making the Business Case • A Merger of Equals • Strategic
Preparation • Unihealth America: Making Time an Asset •
The Mind-set of the Buyer • Psychological Preparation •
The Mind-set of the Acquired • Rites of Passage*

PART III. MANAGING THE MERGER

Chapter 5: Stress, Uncertainty, Anxiety 113

*What Makes a Merger So Stressful • Top-Level Leadership
• Helping Employees Manage Stress • Communicating to
People • Involving People • Caring for People • The Role of
Line Management*

Chapter 6: Managing Integration 143

*Crisis Management • Two Approaches to Integration •
Creating NEWCO • Managing the Integration Process •
Transition Management Tasks • Speed of the Transition*

Chapter 7: The Clash of Cultures 169

*What Is Culture? • Culture Clash—Graphic Controls •
Stages of the Culture Clash • Managing the Clash of
Cultures • Levels of Acculturation • Strategy Versus
Culture • Creating a Unisys Culture • Culture-Building
Ceremonies • Cultural Resistance*

PART IV. THE POSTCOMBINATION PERIOD

Chapter 8: Winners, Losers, Survivors 199

*Postcombination Status • Management Appointments •
Retaining Top Talent • Downsizing After the Deal: Letting
People Go • Layoffs in High Tech • Lessons on Managing a
Downsizing • Survivors • Helping Survivors Cope • Stages
of Personal Adaptation to Change • Factors Affecting
Postmerger Morale*

**Chapter 9: Rebuilding the Business:
Teamwork 225**

*Understanding Postmerger Mind-sets • The Challenges of
Team Building • Training for Team Building at AT&T •
Team-Building Tasks • Team Building Top Down • Team
Building Through the Ranks • Managing Your Own
Transition*

Chapter 10: Reculturation 251

*Magnitude of Postmerger Change • Transformation: Unisys
• 1987-1988 • 1989-1990 • Culture Change at GC •
Replacing the CEO • Feeling the Elephant • Reculturation
at GC*

PART V. SPECIAL TOPICS

Chapter 11: Tracking the Combination 281

*Why Track Change? • What to Look For • How to Track
Progress • Case Examples*

Chapter 12: International M&A 297

*International Deals: Scale and Scope • Molson–Carling
O'Keefe • International Buying and Selling • Multinational
Merging • Postmerger Management • Culture Clash in
International Mergers • Global M&A*

Postscript: Winning Hearts and Minds 315

*Building Through M&A • Leadership from the Top: Theory
and Practice • Realism in the Ranks • Charting a Better
Course*

Appendixes 331
References 341
Index 361

LIST OF FIGURES

Figure 1.1 Merger Stress as Depicted by
Acquired Manager 13

Figure 1.2 Charting a Better Course 16

Figure 1.3 12 Signs of the Merger Syndrome 19

Figure 1.4 A Successful Combination as Depicted
by Merged Manufacturing
Management 24

Figure 2.1 Mergers and Acquisitions of Publicly
Traded Companies 31

Figure 2.2 Rules of Engagement in M&A 37

Figure 2.3 Merger Images of Love and War 42

Figure 2.4 Merger and Acquisition Scripts 44

Figure 2.5 What Are Today's Executives Greatest
Anxieties? 52

Figure 2.6 Employee Attitudes After a Merger or
Layoff 54

Figure 3.1 Organizational Fit—Hewlett-Packard
and Apollo 73

Figure 3.2 When Companies Don't Fit Together
as Depicted by Acquired
Company 74

Figure 4.1 Merger or Acquisition? As Depicted
by Acquired Employee 89

Figure 4.2 Pacing of Integration in a Merger 92

Figure 4.3 Degree of Integration Between
Companies 93

Figure 4.4   The "Savior" Expectation Following a
              Merger or Acquisition 106
Figure 4.5   Acquired Company's Reaction to
              Possible Sale—Top 40 Senior
              Managers 108

Figure 5.1   A CEO's Ten Commandments of
              Merger Leadership 124
Figure 5.2   Managing Merger Stress: Symptoms
              and Remedies 130

Figure 6.1   Two Styles of Integration 148
Figure 6.2   NEWCO Transition Structure 151
Figure 6.3   Hardware Product Development:
              Hewlett-Packard Versus Apollo 161
Figure 6.4   Merger Implementation Plan—
              Customer Service 166

Figure 7.1   Times Mirror–GC Cultural
              Differences 172
Figure 7.2   Manager in Midst of Culture
              Clash 179
Figure 7.3   How Time Sees Warner/How Warner
              Sees Time 181
Figure 7.4   Combination Planning Protocol—
              Savings Versus Organizational
              Fit 187
Figure 7.5   Integration: Benefits Versus Ease 188

Figure 8.1   Redeployment Strategy at Merged
              Company 211
Figure 8.2   Recipe for Integration Stew During a
              Downsizing (circulated through
              acquired company) 215
Figure 8.3   Welcoming Relocated Employees 220

Figure 9.1   Recognizing People's Current
              Emotional States 227
Figure 9.2   AT&T Graduates' Diploma from
              Seminar on Managing
              Transitions 234

Figure 9.3 Stages in Building a New Team 236
Figure 9.4 One Manager's Picture of Post-Merger
            Team Building 247

Figure 10.1 Magnitude of Postmerger Change 253
Figure 10.2 Change Versus Transformation 255
Figure 10.3 Cultural Transformation at Unisys 257
Figure 10.4 Unisys Results—1986–1988 263
Figure 10.5 Unisys—Postmerger Attitudes 264
Figure 10.6 Deculturation at Graphic Controls—
             Feeling the Elephant 274
Figure 10.7 Data on Reculturation at Graphic
             Controls—Family Again 277
Figure 11.1 Cartoon in Employee Paper Depicting
             Merger Stress 290

Figure 11.1 Postacquisition Employee Survey—
             Graphic Controls 294

Figure 12.1 Merger Committees: HP and Apollo—
             Europe 308

Figure 13.1 Views of Merger Management in
             Theory and Practice 319

PART ONE

MERGERS AND ACQUISITIONS

CHAPTER 1

What It Takes to Succeed

There is a right way and a wrong way of handling the implementation. Both take the same amount of time and effort. The difference is that one is usually successful, while the other is not.
　　　—Chief executive, consumer products company,
　　in *Acquisitions—The Human Factor* [1]

Right after the acquisition we were kept in the dark. Then they covered us with manure. Then they cultivated us. After that, they let us stew. And, finally, they canned us.
　　　—Isadore Barmash, on the "Mushroom Treatment," *Welcome to Our Conglomerate—You're Fired* [2]

Disbelief. How could this have happened? Uncertainty. What does it mean for me and my company? Anxiety. Can I deal with what might happen? These are the initial reactions of executives facing a bid for their company—often followed by rage and fear as the sale is completed. People who go through a combination react in much the same way as those who suffer illness or tragic loss. First, there is denial. This may entail wishful thinking—that the buyer will "save" the acquired company or that things will pretty much stay the same. When it is learned that change is inevitable, and likely painful, anger takes hold. Employees point the finger at their own management asking, "why

didn't we buy a company?" or, in this era of golden parachutes, concluding, "the bosses lined their pockets and sold
us out." Then they turn their anger on the new owners.
Next, they "bargain" with their families and colleagues,
with their old bosses and new ones, in a desperate attempt
to clarify their fate and sort things out. Finally, they come
to some resolution in order to get on with their lives. A great
many executives choose to leave their firms. A study by
Lamalie Associates found that nearly 50% of top managers
in target companies voluntarily depart within one year. Another 25% leave within three years.[3]

There are, however, executives who stay with their
companies, who defend their people and ways of operating,
and who successfully influence the terms of the combination. William M.E. Clarkson, former CEO of Graphic Controls Corporation (GC), was a "wounded leader" following
his firm's acquisition by Times Mirror in the late 1970s.
GC, a thousand person manufacturer of recording charts
and instruments, was hit by an unfriendly takeover attempt
and then purchased by Times Mirror, a multi-billion dollar
conglomerate thirty times its size, in a "white knight" acquisition. Clarkson was a vigorous, task-oriented leader
right after the takeover bid and, according to peers, "the
leader we like him to be" in his first dealings with Times
Mirror. Then he went through weeks of depression, suffering from the loss of personal authority, the break up of
his Board of Directors, and constant challenges to his
company's autonomy. One morning his wife called a GC
officer and fitfully reported that "Will just doesn't want
to get up today."

Clarkson and his top team knew that they had to come
to grips with the situation, regain the confidence of their
anxious managers, and reassure worried employees. This
would require individual soul searching, the mourning of
loss, and collective commitment to see the combination
through. GC's top team would have to re-orient their thinking, respond proactively to the new situation, and represent
themselves purposefully and with determination to the leadership of Times Mirror.

RETAINING GC'S INDENTITY

A sense of shock permeated GC's top executives after their sale to Times Mirror. They had attempted, months before being hit with an unfriendly takeover attempt, to defend themselves against such a bid. Meetings with attorneys and investment bankers yielded a roster of defensive measures ranging from staggering elections to the Board of Directors to putting more shares of stock in friendly hands. But none of these measures were implemented. Why? Good reasons in every instance, but complicated by *naivete*. As one manager put it: "We just couldn't imagine someone trying to buy us without our consent."

Meanwhile, Time Mirror, with "more money than it knew what to do with" had begun a vigorous acquisition program. Robert Erburu, Times Mirror's president, and Chuck Schneider, a group vice-president, contacted GC as part of its search for possible acquisition candidates. GC mangers were cordial to Times Mirror but cool to the idea of an acquisition. Needing funding for future growth, they instead opted to sell off an unprofitable business and recapitalize the company.

Then came the unfriendly bid. Clarkson first received a call from a New York acquisition specialist who informed him of a buyer's interest in his company and subsequently met the prospective buyer face-to-face. Clarkson told him "GC is not for sale." On Friday, a month later, came news that GC's stock, traded over-the-counter, was moving like "wildfire." A call from the bidder confirmed that an unsolicited tender offer was underway.

GC's top managers lurched into round-the-clock activity over the next five days. Calls to consultants and brokers revealed the unfriendly bidder to have had a history of playing "fast-and-loose" with subsidiaries. Evidence of inside trading on the part of some investment bankers was unearthed. But Board members and attorneys advised Clarkson the GC had to sell. After a high pressure conference call, involving Board members, advisors, and GC's top mangers, it was agreed to approach Times Mirror and solicit a counterbid.

Times Mirror's offer, two-and-one-half GC's stock price, was pre-emptive and the unfriendly bidder withdrew. Two weeks later, 90 percent of GC's stock was in the hands of a new owner. Clarkson emphasized, in meetings with managers and in letters to employees, that Times Mirror had been honorable in all of its dealings and had promised to give GC the freedom and running room needed to direct its own course.

One month later, however, feelings of injustice and anger were rampant in GC. Accordingly, Clarkson, working with consulting psychologist James Gillespie, proposed that his top team hold a "grieving meeting" to mourn their losses and expiate their guilt over failing to defend the company. He recalled, "So few people understand what the trauma is all about. I could hardly bear to talk with them...they (say) you're crying all the way to the bank. So few people understood our mission, our community, our value system... You can't just dismiss all we accomplished and say, well, here today and gone tomorrow."

The grieving meeting began with each member of top management sharing his personal losses and guilt at not being able to prevent the takeover attempt. One by one, team members shared their fears, disappointment, and frustrations and collectively expressed their anger at the "shithead" who had tried to take them over and forced them to be acquired by a White Knight.

Then the tone and character of the meeting shifted. GC had been "bought"—management had not "sold out." Clarkson was credited with making a "hell of a deal" and saving GC. Times Mirror top executives might, after all, be honorable men. Perhaps GC could even become a "guiding light" for its new owners. In one sense, GCers were working through their loss and anger and preparing to "bargain" over the terms of integration. In another, they were re-purposing themselves.

To succeed, it was agreed, GC would need a "good forward-looking plan." One executive called for a no-quarters-given strategy whereby GC would fight any and all "technocratic steering." Clarkson redefined this as a commitment to "hold on to what we value." They then concluded the meeting by burning in effigy a figure of the raider that had put their company into play. The top team was resolved to maintain their company's identity in the months ahead.

This sacrificial rite marked a change in Clarkson and his top team. To this point, it had been "every man for himself." After the grieving meeting, by contrast, managers and supervisors were gathered together for "town meetings". Here traditional values were reaffirmed and strategies were developed for working with Times Mirror. The charge was to act politely and cooperatively while looking at the merits of integration decisions in light of GC's values. One manager noted that the "enemy is us"—not one of Times Mirror's "fat cats." Conflicts, he proposed, could be managed so long as people understood their emotions and tried "walking in the other guy's shoes."

THE CEO AS HERO

The emotional set of executives on the other side of a merger as quite another story. Winners savor, for a time, the thrill of conquest. W. Michael Blumenthal oozed confidence and self-satisfaction the day after his company, Burroughs, a mainframe computer maker, launched a second and successful bid to purchase Sperry, a competitor, in 1986. Blumenthal had spent months plotting the takeover attempt and had a clear vision of how the combined company, with ten billion dollars in sales and over one hundred thousand employees, would succeed in the marketplace. Still, he would have to contend with fearful managers on the Sperry side and with his own top executives who were readying themselves for what one salaciously termed the "raping and pillaging."

Psychologist Harry Levinson reports that buying companies are impelled to consolidate their gains after a successful bid, for fear a subsidiary will turn on them.[4] Right after Burroughs won the takeover battle, its executives began to denigrate their counterparts and plot their conquest. But Blumenthal was preaching a different message—promising there would be a partnership between the two companies. He wanted to create a new company, with a new identity, to be staffed by a new team that drew from the best of both organizations. One Burroughs executive lamented, "Mike spends all his time with Sperry and is bending over backwards courting their executives." Many others felt betrayed.

Blumenthal had nights of sleeplessness. Top Sperry executives had generous golden parachutes and could leave, profitably, at any time. His own executives began to lobby for decisions that would grant them new powers and more sway. Could he get people to work together? There were also organizational challenges to face: putting functions together; making divestitures and staff reductions, and satisfying customers nervous over the future product line, upgrades, and service. Vacations were canceled; workdays were lengthened, and executives from both companies were organized into a crisis management mode. Top people understood that they were on trial and that the next few months would make or break their careers in the new company. Meanwhile, rumors flew through both companies, misinformation was in good currency, and the thrill of victory gave way to a protracted period of nerve-wracking tension and mind-numbing work.

Clarkson and Blumenthal were each facing crises: one struggling to preserve his company's and his own integrity and the other trying to combine his company with another to create a new and more competitive enterprise. There are many conventional notions, such as "when the going gets tough, the tough get going," that executives draw from when facing such crises. Be tough, logical, crisp, decisive, and so on go recommendations for personal conduct. And cover all the bases, leave nothing to doubt, and hold feet to the fire constitute the received wisdom for how to go about restructuring the business.

These images appeal to top executives who have likely risen to the top because of their intellectual prowess and political savvy. They also validate "masculine" definitions of heroism under fire and affirm the leaderly self-image. They are not sufficient, however, for managing the challenges posed by corporate combinations where emotions are raw and uncertainty reigns.

Sure leaders have to rally doubters and credibly communicate the larger purpose behind the deal. Otherwise it looks as though only the bankers, stockholders, and top dogs will make out. But they also need to get into the trenches.

This means creating a transition management process where both sides get together and sweat through integration decisions fraught with ambiguity. Finally, they must care for and counsel people, some of whom will inevitably be casualties. This means otherwise tough and emotionally checked executives have to open themselves to the highs and lows experienced by those whom they lead—if only to lead by example. Clarkson preserved, for the most part, GC's independence and way of life through personal pain and passion while realigning his company into its status as a "subsidiary." Blumenthal united Burroughs and Sperry, forming Unisys, through vision and vigor. Both men were under stress and surrounded by stressed-out executives. Both faced repeated crises in combining companies. And both had to contend with the many we/they and win-lose types of conflict that racked every integration decision.

A VISION OF PARTNERSHIP

When Blumenthal took control of Burroughs in 1980, it was mired in the computer industry "BUNCH," along with Univac (Sperry), NCR, Control Data, and Honeywell. His aim was to build revenues to a point where Burroughs could emerge as the clear alternative to industry leader IBM. In five years as chairman and CEO, he brought in a new top management team, acquired Systems Development Corporation and Memorex, and led an impressive financial turnaround that doubled revenues and tripled profitability. Still, as Blumenthal reported, "Burroughs was a $5-billion-a-year company, the 72nd largest in the U. S. and the third biggest computer company in the world with a track record of 100 years. But IBM is so dominant that customers needed my personal assurance that we would be around in five years."[5]

Frustrated by the paradox of offering a highly respected product to a very hesitant market, and unable to grow internally, Blumenthal turned to merger to achieve the size needed to compete with IBM. "There was a consensus," noted one top executive, "that the company could not remain status quo and survive over the long run." Blumenthal's designs on Sperry date back to June 1985 when Burroughs first proposed that the two computer giants merge.

At that time, Sperry was also on an upswing, having jettisoned its farm implements business and focused on information systems. Flush with cash, the company was an attractive takeover target—"a gussied up streetwalker," according to one interviewee. Accordingly, Sperry had sought some defensive acquisitions of its own and had done some preliminary negotiating with ITT. Burroughs' proposal of a "stock swap" was "entirely unexpected and unwelcome." Sperry thereupon launched a strong public relations campaign stressing customers' worries over the continuity of its product line. When Burroughs' stock took a beating on Wall Street, the merger proposal was dropped.

Or so it seemed. In truth, Burroughs' investment bankers began lining up $3 billion in credit to finance a cash offer for Sperry. Blumenthal and key executives made an intensive study of the affordability of retaining both companies' incompatible product lines (Burroughs had four different computing architectures and Sperry had three). Chief Financial Officer Jim Unruh scoped out the financials and legal counsel Kurt Hessler previewed legal manuevers. On Monday, May 5, 1986, Burroughs launched its second bid for Sperry—in cash. As the press described it, "Blumenthal put a 'bear hug' on Sperry."6

Sperry President Joe Kroger resurrected customers' worries, and the industry press reported that the merger would create a "Digital Tower of Babel." But Blumenthal and his team had done their homework and prepared financial forecasts, based on continuity of the two companies' product lines, that made the bid "attractive." This time Burroughs' stock price shot up as did Sperry's. "This Time," headlined the financial press, "Burroughs Won't Quit."

After ten days of legal wrangling, shark attacks (Ivan Boesky made $19.6 million in the bidding war), proposed asset sales, overtures to white knights, and other moves and countermoves, the Sperry Board met and proposed a complex stock buy-back arrangement. Wall Street analysts interpreted this as an invitation for Burroughs to "come back" with a higher bid. Subsequent face-to-face negotiations between Blumenthal and top Sperry executives led to hard bargaining and hard feelings. For 12 days, Burroughs made "take-it or we'll-take-it-to-your-stockholders" offers, and Sperry countered with charges of "bad faith" bargaining.

In the end, of course, the Sperry Board took Burroughs' final offer, but reactions in the two companies were as different as night-and-day. On the Burroughs side, one manager commented, "Last time it was friendly. This time it's our show." On the Sperry side another said, "When we rejected the first bid, there was relief, even some elation. We got cocky that we could remain independent. Reaction to the success of this second bid is anger and dismay."

Blumenthal was ready for these reactions and immediately after the sale issued a pamphlet entitled "The Sperry/Burroughs Partnership." The juxtaposition of the buyer's and seller's company names and the characterization of the hostile takeover as a partnership signaled his intentions to make this a "friendly" combination. The text, drafted in evocative language, announced that "Great companies are built by people willing to make bold moves, who take events into their own hands and dare to act of their vision....we are in the vanguard of a movement that is sure to redirect the course of the computer industry." This was meant to be more than "PR" and self-aggrandizement: It invited people from the two companies to venture forth on a new course.

From the outset, Blumenthal was giving people a sense of purpose. Industry analysts had characterized the merger as "two male dinosaurs attempting to mate" (old companies with incompatible computing "architectures"). Brochures sent to stockholders, employees, and customers carried a different message. By continuing two product lines, the new company could serve two customer bases and soon engage in cross-selling, thereby giving current and future users more product options and better services. This also sent a message to technical and sales people in both companies that they would have many more opportunities in a larger and stronger enterprise.

Blumenthal set out on a worldwide tour of former Sperry plants, sales offices, and user groups shortly after the sale was completed. A video of his vision of the combined company was seen by thousands of Sperry employees. Public speaking was one of Blumenthal's strong suits but even more important were his candor and openness to give and take.

All of his speeches were followed by question-and-answer sessions where he laid out the facts about impending staff reductions and emphasized that no one yet had the "answers" about individual jobs or functions.

In a sense, Blumenthal was *telling it like it is.* This distinguishes him from many top company executives who issue bland promises that "nothing will change" or who try to finesse or smooth over issues that are troubling and promise disruption. At the same time, he was telling it *like it ought to be.* Credible statements of vision address more than an idealized image of the future: They provide a blueprint that makes it concrete and seemingly within people's grasp. "I didn't know exactly how to get from here to there," Blumenthal recalled, "but I visualized the process from the beginning as a series of steps leading to some desired result."

All of this front-stage work focused people's attentions on the prospects, rather than just the problems, of partnership and defined the steps that would be taken to bring the new company into being. Meanwhile, Blumenthal was backstage counseling his managers. "People really get scared in this situation, they're anxious," he said, "You have to be able to relate to that and you have to be able to say to yourself 'I have to be tolerant, and I have to assuage it and channel it constructively....' " Seminars on the human elements of mergers also helped executives from both Burroughs and Sperry to understand people's emotional reactions to a takeover and to open up about their own feelings.

Blumenthal then defined guiding principles for putting the two companies together including *meritocracy* and *unity.* These principles would govern the combination where by design functions would be crashed together and systems and people would be integrated. They promised, however, that integration decisions would be based on trustworthy analyses of the strengths and weaknesses of each company and that the most able people would be chosen to lead and staff combined functions.

MANAGING MERGER MADNESS

The leadership of Clarkson and Blumenthal, as well as that of several other executives, middle managers, and human resource specialists will be reported in this book. From the outset, however, a key point needs to be made. It is that success in these endeavors depends on the efforts of many people who have to work long hours; contend with great uncertainty; handle conflict and upset; make important decisions; and get along with people whom they don't know, may not trust, and could be in competition with them.

A merger or acquisition generates its own turbulence that produces stress, threat, and emotional disequilibria. We've seen cartoons make the rounds that depict brides being menaced by dragons and executioners wielding the axe. Signs of stress are palpable, ranging from tension headaches and sleeplessness to excessive smoking and irritability. As one executive put it: "Merger stress is a 10" (see Figure 1.1).

When merging commences, middle managers and employees are preoccupied with impending change and vigilant to signs of what it all means for themselves and their work areas. They get nervous and edgy, cloy together with peers, and get clammy when facing superiors and subordinates—all the time sorting themselves out as possible winners, losers, or survivors.

Figure 1.1
Merger Stress as Depicted by Acquired Manager

Under such intense stress, people revert to basic behaviors—their "backup" style. Some will backstab their peers and bad-mouth their competitors to secure their own jobs. It is commonplace to hear people say "Who would have thought that about (so-and-so)?" during this tension-filled period. Theft, violence, and even sabotage increase markedly following some mergers. In one case, airline baggage handlers sent some 15,000 bags to the wrong destination in the months following their company's acquisition. It was their meaty way of getting back at new owners who proposed to "trim the fat." Even survivors act up: Some will lay low, others will glad-hand, and many will be surreptitiously looking elsewhere for a job.

Top managers are not immune to merger madness. It can fill normally confident executives with self-doubt and cause even battle-tested leaders to shoot themselves in the foot. One acquiring chief financial officer (CFO), for example, promised that change would be introduced smoothly and with consultation. Then his team charged in and crippled the newly purchased subsidiary. It seems they had encountered "resistance" and the CFO felt it necessary to show local management who was "boss." In another instance, an experienced CEO pronounced that staff reductions would be taken care of through "normal attrition." Then 700 people were laid off.

Neither of these men were guileful. The simple truth is that when called upon to be at their best during a merger, many top executives are at their worst. They fail to understand what is happening to themselves or their people. Their built-in bias for action bowls over careful planning and preparation. And their drive for results subverts the very processes of problem solving and commitment building necessary to achieve them.

The key to countering merger madness is to manage the human processes effectively—before the sale, as the companies combine, and in the aftermath.

WHAT HAS TO BE MANAGED?

Peter Lawton, a colleague with Temple, Barker, Sloan in Toronto, suggested that we develop a "map" to illustrate many of the problems that have to be managed over the course of a merger (see Figure 1.2). To "chart a better course" managers must travel from the Sea of Uncertainty across an island bisected by a River of Reality to reach the lighthouse at Safe Harbor.

As depicted, this involves navigating the Sea of Uncertainty to find a compatible partner and get people ready to merge. Otherwise, the deal leads to a "black hole" from which there is no escape. Once the combination is underway, the map warns, there is anger, rumors circulate, and people suffer from loss, sometimes leading to depression. Employees can be lost at Cape Fear and eventually be adrift in the Survivors Sea. Meanwhile, merger managers do battle on the Plain of Power Plays and watch top performers crank out resumes.

As the combination proceeds, people enter the Valley of Lost Dreams. Some can see the Ocean of Opportunity. But many ride the rapids in Culture Clash Creek. Often combining companies also have to travel the River of Reality when mounting debt and redundancies requires cutbacks and layoffs and, in some cases, divestitures. The return trip travels through Guilt Gulch and can lead many into the Desert of Despair. The hike to Mount Momentum necessitates rebuilding the business and reforming work teams. Along the way, competitors are watching, and there is the potential to be waylaid on Blood Bath Beach. Companies that succeed reach Cape Hope by following the Beacon of Light. Here combined peoples and companies develop a new way of life.

We help managers undertake this journey. It is important to recognize, however, that the map is *not* the terrain. Every combination has its own contours, and many pitfalls, difficult to foresee, await merger managers. With that said, there are some predictable problems that need top level attention.

Precombination Processes. Companies that succeed at M&A know what they want from a deal. They study industry trends, competitive dynamics, and financial considerations. Their search for a partner is guided by well defined objectives. The most successful ones also assess what capabilities they

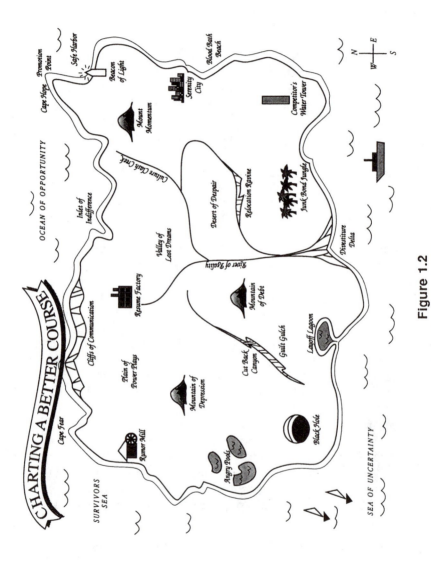

Figure 1.2
Charting a Better Course

14

bring to any particular combination—capital, technology, products, distribution channels, marketing acumen, reputation, and so on—and what they need from a partner. All of this informs the "theory" behind the deal and is fleshed out in an integration strategy.

Our concern is with the human and situational factors that cause executives to mismanage strategy setting and to misjudge the competencies that they and their partners bring to a combination.[7] On the buyer's side, for example, staffers in corporate development often have different preferences in the choice of a partner than do line managers. They are typically preoccupied with "financial fit" and scarcely attend to organizational and cultural factors. In turn, managers in sales, manufacturing, and R&D have their own agendas to advance. As a result, many deals commence with buyers lacking a clear and consistent image of what they want and uncertain of exactly what they are buying.

Acquired managers, who may or may not have wanted to be acquired, can be equally divided and as uncertain of who bought them. They expect clear direction and can't countenance their owner's confusion. Many are convinced that there must be a "secret plan" and begin to, as one manager put it, "circle the wagons."

In principle, rational executives, guided by goodwill, can sort through internal conflicts and the many "misfits" between companies. And then, when they come together, arrive at an agreeable framework for integrating the firms. But, in practice, many are neither rational nor agreeable to compromise. Buyers often exude superiority and hubris— "after all, we bought you." They also want their partners to conform to their ways of doing business. In turn, acquired managers will resist sensible requests and ideas, fight tooth and nail proposals for change, and threaten to leave should their autonomy be challenged.

The upshot is that good deals don't necessarily lead to good combinations. Both buyer and seller need to be prepared strategically and psychologically to join, and they need to define and enforce sensible guidelines for integration. This isn't easy. Clarkson and his team, for example, had hoped to participate as coequals in integration decisions with Times

Mirror. Instead, they learned that their new owner had its own approach for integrating subsidiaries and more or less expected to find a "yes, sir" attitude. This led to months of battling back and forth between the two companies over matters of policy and principle. GCers found Times Mirror's procedures bureaucratic and inflexible. The parent company's modus operandi clashed with GC's more freewheeling and participatory style. Worse, it was being imposed on them.

The Merger Syndrome. In the first several months of a combination, merger-related dynamics can unsettle executives, put the two firms at odds, and set the combination on the wrong course. Employees are consumed with the goings-on—their emotions ranging from elation to fear. Countless crises overwhelm strategic calculations, and integration planning exercises devolve into conflict. Each side begins to stereotype and put down the other, and harbored hopes give way to a sense of betrayal. There is a pattern in the human reactions to a combination that we call the merger syndrome (see Figure 1.3).[8]

Signs of human stress are present in all combinations, even the friendliest and best managed ones. The first sign of merger syndrome is heightened self-interest—people become preoccupied with what the deal means for themselves, their incomes, and their careers. They develop a story about the implications, but often it is a mix of fact and fantasy. No one has real answers and, if they do, the answers are apt to change.

Then the rumor mill starts and people trade on worst case scenarios. At the headquarters of an acquired optical products company, rumors spread that 3,000 people were to be laid off. Interestingly, only 1,700 were employed at the site! All this adds up to distractions from job performance. And stress takes its toll in people's psychological and physiological well-being.

Figure 1.3
12 Signs of the Merger Syndrome

Immediately after the sale is announced...

1. **Preoccupation.** Are people obsessed with the merger and speculating about what it might mean for them? Is this distraction leading to poorer performance on the job?

2. **Imagining the Worst.** Is the company rife with rumors about the sale? Are people developing worst-case scenarios about what might happen?

3. **Stress Reactions.** Do people seem tense and anxious? Are there psychological reactions—fear, aggressiveness, withdrawal—or somatic reactions such as headaches, sleeplessnes, increased smoking?

4. **Crisis Management.** Is there an air of tension and chaos? Have executives retreated into war rooms and adopted a combat mentality?

5. **Constricted Communication.** Are most employees in the dark about what is going on? Are top executives making decisions on their own and restricting contact with the rest of the company?

6. **Illusion of Control.** Does top management assure people that there is a master plan for the combination and promise that change will be handled smoothly and without much pain? Do people doubt the credibility of these promises?

As the two companies combine...

7. **Clash of Cultures.** Do people see big differences between how the two companies are organized and do business? Do they see differences in management styles and values?

8. **We vs. They.** Do people focus on the differences rather than the similarities between the two companies? Do these perceived differences become sharper?

9. **Superior vs. Inferior.** Do people evaluate the differences between companies in terms of good and bad? Do they see their company as superior?

10. **Attack and Defend.** Are people in the company plotting ways to advance their positions or defend them? Do they see people in the other company doing the same?

11. **Win vs. Lose.** Are people keeping track of decisions to see whose side wins each skirmish? Are some, who see themselves as winners, rushing to impose change? Are others, who feel like losers, revising their resumes and talking to employment recruiters?

12. **Decisions by Coercion, Horse Trading, and Default.** Does one side force most decisions on the other? Are other decisions made by horse trading or default rather than mutual problem solving?

To cope with the many tasks of combining, teams of executives in both companies typically lurch into a crisis management mode. The experience is stressful yet exhilarating, and many liken themselves to "generals" in a "war room." Decision making in these top groups can be crisp and decisive. However top management is generally insulated during this period and often prepares self-defeating gambits. Top teams misestimate or wholly ignore the other side's priorities and counterstrategies. And they cut themselves off from relevant information and isolate themselves from dissent.

All of this is symptomatic of what psychologist Irving Janis terms "groupthink"—the result of accepting untested assumptions and striving for consensus without "reality testing" the possible consequences.[9] Crisis management only gives executives the illusion that they are in control. In truth, they have set themselves up for trouble.

Meanwhile, people in one or both organizations are adrift. Decision-making powers are centralized. Downward communications are formal and unsatisfactory. Official reassurances that any changes will be handled smoothly and fairly ring hollow to a worried work force. Everything seems to be up for grabs.

Then, as they are charged to work together and integrate the businesses, executives from both sides jockey for position and fight for their budgets, their projects, and their power bases. Rather than cooperate, they attack and defend. Studies of how to integrate operations are mired in controversy. Clout and connections determine who runs what and what combined functions will look like. Meanwhile employees update their scorecards, chart "wins" and "losses," and begin to sort themselves out. This can turn a corporate marriage sour and make the honeymoon hellish.

All of this is exacerbated by the "clash of cultures." By their very nature, mergers produce a "we versus they" relationship, and there is a natural tendency for people to exaggerate the differences as opposed to similarities between the two companies. What is noticed first are differences in the ways the companies do business—maybe their relative emphasis on manufacturing versus marketing, or their predominantly financial versus technical orientation. Then differences in how the companies are organized, say, their centralization versus decentralization, or their differing styles of management and control are discerned. Finally, people ascribe these differences to competing values and philosophies—with their company seen as superior and the other as backward, bureaucratic, or just plain bad.[10]

What can be done to help people cope with merger-related stress? Research shows that when hospital patients are forewarned about the pain of an operation and given a realistic portrayal of the steps involved in their recovery, they heal more quickly and have fewer complications than do those given an unrealistically rosy preview.[11] Companies can take steps to prepare executives realistically for change, sensitize them to the human stresses, and develop sensible communications that let people know what they should expect from a deal—and what is expected of them. Thereafter, care, counsel, direction, and involvement are all essential.

What can be done to help management teams cope effectively with crises? To bring them together to make integration decisions? In the case of Burroughs and Sperry, a

Merger Coordination Council was formed, staffed by top executives from both sides, to oversee a study of the comparative strengths and weaknesses of the two companies and to make recommendations about how to merge the firms. Task forces, cochaired by managers from the two companies, prepared indepth analyses of every function and participated in several off-site reviews to coordinate their integration plans. Hundreds of employees were involved in fact-finding. The aim of this transition management process was to cultivate the "best thinking, ownership, and participation" as Blumenthal put it.

It would be mistaken to conclude, moreover, that the merger of companies with different cultures is doomed to fail. The key is to sensitize managers on both sides to these differences and take account of them when making integration decisions. In the case of Burroughs and Sperry, again, managers educated one another on their respective approaches to doing business and then socialized to the point where cultural differences became less divisive. Blumenthal introduced a symbol of togetherness when he passed out red baseball caps, bearing the Sperry and Burroughs logos, at one executive retreat. Whenever one or the other organization was being criticized and a we/they mentality was emerging, executives would have to put on their hats and think like "one company." The meaning to top executives, as one observer put it, was that "all notions of takeover, of victor and vanquished, were dismissed." The broader implication was that "old" Burroughs and Sperry cultures would have to die and a new company culture would be born.

Postcombination Problems. Postcombination problems begin the day top executives declare that the merger or acquisition is complete. They have suffered their stress, worked through conflicts, secured their assignments, and set their minds on their next strategic moves. But middle managers and supervisors must still contend with the "details." And they have to handle their own versions of combination crises, conflicts, and culture clashes.

As a result, the best laid plans are often greeted with skepticism down the line and implementation is marred by second-guessing and resistance. A host of unresolved issues comes to the fore. What are the proper procedures? And who do you go to get a definitive answer? It takes time to work things out; old rules and relationships are in flux. But top executives won't give people the time, or space, or support. Instead, they press for "results" and begin to point the finger. Meanwhile, there may be layoffs and staff reductions. Some managers will be kind and others cruel. Are all these layoffs necessary? Isn't there an alternative? What about age discrimination? Mismanaged reductions in force send a message to all employees about management's real priorities and leave a bitter aftertaste. Top executives too often put the onus on the personnel function to handle the reductions and then have a ready scapegoat when things go wrong. Nobody coaches middle managers on how to handle people. And top management is too busy to meet with longer-service employees who must go.

And on and on it goes. Functions are not aligned. Systems and procedures are out of sync. Costs are cut, but not as much as anticipated, and the top line shrinks as the sales force revolts. Add another wave of layoffs, maybe a second-stage reorganization, and perhaps some selective management dismissals and the combination is doomed to failure. One merger veteran commented on the process problems concisely, "We screwed up the acquisition; we screwed up the integration; and now we're screwing people and the business. At least we're consistent."

What does it take to rebuild the business? The basic building blocks are its work teams. Managers need to sign people up, unit by unit, and mold them into a team. This requires helping people "let go" of the past and getting them excited about the future. Organization building complements team building. While middle managers build their teams, top executives and senior staff have to ensure that strategies are being advanced and combination goals realized. This means managing upward, downward, and sideways.

But, even when all the foregoing challenges have been met, there remains the crucible of building a new post-combination culture. Katy Stone, a vice president of manufacturing at Alpha Electronics (a pseudonum for a company requesting anonymity), faced the daunting prospect of integrating her operations with those of an aquired firm, following the layoff of some 500 employees. "Neither company had the best," she recalled. "Rather than fight over our two

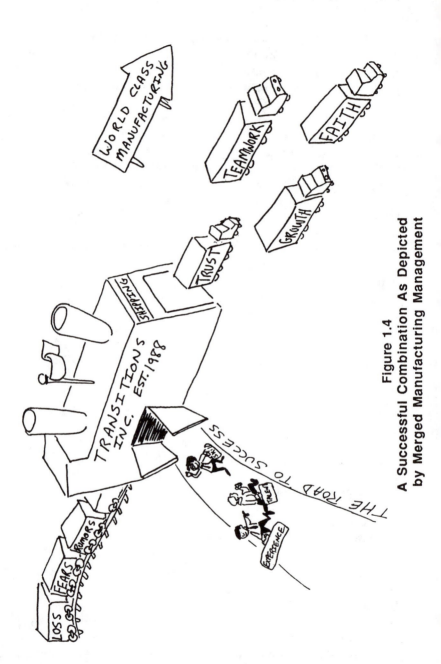

Figure 1.4
A Successful Combination As Depicted
by Merged Manufacturing Management

22

weaknesses, we set about building a world class operation. People could get behind that. Sure there were doubts and some guilt over losing people. But now there's excitement about where we're headed." (See Figure 1.4.) Culture building is an ongoing activity. Once new teams and structures are in place, they need to be anchored in a combined company philosophy and culture. Otherwise, the new organization will crumble and people will lose faith. Culture building takes time. What people think of their new company depends on how winners, who gain responsible posts, take charge; how losers, who are laid off or retire early, are treated; and, crucially, how survivors, the bulk of the work force, evaluate their prospects and opportunities. Successful companies thoughtfully manage these three classes of employees and build a new cultural identity.

PROCESS IS THE PRESCRIPTION

These prescriptions for success address the process for making mergers work. We develop them in Parts II, III, and IV, which address the precombination period, the integration of companies, and the postcombination phase. Part IV then looks at how to monitor a merger and at international M&A. A postscript shows how the prescriptions we offer, taken together, give combining companies a better shot at success.

As we shall see, high-minded leadership was integral to the success of Blumenthal and Clarkson, along with their vision and energy, their ability to give and get support, and their honesty and collegiality with people. All of these attributes, plus a measure of charisma, constitute what consultant David Nadler calls "the magic leader."[12]

But leaders at all levels also have to attend to the more mundane but no less important job of managing the combination process. One "magic" CEO, for example, formed cross-company task forces to plan the integration of another company with his firm. Within a few weeks, however, his financial group shoved through their recommendations and launched a full-scale assault on their counterparts. Key order entry and product tracking systems were "unplugged," making them conform to the parent company's systems, but creating chaos in the smaller firm. Meanwhile, the integration plans formulated for service and sales were uncoordinated. Service people began shifting territories and accounts well in advance of salespeople who heard the news first from their customers.

A leadership failure? The vision was there and the CEO delivered several impressive and credible speeches that got people worked up. He had a close and candid relationship with his direct reports and gave the task forces clear guidelines for putting the companies together in a sound and sensible way. But the finance people were caught up in the "thrill of victory" and were never reined in. Moreover, the work of sales and service teams was not closely tracked or controlled, and other senior managers didn't feel accountable for the resulting screwups.

Managing a merger is not a matter of "magic." And there are no easy shortcuts or esoteric tricks of the trade. In this case, the CEO finally got on top of the situation when he appointed a combination "czar" to track, oversee, and coordinate reorganization activities; hosted breakfast meeting reviews for top executives from both companies; personally counseled wayward and turf-hungry subordinates; and dedicated himself to the everyday but essential tasks of making the merger work.

GCers, by comparison, managed the process as a true team. One year after the forced sale of their company, they met to review the "wars" and lick their wounds. Clarkson set the new tone: "Why fight a battle that you're never going to win...just to preserve your own sense of pride?" From this emerged a discussion of integration factors over which GC had "minimal or no control." These would have to be managed "skillfully and well." With that, top management could focus time and energy and creativity on areas where they had "degrees of freedom."

It was agreed that good results were mandatory and that GC middle managers should cultivate better relationships with their counterparts. Once the norm had been "don't fraternize with the enemy." Now it was to seek "acceptance and encouragement." This would mean relating to counterparts without "overdramatizing differences" and showing more "sensitivity" to the values of Times Mirror.

MERGER MANAGEMENT:
THEORY AND PRACTICE

No single theory can explain the varied and complex dynamics of human and organizational behavior during a merger or acquisition. But several help in interpreting what is going on and suggest prescriptions for management on both sides of a deal. Our views on merger management are steeped in an eclectic but complementary set of theories:

1. The Strategic-Management Perspective. This perspective reflects the "rational actor" model of behavior so prominent in microeconomics and business school classrooms.[13] It treats managers as *information processors* who scan their environment to identify problems and opportunities, formulate strategies and tactics to address them, and then plan activities and organize their people to achieve desired results. Strategy implementation, in turn, is based on the assumption that top-down leadership, goal setting, feedback, and the judicious application of rewards effectively guide behavior in organizations.

Proponents of this "perfect world" model acknowledge its limitations. For example, managers operate in a world of "imperfect" information. Thus their plans and actions are constrained by the quality of information available to them. Second, managers will "satisfice" rather than optimize when it comes to attaining goals. This means that they will make compromises, scale down expectations, and live with acceptable but not optimal results.

The model is a workable *approximation* of human behavior in a merger. In our experience, most merger managers are quite rational—in intention and execution. And combining companies are often guided by a sensible top-down strategy—in their selection of a partner, in the integration of functions, and in the rebuilding of the combined business. But, as we shall see, rational strategies can also be flawed; integration often goes off course; and managers get caught in unexpected conflicts, lose their following, and inflict unnecessary suffering, on others and themselves, through the process of a combination. Hence we need to draw upon other theories to explain why.

2. The Political Perspective. This model contends that organizations operate through various "interests" that strive to maximize their power and resources.[14] Whereas the strategic management model assumes top-down rationality, this perspective suggests that the more discrete strategies and goals of combining businesses, business units, functions, and coalitions determine what goes on in mergers and acquisitions.

The political perspective is commonly used to explain the power moves of the lead company in a combination and its proclivities to dominate integration. It also helps to explain power plays of parent company staff groups when dictating new methods and procedures in an acquired subsidiary. Finally, it is useful in diagnosing conflicts of interest that pit function against function and often manager against manager.

However, the political perspective continues to emphasize "rational" goal directedness, albeit in a complex web of competing interests and people. What it does not account for is the level of uncertainty and stress that arises during a combination that leads functions and managers to work against their seeming interest. Nor does it take account of the emotion and energy that is unleashed—which can alternatively wreck a sound deal or salvage managers from some stupid moves. To get to this, we need to move from the heights of grand strategy and the dispassion of political analysis to ground-level action and the heat of the moment.

3. The Psychological Perspective. The psychological perspective explains why so many mergers miscarry. It posits that strategies and plans are constantly being informed and revised based on managers' own emotional states and those of the people around them. Reckless and self-defeating moves and countermoves, otherwise inexplicable in the rational or political calculus, can be understood through the psychological perspective as reactions to threat, loss, or perceived injustice. In the same way, acts of cooperation, in situations rife with conflict, and assertions of commitment, in cases that predict cynical indifference, all attest to the positive potential of human behavior in a merger.

The psychological perspective, as we use it here, includes consideration of group dynamics—as the work of negotiating a deal, of devising an integration strategy, and of physically joining people and processes is undertaken by groups of managers from both combining companies. This focuses attention on managers' tendencies toward cooperation versus conflict in working with their counterparts or toward participative versus authoritarian modes of decision making. What complicates a combination is that merging groups may have different norms or practices, and putting them together generates new group dynamics. To gain a more complete picture of this requires consideration of cultural factors.

4. The Cultural Perspective. Each of the two companies involved in a combination has its own definition of rationality, politics, and appropriate behavior. The cultural perspective explicates how these definitions—expressed in cultural beliefs and values—serve to explain and justify behavior in a merger. It is what we term the "clash of cultures" that leads to so much miscommunication and misunderstanding between the companies and to so much righteous finger-pointing when problems occur. The problem: What looks rational to one company seems political to the other one. And what is experienced as a psychological shock in one company looks to be a natural aspect of doing business to the other.

The cultural perspective extends beyond the clash of cultures to larger themes of human life. Throughout the text, we use images of war and love, of occupation and migration, and of death and rebirth. These are *not* literary techniques— they come from managers' descriptions of their experiences in a merger. Like the managers we have studied and worked with, we regard mergers and acquisitions as something other than "business as usual." Hence we put particular emphasis on the processes of acculturation wherein people participate in events and gain experiences that alter fundamental beliefs about themselves, about other people, and about how things work.

This draws our attention to combination scripts, which delineate the roles of the two combining companies and their intentions toward one another, and to the type and character of their integration, which directly influences the cultural consequences for one or both companies. It also draws us to acts of heroism (and cowardice) and to cultural affirming rituals (and cultural conquest). What impresses is how the very best merger managers transcend seemingly preordained scripts and lead their people through a symbolic death and rebirth.

Our work, as the book describes, is to help managers to think more clearly as rational actors, to open up the political process to scrutiny and influence, and to help people cope with the psychological trials and trauma of putting companies together. We also lend a hand in staging events, scripting communications, hosting rites of passage, celebrating triumphs, and healing people from their defeats. This is our way of helping managers make their mergers work.

CHAPTER 2

Contested Terrain

When those states which have been accustomed to . . . freedom under their own laws are acquired, there are three ways of trying to keep them. One is to destroy them, the second to go and live therein, and the third to allow them to continue under their own laws, taking a tribute from them, and creating within them a new government of a few which will keep the state friendly to you.
—Niccolo Machiavelli, sixteenth century, *The Prince* [1]

One Thursday morning a company . . . unexpectedly announced its plans for merger over the company intercom. People could be seen standing about in the lobby and halls in small groups as if in shock. The only other time I'd personally observed people in similar states of disbelief was shortly after the announcement that President John F. Kennedy had been shot. Then, as in this case, people stood about numbly, some with tears of disbelief in their eyes. Days, weeks, months later they referred back to that original moment in ways that said, "I still remember what I was doing during that tragic announcement—I can still feel myself turning numb . . . ." Employees referred to the sudden merger announcement as "Black Thursday."
—Psychologist Marsha Sinetar, twentieth century, "Mergers, Morale, and Productivity," *Personnel Journal* [2]

Machiavelli had studied the rise and fall of the Greek city-states and Roman empire and observed the shifting alliances between Italian republics when he offered his advice to the Venetian prince. His views on statecraft read like a primer on how some corporations do business today. The press is filled with stories of raids and defensive restructurings. Hostile tender offers turn executives into modern day militarists, and arbitrageurs, in league with lawyers and investment bankers, are the Machiavellians of today. "It's the closest thing to combat I've seen since World War II," says R. Eberstadt, Jr., whose company, Microdot, Inc., was the target of a raider.[3]

Even friendly deals are frenzied. The buyer's corporate development department may seem to hum with routine efficiency—like a peacetime army—but when it's time to commence dealing, the pace is frenetic. Accountants run the numbers, lawyers prepare opening gambits, and all are sworn to secrecy in order to keep other bidders from moving on the target.

The tumult is magnified in the case of large scale mergers, opportunistic tender offers, and unfriendly takeover attempts. Teams of accountants are immersed in valuation and due diligence; a phalanx of attorneys studies antitrust regulations and antitakeover laws, silken senior partners of investment houses and law firms pore forth advice; and the blood of top executives is stirred. Making a bid is heady business. And there is headlong momentum to get this business done.

In the aftermath, "Black Thursday" is often a harbinger of darker days to come. Studies show that employees spend hours of their workday, for several months following a combination, speculating over its rationale, trading on rumors and gossip, and obsessing over what it means for themselves and their futures.[4] Day-to-day performance plummets, and companies go through a protracted period of "post merger drift".[5] Turnover is rampant, with the best performers leaving first, and many who stay feel like survivors, rather than winners, or like damn fools for not jumping ship.

This chapter surveys the contested terrain in mergers, acquisitions, and takeovers. It begins with a description of today's merger environment and then summarizes the history of M&A in American business. This is followed by an analysis of the new rules of engagement between combining companies. The chapter concludes with an account of how Blumenthal and Clarkson conceived of their challenges and, more broadly, what these new rules mean for merger managers.

MERGER MANIA

The 1980s witnessed nearly 35,000 combinations of publicly traded firms at a cost of $1.3 trillion.[6] There were many more deals involving privately owned companies. Described as "merger mania" in boardrooms and a "feeding frenzy" on Wall Street, the M&A game introduced a new vocabulary into business, replete with images of "pirates" or "raiders" leading takeover attempts aided by "hired guns," who identified targets of opportunity, and financed by "junk bonds," which paid out when "unproductive" assets were sold off and "deadwood" was eliminated from the company payroll (see Figure 2.1).

Figure 2.1
Mergers and Acquisitions of Publicly Traded Companies

Year	No. of Transactions	Value ($billions)
1980	1,560	$34.2
1981	2,328	70.0
1982	2,298	60.4
1983	2,391	52.7
1984	3,163	126.0
1985	3,463	145.5
1986	4,363	206.4*
1987	3,908	176.5**
1988	4,026	230.5
1989	3,766	245.4***
1990	3,972	171.4

*Increase attributable to "rush to close" before new tax law took effect.
**Stock market crash depressed rate.
***Fewer deals but larger transactions

Young MBAs and Yuppie stockbrokers gravitated to the big money game, sometimes sacrificed their scruples and, as the recent wave of insider trading scandals intimates, also broke the law in search of the "big score." A group of Columbia MBAs didn't even have to graduate to get into the fray. Asher Edelman, a well known arbitrageur serving on the Columbia faculty, offered his students bonuses of $100,000 for identifying "pigeons" whose stocks were undervalued and whom he might "pluck."[7]

With the collapse of the junk bond market and bankruptcy of some well-known raiders, however, deal making in the 1990s appears to be entering a saner phase. Today the emphasis is on strategic deals where the buyer is interested in running the company, not simply milking its profits. This means there will be more mergers and acquisitions involving companies in similar or related businesses. The recent rash of deals within the food, financial services, media and entertainment, pharmaceutical, and energy industries all bear witness to this trend.

Global competitiveness requires size, reach, and multinational presence. Hence many more companies will be going global through international deals as Philip Morris Co.'s $3.8 billion purchase of Jacob Suchard, the Swiss candy maker, suggests. The number of announced acquisitions of foreign companies by U.S. firms doubled in the 1980s and should double again by 1995. This, of course, works both ways: Foreign acquisitions of U.S. firms increased 500% during the decade past and continue to climb dramatically.[8]

Although deals today look more sensible to financial and business analysts, they still pose formidable problems to managers who have to execute their strategies and to employees who are increasingly suspicious of management's intentions. One executive, taking charge of a subsidiary, lost most of the newly acquired top team within a month. They pulled their golden parachutes. Middle managers who remained scoffed at his pledge to grow the business. Copy machines turned out fresh résumés and phone lines buzzed with calls to headhunters. The new boss was left with a skeleton crew at the top and rebellion in the ranks. "I've never seen anything like it," he opined; "I've been through mergers before but never faced anything like this." "That was the old days (ten years ago)," counseled a colleague; "you're in a political war today. Don't you understand, this is a contest for hearts and minds," he added, "and you're losing."

MERGER ACTIVITY IN AMERICAN BUSINESS

Mergers and acquisitions have played a prominent role in shaping 20th century corporate America. They enabled industrialists to dominate their markets in the early part of this century and to develop and control supply and distribution channels through the 1920s to 1950s. To an extent, this put business against business in the competitive marketplace. But, on a grander scale, it also pit private against public interest because as business gained advantage, government would regulate trade, and then business would come up with new combination schemes. Conglomerates were created via mergers and acquisitions as a hedge against the boom-and-bust post–World War II economy and to balance out business cycles. And today, the dubious financial track record notwithstanding, the "urge to merge" is a dominant business impulse.[9]

The surge of combinations in the 1980s affected upward of 10 million people. America's largest firms have been a party to megamergers or sought as takeover targets. A brief look at American merger history shows how today the terrain is contested as never before.

Three Merger Waves: 1890–1975

First Merger Wave. The first merger wave commenced with the passage of the Sherman Act in 1890 that prohibited collusion in restraint of trade. While this outlawed price-fixing between firms, it prompted thousands of horizontal mergers, joining companies in the same industry. As a result, the wealthiest and most acquisitive business leaders were able to minimize competition, erect substantial barriers to entry into their fields, and gain control over entire industries. Small and medium-sized firms combined to form such dominant companies as United States Steel, Standard Oil of New Jersey, DuPont, and General Electric.

Teddy Roosevelt's election completed a populist wave of protest over these industrial trusts. Two bills passed in 1914, the Clayton Act and the Federal Trade Commission Act, intensified government enforcement of antitrust provisions and brought the most blatant monopolization efforts to an end. Over time, however, the antimerger provisions of these legislative acts were gutted by court decisions that found that most mergers did not violate the technical provisions of the law. Then a heated-up economy commenced a second great wave of buying and selling from 1925 through 1931.

Second Merger Wave. *Vertical* combinations, in which a buyer acquired a major supplier or customer, were common in this second merger wave. A baked goods company, say, might acquire a flour miller to control costs and ensure raw material (backward integration) or buy a trucking company or chain of retail shops to assure distribution and markets (forward integration). American Cyanamid, Radio Corporation of America, and General Foods were built through vertical combinations during this era.

The Great Depression following the stock market crash stifled the frenzy of buying and selling, but, again, it was stiff government action some years later which brought an end to this second merger wave. The passage in 1950 of the Cellar-Kefauver amendment to the Clayton Antitrust Act gave government regulators the power to scrutinize both horizontal and vertical mergers for competition-inhibiting or monopoly-creating potential. This act survived judicial scrutiny. In 1962, for example, the U.S. Supreme Court ruled that Brown Shoe could not acquire G. R. Kinney Co. Although the combined operations accounted for just 2.3% of existing retail shoe outlets, the court determined the merger would lessen retail and wholesale competition.

Third Merger Wave. A strong postwar economy through the 1950s and 1960s led large corporations to seek new avenues of growth. With government regulation and its enforcement inhibiting deals within industries, motivation and money were redirected toward diversification. *Conglomerate mergers*, linking firms having different customers and technologies, and often in different industries, defined the third merger wave.

This wave swelled in the 1960s with the rise of inflation and the pre-eminence of portfolio models of corporate finance. Business leaders were advised to diversify and manage their empires via a holding company structure. Between 1961 and 1968, Litton Industries made 79 acquisitions, Gulf & Western made 67, and Teledyne, which had no assets in 1960, took over 125 firms.

Those at the helm of conglomerates were financiers, not the operations men and marketeers who had led the earlier merger waves. Their style was epitomized by ITT's Harold Geneen, master of the multibusiness holding company, who would digest the daily financials of each of his companies and take cardboard boxes filled with reports and data to his regular meetings with subsidiary managers. Geneen and others like him were not identified with particular products, markets, or industries. They managed "results" and could, in their opinion, run any kind of business.

Fourth Merger Wave.

Mobil's $1.6 billion takeover of Montgomery Ward (then part of Marcor) in 1974 and GE's 1975 acquisition of Utah International for $1.9 billion ushered in the fourth wave of merger activity and changed, fundamentally, the scope of deal making. First, the size of deals reached previously unimagined levels. The Marcor and Utah International takeovers alone exceeded the billion dollars in assets acquired in all of Teledyne's and Litton Industries' deals between 1961 and 1968. Nowadays deals of this size occur every few months. And, with Beecham Group's purchase of SmithKline Beckman and Kohlberg Kravis Roberts' takeover of RJR Nabisco, records for the largest deal continued to be broken.

Deal making of this sort has occurred while government regulators have, for all intents and purposes, ignored antitrust restrictions on mergers between firms in unrelated markets and eased up on their oversight of deals within an industry. Former Federal Trade Commission lawyer Kenneth Davidson writes, ". . . antitrust laws no longer have any intentional impact on corporate size or growth. These policies almost bring the antitrust prohibitions full circle, that is, back to where they were before the Cellar-Kefauver Act."[10] Furthermore, following the deregulation of banking and transportation, government regulators have generally assented to massive consolidations in insurance, banking, and investment houses, as well as in airlines, trucking, and shipping.

Second, while some conglomerates rose out of obscurity through the merger process of the 1950s and 1960s, megamergers involve already well-known, successful firms such as GE and RCA, Time and Warner, Philip Morris and Seven-Up, and R. J. Reynolds and Nabisco. Many conservative, old-line giants have combined causing the collapse of long-standing corporate cultures and threatening the security of millions of heretofore cradle-to-grave employees.

Finally, the current merger wave features new players and new tactics in the contest for corporate control. Corporate raiders, for example, have decried the self-indulgence of senior management who enjoy bloated salaries and handsome perks while allowing share prices to fall well below their potential value. The most opportunistic raiders purchase these undervalued shares and reap profits by pumping up prices through bidding wars, and then get paid off in "greenmail" or by selling their shares at a premium to "white knights." The more salutary raiders, to their lights, aim to restructure and downsize their conquests. They reap their dividends by selling off prime assets (break-up raiders) or by taking over control from management and whipping firms into shape (discipline raiders).

Like those before it, this fourth wave of merger activity has greatly altered the corporate terrain. Some 250 of the firms on the 1980 *Fortune* 500 have not survived, intact, on the 1990 list. The October 1987 stock market crash led many analysts to predict that the fourth merger wave had crested. Instead, it has gathered momentum from collapsed stock prices, increased foreign investment, and the willingness of companies to spin off unwanted businesses leading to more and larger deals.

THE NEW RULES OF ENGAGEMENT

Beyond *quantitative* changes in the number and size of deals, there are also *qualitative* changes in how people operate in the M&A game today. Consider the old versus new rules of engagement (see Figure 2.2).

Figure 2.2
Rules of Engagement In M&A

Old Rules	New Rules
Gentlemanliness of deals.	Respectability of hostile deals.
Careful pace of deal structuring and decision making.	Rapid pace of deal structuring and decision making.
Limited role of outsiders.	Hired M & A experts on commission.
Isolated deals.	Entire industries put in play.
Stock swaps.	Cash deals.
Company perspective.	Asset perspective—Divestitures.
	Defensive restructuring/LBOs.

Hostile Dealings. Until the most recent wave, for instance, mergers tended to be "gentlemanly" deals. Parties from the two sides, usually the CEOs, mutually negotiated the price, terms, and integration plans. These were top executives who knew one another—maybe through industry associations or memberships in the same clubs—or who were introduced by familiar third parties such as trusted legal or financial advisors. They moved slowly, got to know one another and gained a feel for one another's needs. If personalities or styles clashed, the dealing would cease with a polite "no, thank you."

Today, by comparison, hostile takeovers, although the exception not the norm, have become fair play. No longer a tactic associated with raiders or mavericks, the CEOs of "respectable" firms are making uninvited bids. W. Michael Blumenthal, for example, had no "second thoughts" when his company, Burroughs, put a "bear hug" on Sperry. "Friends advised against it," he recalled, "they cautioned: 'Do you want to be known as a raider?' " As he looked at the condition of his company and the industry, however, his moral compass dictated that he act. "Otherwise," he added, "You are presiding over the decline of the organization and in the end you hurt everybody."

Faster Pace. Though involving larger companies and more complex transactions, today's merger deals are also executed at a much more rapid pace than were those in years gone by, compressing the time frame in which decisions can be made. Executives must act and respond quickly to bids and counterbids, raiders and rescuers. Even in uncontested cases, they are hurried by investment bankers and other external advisors whose commissions will be the same whether the deal takes five days or five months to negotiate.

The rapid pace prevents the two companies from getting to know one another during negotiations and often leads to the merger of incompatible companies. In the case of Graphic Controls, to compound matters, management was "hit by a truck" when raided and had to settle on the terms of its acquisition by Times Mirror quickly. "In just six calendar days, without any choice in the matter," GC's Will Clarkson recalled, "we went from being a public company, with 2500 stockholders, trading 500,000 shares annually, to becoming a subsidiary of another public company many times our size." "Instead of reporting to a seven-person Board," he added, "I had a new boss."

More Players. Lipper Analytic Services estimates that 50,000 people from investment banks, commercial banks, and law firms were involved in deal making in 1988, compared to 10,000 five years earlier.[11] Nowadays, specialists on both the offensive and defensive sides, with tactics ranging from two-tiered offers to poison pills, are brought in at the slightest indication that a company is in play.

In his account of the days following an unsolicited takeover offer by Diamond Shamrock in May 1983, former Natomas Company Chairman Dorman L. Commons listed among his company's advisors: lawyers on retainer from local (San Francisco) and New York law firms, the New York managing partner and San Francisco managing director of Salomon Brothers, a managing partner from another investment bank, and a representative from the New York branch of a public relations firm. It is the norm, now, for major firms to keep takeover lawyers, bankers, and advisors on retainer.

Because of the potential of a surprise attack, key advisors are available on an "on call" basis around the clock, seven days a week.[12]

Industries in Play. In today's business environment mergers beget even more mergers. In many industries, one deal prompts an avalanche of bids, battles, and buyouts. Soon after Capital Cities succeeded in its bid to take over ABC, GE acquired NBC's parent RCA, and Ted Turner launched the battle for CBS which eventually placed Laurence Tisch in control of the media giant. Entire industry sectors have become reconfigured by merger mania. The smile on PSA airplanes, Republic's goose, and Western's "only way to fly" are nothing more than artifacts of a bygone era of airline travel.

As a result, many CEOs are compelled to "eat" before "being eaten." Only one firm in the farm equipment manufacturing business, John Deere, has not changed hands in the past several years. Navistar International, formerly International Harvester, sold its farm equipment business to Tenneco in 1985, the same year that West German manufacturer Klockner-Humboldt-Deutz bought Allis-Chalmers' farm unit. The next year, Ford acquired Sperry's farm implements division and Massey-Ferguson was later restructured as Varity Corporation.

Cash Deals. Also changing is the way in which deals are structured. Many mergers used to be transacted through stock swaps or the exchange of securities. More recently, cash has been the principle means of payment. Heinz CEO Anthony J. F. O'Reilly notes that in 1988 alone, his company spent more on acquisitions—$500 million—than in the previous ten years. "Cashing out" also symbolizes a clean break for former owners and executives, who no longer have to stay on as partners—at least with security holdings.[13]

Divestitures. Merger activity is also being redefined today by what some term a new corporate "methodology." In the old days, buyers and sellers acted with reference to entire companies. Today the focus is on assets. "You're not just buying a company to hold it and merge it anymore," says Frederick Sturdivant, of the MAC Group, "You're looking at is as a mosaic—there are some pieces to keep if they fit and some pieces to be spun off to get more value." As a result, a buyer may focus on a segment of its business mix, keeping what it wants, and sell off the rest. Fully one-half of all corporate acquisitions in the 1980s were units divested by prior owners. By contrast, during the 1970s, divestitures made up less than 15% of all acquisitions.[14]

Defensive Restructuring/Leveraged Buyouts. Once viewed only as offensive tactics to build company vitality and productivity, an increasing number of deals are born of a defensive rationale. To fend off Sir James Goldsmith's hostile bid, for example, Goodyear CEO Robert Mercer went on a selling spree, divesting the company's oil and gas division, aerospace operations, and other units, keeping little more than the tire business and the Goodyear Blimp. The sales gave Mercer the money needed to buy back company stock but otherwise thwarted his strategy to reduce the company's reliance on the volatile tire market. The price tag for this defensive maneuvering was $1 million a day in interest payments and a loss in earnings of $100 million from the sale of money-making subsidiaries.

RESTRUCTURING AND DOWNSIZING

The current merger wave has completely transformed how corporate leaders and employees approach their work. Managers who spent careers thinking about how to wrest market share away from other companies now strive to preserve control over the operations of their firm. Peter Drucker writes,

> An ever increasing number of businesses—large, medium-sized, and small—are not being run for business results but for protection against the hostile takeover. The fear of the raider is undoubtedly the largest single cause for the increasing tendency of American companies to manage for the short term and let the future go hang. The fear of the raider demoralizes and paralyzes. The impact on the morale of management . . . and of professional people in the company can hardly be overestimated.[15]

Many company leaders heed the battle cry "do unto yourself before someone does it unto you" and take action to reduce the likelihood of an unwanted bidder moving in. Some sell off their own assets and pass the gains onto shareholders in the form of special dividends. Others increase stock prices by cutting headcount, budgets, and R&D expenditures, by restricting pay raises and requiring unpaid vacation, and, in general, by investing less in the business. A recent study by Employment Management Association found that 79% of the 260 companies studied reduced their staff for economic reasons in the past five years.[16]

Restructurings, downsizing, divestitures, and other such corporate makeovers all change the strategy and direction of a company and, in today's business situation, are closely linked to mergers and acquisitions. On the one hand, they are sometimes undertaken to prevent takeovers. On the other, they many times come in the aftermath. For example, massive debt loads created by cash transactions require many companies to sell off assets simply to pay for the deal. Otherwise, redundancies and strategic requirements dictate wholesale change. An American Management Association study of 100 acquisitions found that over one-half led to major internal reorganizations and over one-third led to significant downsizing and reductions in force.[17]

Certainly there are distinctions among each of these types of strategic change. Yet, they all disrupt established ways of doing business, threaten people's near-term job security and long-term career opportunity, and turn executive and employee attention away from team performance and toward self-survival.

LOVE AND WARFARE

Behind these new merger strategies, methods, and practices, there are age-old factors that influence the course of a combination and the impact on the people involved. Professors Paul Hirsch and John Andrews note that the language of deals today draws from such popular genres as the Western (with ambushes and shootouts), piracy (with raiders and safe harbors), chivalry (with rescues of damsels-in-distress), and, of course, love affairs and marriage.[18] Through this symbolic use of language, they assert, we represent the roles of the two companies and their respective relationship. (See Figure 2.3.)

Broadly speaking, the combination is shaped by the power of the parties (whether equal or unequal) and their intentions toward one another (whether love or war).

Figure 2.3
Merger Images of Love and War

	Images of Courtship, Love and Chivalry	Images of Warfare, Conquest and Violation
Principals	Suitor Beauty Matchmaker	Raider Pigeon Hired guns
Negotiations	Dancing Playing coy	Bear hug Throwing up flak
Tender Offer	Courtship Proposal Bringing to the altar	Ambush Shootout Rape
Failed Bid	Sex without marriage	Safe harbor
Another Buyer	White knight	Black knight
Aftermath	Afterglow Honeymoon	Wounded list Living hell

Power Parameters

The relative power of two combining companies is often dictated by size and by who buys whom. Typically, their combination takes either the form of a merger (joining two similar size companies) or an acquisition (where a larger company buys a smaller one). But, no matter how the combination is structured, psychologist Joan Rentsch finds that the two parties have distinct going-in assumptions about their roles. Acquirers, she reports, have strong expectations of asserting their powers, whereas acquirees anticipate less autonomy and job security. This dominance/submission scenario is built into deals involving big companies and

small ones. Yet, even in true mergers, one or the other company expects to take the lead.[19]
However, size alone does not establish the superiority of a company. In Capital Cities' purchase of ABC, for example, it was the buyer, rather than the media company three times its size, that had the upper hand. And a takeover, whether initiated by an equal-size company, or larger or smaller one, puts the lead party in charge. Furthermore, there are "reverse mergers" where business units that are part of a lead company's portfolio undergo more dramatic change and dislocation than those in a smaller concern. After AT&T succeeded in its protracted bid for NCR, the lead company's computer systems group was integrated into the target, which became a unit of AT&T.

A second factor that shapes the relationship concerns the intentions of the two companies. To an extent, this is prefigured in the friendliness of mutual negotiations versus the hostility of a bidding war. More generically, however, there is a lead party and a target in almost every combination, whether the scenario is a parent company making a small acquisition, one firm looking to merge with another, or a raider trying to take over a target. This means that the lead company has likely studied the marketplace, has more or less predetermined what it wants from a combination, and has some image of how it will integrate the firms that it buys. These plans, of course, may or may not match the expectations of a prospective partner or serve the best interests of the combination.

What ultimately determines the relationship between parties is their relative *degree of influence* over how the companies are put together or integrated. Compare, for example, the integration tactics of two different "white knights" of targeted oil companies: DuPont "rescued" Conoco from an unfriendly bidder and then unilaterally consolidated corporate staff functions and moved its headquarters to Delaware. By contrast, USX's Chairman David Roderick saved Marathon from Mobil and then worked closely with Marathon's top team to establish a mutually agreeable relationship. Marathon retained its own management and policies, its own headquarters and staff, and, importantly, was free to steer its own course.

Combination Scripts

For the sake of simplicity, we offer four combination "scripts" based on the relative strength of the two companies and their influence over integration decisions (see Figure 2.4).

Marriage. When the two companies are of equal size and power and combine based upon mutual influence, the result can be termed a "marriage." The CSX/SeaLand merger joined land and sea shipping companies to create a worldwide distribution capability ("one-stop shipping"). The two sides mutually agreed on a plan that partially integrated them and redefined the combined company in the marketplace. What made this a happy marriage was that the intentions of both parties were mutual and compatible, there was a prolonged and intense courtship period, and the degree of integration was deep and, by all accounts, mutual.

Figure 2.4
Merger and Acquisition Scripts

	Mutual Influence	One-Side Dominates
Two Companies of Equal Size and Importance	Marriage	Conquest
One Larger and More Important than Other Company	Adoption	Occupation

The merger of Allied-Signal and Bendix corporations is a story with a "happy ending" from inauspicious beginnings.[20] Edward Hennessy, Allied's chairman, found himself in a bidding war with United Technologies and Martin Marietta all pursuing Bendix. When Martin Marietta executed a "PacMan defense" and began to buy up Bendix stock, Hennessy seemed intent on buying both companies. Ultimately, he purchased Bendix and sold Martin Marietta back its shares. And then he set about improving performance and raising Bendix morale above premerger levels. How did he do it? From the start, he emphasized that both companies would influence the integration process and appointed managers from both sides to merger planning teams. He also proved to be a tireless cheerleader, personally greeting Bendix employees and rallying them to the cause, while counseling skeptical executives and holding his own managers in check. Finally, Hennessy held off on budget cuts until both sides could complete detailed studies of need and thereafter treated outplaced employees with generosity and care.

Companies need not "get into bed" to have a mutual relationship. For example, USX and Marathon operated as more or less separate companies following their merger. And our interviews in Marathon found that most managers were unaffected by the deal. Sure there was some second-guessing, but USX Chairman David Roderick promised that his people would keep their "hands off" of Marathon. Perhaps he had learned this lesson the hard way based upon the company's mismanagement of and meddling in its chemical subsidiaries. In this case, by comparison, USX "respected our autonomy," said Marathon's executive vice president Elmer Graham, and "kept to its promises." The secret? According to another Marathoner, Roderick's willingness to "call off the (corporate) dogs."[21]

Adoption. Congenial big company/small company acquisitions are most often represented in family terms with the "parent" adopting a subsidiary. The model works best when the junior partner has some say-so over integration or operates rather autonomously. Often the larger company gains new products or markets and, in turn, gives its partner access to more capital, borrowing power, and systems support. Delta's acquisition of Western Airlines, well conceived and carefully managed, is an exemplar.

Many of General Signal's acquisitions fit the adoption scenario.[22] This operating and holding company can be generous with capital and support, but gives its acquirees plenty of running room. Yohan Cho, head of a small telephone testing equipment manufacturer acquired by General Signal remembers getting the message: "You guys are the entrepreneurs, you know how best to expand your company." At the same time, subsidiary managers are exposed to a variety of corporate training courses and are groomed in the General Signal Club. Ultimately, they are expected to become loyal family members. And these expectations are set from the get-go.

Still, some of the responsibility for making this kind of combination work rests on the acquired company's CEO. When IC Industries bought Pet Inc., for instance, the acquired firm held an annual employee meeting in lieu of an annual report and stockholder gathering. Xerox gave Versatec, a computer disk manufacturer, plenty of freedom, but Versatec's management recognized its responsibilities: "You don't wait for the corporate guys to do it," recalls one acquired executive, "you know that to make it right depends on you."[23]

Conquest. When two equal-size companies combine and one dominates the integration, the result is conquest. High on the list of war-and-horror stories is Connecticut General's merger with INA. CG, a life insurer, based its business on a solid actuarial foundation and was, accordingly, a rather bureaucratic, buttoned-down kind of company. INA, a property and casualty insurer, had no such actuarial base and was more freewheeling in its style. In the initial stages of the combination, CG overwhelmed its partner with new reporting requirements and rigid strictures. Then came the purge.

This was to be a "merger of equals" with the promise of blending "the best of both organizations" to create CIGNA. Early signals were that staff reductions would be minimal. Several months later 4,200 jobs, most in the property and casualty areas, were eliminated. Many long-standing employees from CG's property and casualty group were either demoted, given early retirement, or moved to new corporate headquarters. The reaction was summed up neatly by a cartoon appearing on a bulletin board: "Doing a good job here is like working in a whore house. . . . The better we perform the more often they screw us!" CIGNA's property and casualty business suffered: its income dropped 18% in the first year.[24]

Occupation. When bigger companies acquire smaller ones and set the terms of integration unilaterally, the deal can turn into an occupation. In some cases, this often involves a physical takeover of a company, where new corporate management is installed and reigns. There are also symbolic occupations, as in Cooper's acquisition of Crouse-Hinds, where the acquirer absconded with the subsidiary's board room furniture and china tea service.

Frank Lorenzo, then head of Texas Air, was adept at both these forms of occupation. He took acquired Continental Airlines into bankruptcy to break its union and painted the Continental logo on People Express aircraft the very night of his purchase of the company. In the end, of course, Lorenzo got his comeuppance. His ruthless treatment of Eastern Airlines, leading to highly publicized maintenance scandals and his court-ruled dismissal as head of the airline, is a modern-day morality play teaching that cold-blooded profit taking leads to ruin.

An occupier's mentality can also destroy a well-conceived deal. Mellon Bank's friendly acquisition with Philadelphia's Girard Bank was implemented, according to one Girard staffer, with "all the finesse of the Russian army." Professor Lee Perry notes that Mellon came in with a "clean house" mentality, swiftly overhauled operations, and changed the Girard name and signage. The message to employees and management was that Mellon could run their bank better. It was this kind of hubris, Perry notes, that led the acquisition to ruin and turned employees against their once promising new parent.[25]

The first to experience this betrayal is the subsidiary's CEO. In a study of 200 acquired CEOs, Robert Hayes and Gerald Hoag found that, in cases in which the CEO left, only 18% of the departures were planned retirements. Most of the executives who left unexpectedly did so within two years after the acquisition, before the parent company had developed the necessary experience and management backup to run the company. The authors note that many of the acquisitions were in new markets or industries where the parent company needed to retain acquired top management to be successful.

Why this exodus of needed former CEOs? Hayes and Hoag found that their complaints centered on unsolicited parent company directives and decisions, excessive reporting requirements, and corporate staff interference. They write:

> Managerial autonomy and control is clearly the single most important factor influencing the retention of acquired top management. Over two-thirds of the executives who left their companies following acquisition reported that extensive interference by the parent company . . . was the primary factor behind the decision to leave.

By contrast, the situation among executives who remained with their companies was almost the reverse, with over 75% of the retained CEO's reporting satisfaction with the degree of autonomy offered to them. [26]

WRITING A NEW SCRIPT

It doesn't take much finesse for companies to conquer or occupy. The real challenge is to set agreeable power parameters and to exercise mutual influence over the integration—particularly when the situation dictates otherwise. Let's face it, Burroughs' purchase of Sperry was scripted for conquest. When we first met Blumenthal at his Michigan home, the day after the bid was accepted, we recounted Machiavelli's advice on handling acquisitions and asked him of his intentions. He brushed aside notions that a conquest was preordained in this case and enumerated the reasons why gaining the loyalty of Sperry customers, top managers, and employees was crucial to success.

Next Blumenthal defined his philosophy for the merger, emphasizing the importance of partnership between the two companies and his desires to select the best people and best organizational structures based on merit. Furthermore, he wanted to build a new company, with a new identity, to which people from both sides could transfer their allegiance. When asked, "why should people trust you?" he described his career history and faith in the ability of people to overcome adversity through honesty, hard work, and determination. It was not so much the words, as the conviction, that won us over. This led into a discussion of the human and organizational factors Blumenthal needed to consider to bring his vision to life.

First, there was the matter of external perceptions of the deal. Jeannette Learman, head of corporate communications at Burroughs, had already begun an aggressive public relations campaign justifying the deal as a "procompetitive" merger enabling the combined company to go head to head with IBM. Letters to former Sperry customers were in the mail reassuring them of the continuity of product offerings and promising ongoing service and support. It was agreed that Blumenthal would also have to visit personally with large Sperry customers and user groups.

How about internal perceptions? Learman offered the novel idea that they hold a "name the company" contest and solicit ideas from employees. She also proposed that Blumenthal issue literature and send letters to employees' homes that spelled out the reasons behind the merger and the principles that would be applied to integration. Public relations, however, wouldn't sway top Sperry executives who were covered by generous golden parachutes. Richard Bierly, head of human resources at Burroughs, reviewed these packages and suggested that employment contracts be substituted that would also contain a "release" clause in the event of changes in duties. We countered that money couldn't buy commitment. Hence it was agreed that Blumenthal would have to woo top Sperry executives personally and counsel his own people through the transition phase.

We then talked over the ins and outs of developing a Merger Coordination Council and task forces staffed by executives from both companies. Certainly this would establish a focal point for merger policy setting and planning and hasten the "getting-to-know-you" process among managers. Even more so, it would enable managers to "show their stuff" and test their ability to digest complex information, develop innovative recommendations, and team up with their counterparts. That way Blumenthal could observe managers' strengths and weaknesses and make more informed decisions about top level appointments.

Barbara, his wife, then challenged him to "get in touch" with people's reactions to the takeover. We reviewed symptoms of the merger syndrome and reminded Blumenthal that, at this point, he was the only person who was guaranteed a job in the combined company. It was agreed that we would offer merger sensitization seminars to executives on both sides and track the human reactions to the combination over the next several months. But we also emphasized that Blumenthal himself would have to reach out to people and reach into himself to think and feel like the people he hoped to lead.

Afterward, Blumenthal went on the stump to assuage the concerns of the Sperry customers and to play down the notion that Sperry would be subordinate to Burroughs. He promoted the merger as a "a true marriage of Burroughs and Sperry—a marriage that will create a strong competitor for IBM and the Japanese computer manufacturers." The message to employees was equally upbeat. "Now is our chance. Together we can do things we could not have done alone. It is a new idea. We are a new company. We can take on anybody. We can succeed. Come and join us—let's go." A Sperry manager recalled, "He was able to put himself in our shoes, verbalizing all the doubts and questions people had in their deepest corners. He planted a seed for perceiving this as a new company."

Rewriting the GC Story

The first chapters of GC's acquisition story were already written when we met with Clarkson to propose an in-depth study of management's reactions to the sale and its impact on the work force at large. Had it followed the usual story line, Clarkson would have left GC—taken his money and run. Then the rest of management would have "knuckled under" to Times Mirror. Instead, Clarkson stayed, and he and his team grieved their losses, recouped profitability, and represented their interests effectively to Times Mirror. One veteran summed up GC's early hopes for meeting profit requirements while retaining a sense of independence: "This way it can be exciting and fun, maybe not what we've had, but fun. If we go the other way, and follow their lead, the technostructure will surely immobilize us, and we will wither up and become 'businessmen.'"

However the combination was proving to be neither fun nor exciting for most GC managers when we talked with them several months after the sale. One described himself as "Jekyll and Hyde"—on the face of it acquiescent and responsive but inside burning with rage and self-contempt. Employee surveys would show, in turn, that managers were seen as "two faced" by their people and were failing to lead by example.

We proposed to Clarkson that he involve his boss, Schneider, and other Times Mirror executives in a study of human reactions to the acquisitions. As we looked at the pluses and minuses, however, he and his managers came to the "reluctant" conclusion that the parent company's participation would involve "too much risk." "They've demonstrated no interest, absolutely zero, in the way we do things," Clarkson noted, adding, "and I've already acquired the reputation of something of a 'kook.' " "They find fault with everything," he concluded, "and I'm not willing to risk (a full and honest) study for my sake and especially for the sake of the other managers."

It was agreed, therefore, that we would limit our study to GC's managers and employees and report our findings only to Clarkson and his team. All recognized that this would surely slant our understandings and narrow our effectiveness. Nevertheless, it seemed to us important to help GCers to look systematically at the human aspects of M&A and develop a new script for dealing with Times Mirror based on their long-standing commitment to the "authority of knowledge."

THE HUMAN COSTS OF M&A

The GC study provides a ground-level look at the human toll of M&A. On a broader scale, however, it is clear that merger mania has affected managers throughout the country. A recent poll by Robert Half International finds fear of job loss following a merger or acquisition to be the number one worry among senior executives surveyed in the nation's 1000 largest companies.[27] These fears (see Figure 2.5) are exacerbated by raiders like Carl Icahn who writes,

> One of the hidden 'assets' in many companies is top management: get rid of them and the value goes up.

What's going on in companies these days is absurd. It's
like a corporate welfare state. We're supporting managements who produce nothing. No, it's really worse than
that. Not only are we paying these drones not to produce,
but we're paying them to muck up the works.[28]

This outlook affects everyday employees as well as executives. Gone are the days when employees trusted their
leaders to make a good deal for all concerned. Today they
are savvy to the fact that buying companies take on enormous
debt to finance cash bids and that reductions in force are
needed to making the deal pay off. Cynicism lingers for those
who go through layoffs or forced early retirements—and is
carried over to the next employer. Even those who survive
a combination with their positions intact have reason to
be wary. Employees see monies which would have been
available for pay raises or internal expansion go instead
to interest payments and bankers' fees. And they see top
management running the business for the short run rather
than for future growth.

Figure 2.5
What Are Today's Executives' Greatest Anxieties?

1. Loss of job due to a merger or acquisition	54%
2. Burnout	26%
3. Failure to get promoted	8%
4. Being fired	6%
5. Failure to get a raise	5%
6. Insufficient income to meet living standards and financial obligations	3%
7. Illness	2%

Many companies who deal today are losing the battle
for hearts and minds. Surveys show that employees in companies that have been through mergers and acquisitions are less

secure and satisfied than are those whose companies eschewed the M&A game. And those who have been through a downsizing or witnessed layoffs have considerably less confidence and trust in their employers than otherwise (see Figure 2.6).

Behind the headline-grabbing stories of tender offers, trading, and takeovers, there is the human story. Samuel W. Murphy, Jr., was senior vice president and general counsel for Gulf Corp. when it was attacked by T. Boone Pickens and subsequently taken over by Chevron Corp. "There was room for only one general counsel," he remembered, so he moved to a "stable situation" —at RCA. "I was stunned when I read about the acquisition of RCA by General Electric," Murphy recalled. "I was personally dismayed, but I was also upset at seeing something like this happen to a great institution."[29] Murphy, like so many senior executives in corporate America today, had his career aspirations within his sights and then suddenly "everything was snatched away." Another executive expressed the feeling this way, "Everything I counted on before was topsy-turvy. The things I thought would make me successful—hard work and commitment—didn't pay off. Now I wonder, 'What was the use of it all?'"

These views are important. America's success in coming out of the depression of the 1930s and victory in World War II heralded the age of the modern corporation. Big business built the planes and tanks, marshalled people's talents and managed them effectively, and created the industrial might to make us a world power. Millions flocked to large companies seeking stable employment and the opportunity to contribute on a heretofore unimagined scale.

Today, by comparison, big business is maligned and smaller companies are almost as suspect. Surely merger managers have responsibilities to increase profitability, improve competitiveness, and regain consumer confidence. They also, in our view, have responsibilities to employees. There are signs that well-conceived and crafted mergers can succeed on the financial front. Less certain is victory in the contest for people's hearts and minds. For want of winning that contest, we would contend, the long-term benefits to companies and country could be lost.

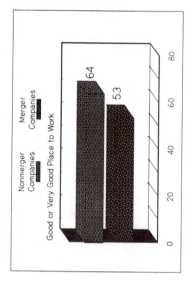

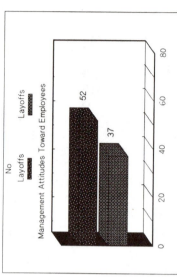

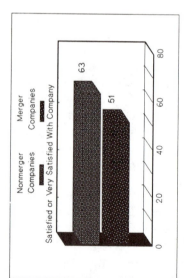

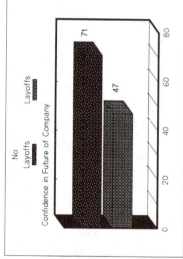

Figure 2.6
Employee Attitudes After a Merger or Layoff

Source: Gantz-Wiley Research Consulting Group. National survey of 2,500 households of employees whose companies have been involved in mergers or layoffs in past 12 months.

PART TWO

THE PRECOMBINATION PERIOD

CHAPTER 3

Organizing to Buy or Sell

"Like a major surgical operation, an acquisition or a merger must be well thought out, prepared, planned and executed.... Of utmost importance are the qualitative steps which are usually neglected. All the financial plans or predictions in the world will be useless if, on announcement, the management and workers leave to look for jobs elsewhere. Without the proper qualitative approach, planning a merger will be like adding one and one and getting zero."
    —Michael A. Carre and Philippe M. Bouvard,
    "The Courtship and Honeymoon of Successful
    Mergers," *European Business* [1]

There are so many stupid decisions. It often seems that executives are playing Let's Make a Deal and trying to guess what is behind curtains 1, 2, or 3.
    —Federal Trade Commission report on mergers [2]

Mergers and acquisitions are premised on the belief that the combined company will have greater value than the two companies alone. This added value is expressed as "synergy" between the firms. The formula is this: 1+1>2! However, when you look at the business of buying and selling, it seems most of the emphasis is on the financial elements in the formula and less consideration is given to the complicated and elusive factor "+."

Typically the dealings are led by the two companies' CEOs, some directors, investment bankers, lawyers, and third parties close to one or another of the firms. Their primary concerns are legal and financial—how much a company is worth, what price to pay, how to structure the transaction, and how to get regulators to go along with it. Balance sheets are scrutinized, projections of demand and capacity are studied, and cost-cutting requirements are contemplated. Most of the analysis concerns valuation and the financial contours of the deal.

Who is testing for cross-company synergy in research and development, product planning, manufacturing, marketing, or sales? Too often the engineers, marketeers, and line managers who will have to create or exploit it are not that intimately involved. Who is looking at the organizational implications, the compatibility of the two cultures, or even the next steps to making the "marriage" work? These subjects are often given short shrift in the analysis phase and finessed in the rush to close.

Sure the *right price* is important. But successful buyers know what they want from a combination and focus their search and attention on finding the *right partner*. Of course, opportunity can knock—when a takeover target seeks a white knight, a restructured firm offers a business unit at a good price, or an attractive, undervalued company might be purchased by the right bid—and the temptation to deal can prove irresistible. Still, it's crucial for the buyer to exercise discipline in its analysis and choice of a candidate.

A bad buy has the potential to affect adversely all aspects of the financial health and operating rhythms in either company with consequences for suppliers, customers, and stockholders, as well as managers and employees. Investment bankers, lawyers, and brokers are there to dot every "i" and cross every "t" in a deal's legal and financial framework. But, as Professor Paul Hirsch notes, there is no "future performance" clause in their fee schedules.[3] Outside advisors are paid for the transaction. It's up to management to make the combination work.

This chapter examines the human and organizational problems that have to be managed to complete a deal successfully. It addresses how the buyer brings its strategy into focus, goes about its search for and screening of potential partners, and handles the human aspects of the transaction. It concludes with a closer look at dynamics on the selling side.

"TEXTBOOK" STEPS IN MAKING A DEAL

The process for undertaking a corporate merger and acquisition involves several steps:

1. Formulating a strategy and criteria for a good "fit"
2. Searching for a partner
3. Sizing up good candidates
4. Preparing a bid
5. Negotiating and closing the deal

Formulating a Strategy and Setting M&A Criteria. Corporate strategy setting begins with self-scrutiny of a company's own competitive and market status, its strengths and weaknesses, as well as top management's aspirations and goals.[4] The results define a direction for increased growth, profitability, or market penetration in existing businesses, for diversification into new areas, or simply for cash investment—which may or may not involve M&A activity.

In successful M&A programs, the CEO, relevant corporate and division management, and various advisors translate these objectives into specific strategic and investment criteria. Most buying companies have standard metrics for evaluating a candidate that include its earnings, discounted cash flow, annual return on investment, and such. They also have objectives concerning the impact of the combination on profitability, the combined company's earnings-per-share, and future funding requirements. Beyond this, every company has its own idiosyncratic considerations in a deal.

Searching for a Partner. It is not unusual for large holding companies to scan the financials of 20,000 firms in an acquisition search. Massive data bases can be accessed to scrutinize publicly owned companies. Several large consulting firms specialize in identifying "hidden sector" private companies potentially amenable to purchase. Industry analysts, trade publications, and business brokers are also consulted along with in-house managers.

Corporate strategy guides the search for an acquisition candidate. Take the approach of Berwind, a fourth-generation, family-owned company that has grown from $30 million to over $300 million in sales during the past 20 years, as an example. Originally an old-line Appalachian coal company, Berwind today is a diversified international business with holdings in natural resources, industrial products, real estate, pharmaceuticals, and health care. The company has clear preferences for acquisitions in narrowly defined growth markets where the acquiree has strong brand-name identification. It prefers cash transactions and seeks companies in the price range of $15 million to $60 million. Berwind is also clear on what it does *not* want: Capital intensive companies and commodity producers are not on its "shopping list" nor are turnaround or tax loss situations. These criteria are contained in a brochure sent to any and all interested (and interesting) candidates.

Oftentimes a buyer's search is focused on specific partners and social contacts between top executives signal interest and test the waters. When interest is mutual (or a takeover is contemplated), the buyer normally formulates a "business case" for the deal that identifies potential financial, product, or manufacturing synergies as well as downside risks. This is followed by a period of fact-finding to "test" the theory behind the case (Appendix A lists areas for investigating possible synergies between companies).

Sizing Up Candidates. Seasoned acquirers use a hand-picked team to scout combination candidates. Firms may initially assign the screening responsibility to a staff executive, the head of corporate development, or a senior executive with broad industry experience, but, as the search narrows, an ad hoc team is typically formed to size up promising candidates.

There are good reasons for getting group management actively involved at this stage. Corporate staff are working to *buy* a company. Group management will have to run the firm. Getting them into the process ensures that they take a close look at several companies. Furthermore, acquisition candidates appreciate dealing face to face with executives whom they may ultimately be working with or reporting to. In the screening phase, accountants pore over the financials of leading candidates. Group executives, when they join the team, scrutinize manufacturing and marketing data. It is important that the acquisition team work together and sort through priorities. No candidate is the perfect partner. Gaining a toe hold in an industry may take several buys. Financial synergies may have to be traded off against possible gains in market share.

Preparing a Bid. Once the team completes its screening, a short list of promising candidates is sent to the board of directors for approval. Firms are prioritized according to their strategic and financial fit with the buyer. What happens next depends on whether a friendly or unfriendly deal is contemplated—will it be courtship or combat?

In a friendly deal, the buyer makes its intent known to the CEO, board, or owners of a potential candidate. This is followed by the normal rituals of corporate courtship—high-level visits, a review of the logic behind the deal, and discussions of the personal and career interests of top executives. As the courtship proceeds, more line managers from the buyer are drawn in, and more target company managers are also introduced to the dealings.

Meanwhile, organizational analysis and financial due diligence continue in earnest. This is the time when executives from the two companies preview possible types and levels of integration. The focus is on how the partners might integrate their business functions or effect the transfer of skills and resources from one side to the other. This is also a time when "chemistry" develops between the partners. Buyers and sellers consider whether or not their counterparts are "our kind of people."

When an unfriendly bid is the chosen course, by contrast, intelligence about the firm being eyed has to be gathered surreptitiously. Investment bankers, industry experts, and financial analysts are tapped to gain a clearer picture of the target. Customers of the target company, vendors, and former employees may be contacted. Once this would have caused a stir and would likely have led to premature leaks about a buyer's interests. Nowadays, with so many industries in play, intelligence gathering is more a matter of course for large companies.

Negotiating and Closing the Deal. Once a candidate has passed through strategic and financial screens, and meets other important criteria, the lead company makes its bid. Generally, in the case of a friendly deal, the negotiations then move ahead to completion. Of course, some deals are contested, and negotiations between the two companies can be carried on for months. Other bids may be offered or solicited. And, if a takeover is attempted, the bidding period can be intense and protracted and white knights may enter into the fray. Friendly or not, once the seller agrees to the terms, and the sale meets shareholder, government, and regulatory approval, the deal is "legal."

These textbook steps make the process of buying and selling companies seem straightforward. Indeed, in a study of eleven acquisitions made by diversified multinational corporations, Professor Philippe Haspeslagh of INSEAD found that most of the companies had *developed* a systematic process for finding acquisition candidates, much like the one just described. He observed, however, that few companies *followed* these steps. Why? Because of internal conflicts in the buying organization, limited analysis of the target, time pressures, and problems in follow-through.[5]

THE POLITICS OF BUYING A COMPANY

To some extent, these impediments to a successful buy have their roots in the political subcultures of a corporation. Strategy making is seldom as crisp and clean as management texts make it seem. Different groups or interests in a company have different stakes in particular strategies and will see unique advantages and disadvantages in one acquisition candidate or another. When unchecked, political infighting can manifest itself in several ways during the search for an acquiree or merger partner:

Mixed Motives. A successful buy is based on sound motivation and strategy. Hence problems begin when buying companies fail to develop a clear, coherent, and agreed-upon course of action. Sometimes conflict emanates from the top when key executives cannot agree on a general corporate direction. More often it arises because corporate staff executives and division managers have differing perspectives on what their company wants (and needs) from a combination. This can lead to haggling over "make or buy" decisions and infighting over acquisition or merger criteria.

Inadequate Screening. A second set of problems concerns the use of competing criteria in the screening of candidates. Analysts and managers employ their own specialized methods and frameworks for evaluating possible acquirees. They also have their own criteria to satisfy in the screening process. Corporate staff, for example, may put more weight on the financial logic of a combination, whereas line executives may put more emphasis on particular manufacturing or marketing synergies. Outside advisors and consultants bring forth additional considerations. When these divergent criteria and interests are brought together in an acquisition team, conflict can erupt. Team members may push candidates that satisfy their own criteria rather than overall company goals. Potentially attractive choices can be passed over because no one champions their cause in the face of disagreement. And the search for a partner may go on endlessly, be narrowed too quickly, or else become polarized around a particular candidate.

Fragmented Picture. Finally, company politics can also prevent a buyer from gaining a complete picture of the combination. Professors David Jemison and Sim Sitkin, of the University of Texas, attribute this to the "fragmentation" of analyses on the buyer's side.[6] Members of the acquisition team focus on the various parts of a target, they report, but oftentimes no one manager or group of managers pulls their information together to assess the whole combination. As a result, the buyer lacks a workable model for integrating the companies. This, in turn, gives isolated functions and managers the license to move ahead on their own self-serving terms.

How can companies counter these political forces? Neither Burroughs' takeover of Sperry nor Times Mirror's acquisition of Graphic Controls provides instructive lessons for buyer and seller. The former was highly secretive and involved two bids. The latter was rapid-fire and culminated in a white knight acquisition. To better depict the complex dynamics of buying-and-selling, we turn our attention to Hewlett Packard's well crafted acquisition of Apollo Computer.

"HEWLETT-PACKARD BUYS APOLLO/ APOLLO BUYS HEWLETT-PACKARD"

This announcement heralded California-based HP's acquisition of Apollo Computer, a Massachusetts manufacturer, while acknowledging equally the smaller company's contribution to the deal. "Together we make a great team," the advertisement concluded. The industry was shocked because "staid" HP, the "grandfather" of Silicon Valley, was making a bold move—its first acquisition in 25 years. The combination moved HP/Apollo ahead of Digital Equipment Corporation and Sun Microsystems to number one in the workstation business.

This April 1989 buy may have surprised the competition but actually culminated 18 months of strategy setting and careful search, screening, and analysis on HP's part. The story behind the deal goes back even farther to the mid-1980s when HP found its customers were substituting workstations for some of its instrumentation products. Accordingly, HP developed its own workstation capability but trailed pioneers Apollo and Sun Microsystems in technology leadership and market penetration.

In early 1988 the Workstation Group in HP committed itself to a "must win" strategy to gain market share. Internal analysts reviewed the company's R&D capability and recommended more investment in networking and graphics. Meanwhile, John Eaton from the corporate development department looked into possible joint ventures (HP had one going with Canon in laser printers) and the option of acquisitions.

During this period, Apollo was wracked with problems. Undercapitalized, with R&D departments pulling in different directions, the company was losing customer confidence and its technological edge. Still, Apollo was very cool when first contacted by HP and other potential suitors. Undeterred, Eaton and Workstation management quietly formed an acquisition team and began to look closely at the financial and strategic implications of buying Apollo. McKinsey & Co., the management consulting firm, was hired by HP to interview Apollo customers and assess its image. By January 1989, HP had developed the "desire to acquire," and Bill Kay, head of HP's Workstation Group, contacted Apollo to show seriousness.

This began an intensive period of analysis where HP tested the business case behind a deal. In February 1988, a "crush" team of financial analysts, hardware and software engineers, and line managers from HP evaluated possible synergies between the companies. Goldman Sachs weighed in with Wall Street's perspective. The results looked promising.

Early analyses showed that Apollo's acquisition would add to HP's market position, offer a short-term competitive advantage in graphics and group computing, and shore up Apollo's financial stability and reputation in the marketplace. There would also be financial synergies: reduced overhead costs and some tax benefits. Consolidation of facilities and manufacturing operations would provide a one-time savings. And sales of HP peripheral products to Apollo customers could be a benefit.

To continue its investigation, HP commissioned several internal task forces to study the financials, assess personnel costs and market conditions, and evaluate the field organizations (domestic and international) of each company. A technical team, comprised of engineers from both companies, determined that the two computing architectures could be integrated on a common product platform. This, according to one engineer, "made the deal."

A thorough review of the task force findings was conducted by top management in March, and the HP Board subsequently reviewed the risks and benefits before giving the go-ahead to a bid for Apollo. The two companies negotiated, and in May 1989 the purchase and sale was complete. HP had done its first deal in decades and was beginning its "second childhood."

LESSONS ON SEARCH AND SELECTION

HP's acquisition of Apollo shows a buyer rather successfully contending with internal politics and competing interests in its search for and selection of an acquiree. Over the course of one and a half years, HP developed a clear and consistent strategy, reconciled many viewpoints in its screening process, undertook a detailed review of the target, and maintained secrecy throughout. Still, fragmentation would complicate the eventual combination. Consider the following:

Set a Clear Strategy. The best way to formulate corporate strategy is to study available options and get agreement to clear objectives. In this case, HP top management initially encouraged debate over the merits of growing internally, forming a joint venture, or seeking an acquisition. When it became apparent, however, that HP would have to "buy" its way to leadership in the workstation business, line management developed unambiguous acquisition criteria: A strong partner to add to its market share, complement its emphasis on open systems and standards, and provide added strength in graphics and network computing.

The larger point is that when they have a voice in and can agree on the merits of a strategy, top executives, corporate planners, and line managers operate from common interest and perspective. To enforce this consensus, of course, corporate leaders need to assert strategic criteria and make sure the acquisition team searches for candidates that fit them.

Thorough Search and Screening. This phase of the process requires finesse. On the one hand, buyers need a team whose members have different skills and who represent divergent interests. On the other, team members need to work together and conflicts have to be reconciled. In this case, HP formed task forces to undertake specialized assessments of Apollo and brought the data together in a series of independent formal screens:

Screen 1: HP Corporate Development and Workstation management reviewed industry profiles and screened out unacceptable candidates. A consulting firm was hired to provide an outsider's viewpoint on the most attractive candidate: Apollo.

Screen 2: A "crush" team, representing senior management, corporate staff, and workstation engineers applied strategic and financial criteria to the acquisition of Apollo. Their focus was on "deal killers."

Screen 3: A series of task forces delved into the technical and operational characteristics of Apollo. Their task was fact-finding, and their charter was to assess whether "theoretical" synergies were "true." At this point, engineers from the two companies talked bits and bytes and managers became acquainted.

Still, HP top management insisted on a full review of the acquisition team's findings and, importantly, demanded careful consideration of downside risks. At this point, concerns over the cost of the transaction and potential problems in putting the companies together poured forth. Accordingly, top management charged Workstation management with formulating its plans for (1) customer retention, (2) employee retention, (3) product integration, and (4) integration of organization and culture.

Pull It All Together. HP chartered various groups to respond to these all-important factors. Corporate communications assessed possible public reactions and customer concerns. Pete Peterson, a top executive in HP's human resource function, led a study of compensation practices and previewed employment levels in the combined companies. Peterson also examined the employment contracts of Apollo's top executives and drafted guidelines for severance agreements for affected employees. Engineering took responsibility for further studying technological integration.

Workstation management, in turn, was asked to develop a plan for how to integrate the two organizations and cultures. Their resulting HP/Apollo Vision emphasized combined product plans and marketing directions. *It did not, however, address the integrated organizational structure and desired culture of the combined HP/Apollo.*

HP had established a good "strategic fit" between the two companies' technologies, product lines, and marketing endeavors. However, Bill Kay, as head of HP's Workstation Group, sales managers in another division, manufacturing managers in a third, and various corporate staff groups had different views of how to capitalize on potential synergies. Thus fragmentation prevented HP from seeing the whole picture. And no one "owned" the acquisition process. What was missing was an appreciation of the "organizational fit" between the companies.

UNDERSTANDING ORGANIZATIONAL FIT

An American Management Association study of over 100 acquirers found that less than 50% had good information on their candidates' budgeting and planning processes and fewer than one-third understood their purchasing, inventory, delivery, or quality control systems. On the crucial matters of computing and MIS compatibility, only half had analyzed hardware systems and less than one-third had adequate information on software and voice and data communication systems.[7]

These were not unfriendly combinations nor was this information withheld for reasons of secrecy. On the contrary, the study found that this information wasn't exchanged because the acquirer never asked for it. The AMA study goes on to show how unforeseen incompatibilities led to problems in integrating financial systems and unwelcome increases in computing expenses.

Important Dimensions to Consider

Size and Shape. The most basic aspects of "organization fit" concern the two companies' size and shape. Superior size, for example, can exacerbate a buyer's natural inclinations to conform subsidiaries to its organizational structure and reporting systems. Some blame Exxon's failure in office systems to the way it "squashed" three small firms together and imposed its corporate bureaucracy. More broadly, a study by analyst John Kitching found that 84% of the failed acquisitions involved cases where the acquired company had less than 2% percent of the sales volume of the parent.[8]

Differences in organizational structure can also presage problems. Professors Anthony Buono and James Bowditch report that a "merger of equals" between a centralized urban bank and decentralized suburban bank devolved into conflict when the suburban bank resisted new reporting relationships and fought off intrusions from the "home office." Differences in size and shape, however, need not doom a combination. Buono and Bowditch show how these differences proved negligible in the case of a food company acquisition where the larger parent gave the "adopted" company plenty of room to grow.[9]

Management Control Systems. A.D. Little analyst Richard Davis cites horror stories where an acquirer's conservative budgeting and control systems forced a subsidiary to drop several speculative ventures and ultimately lose market share, where a parent company's standard compensation package hampered innovation and reduced motivation in an acquiree accustomed to more variable incentives, and where a buyer's complex planning and targeting regimens led to the departure of top technical talent to a competitor where they found a freer hand.[10]

To further the point: The AMA study of more than 100 acquirers found that it took companies nearly twice as long to integrate incompatible versus compatible general ledgers and purchasing, order entry, and distribution systems. The human consequence was twice the rate of turnover.

Human Resources. "People problems" inevitably disrupt a combination whenever the two companies have different approaches to job grading, training, performance appraisal, career development, and other aspects of human resource management.[11] In a case we studied, the merger of Milwaukee's Mt. Sinai and Samaritan hospitals went off course when combined management attempted to regrade jobs and relevel salaries between the merged nursing staffs. A common performance appraisal system was also introduced. Each company's systems had been adapted to different labor markets and nursing skill sets. The merged system, according to one nurse, "didn't satisfy anyone but the 'bureaucrats'."

Again, the AMA study found that combined companies having significant problems with productivity and turnover were three times more likely to have encountered differences between their human resource systems than do those with fewer postmerger problems.

Auditing Organizational "Fit"

Admittedly, it is never easy to conduct a full-scale organizational audit of a candidate (Appendix B provides a list of criteria). Still it is useful for a buying company to develop a framework, understood by members of the search team, that identifies organizational factors that might be critical to the success of the combination. Certainly, a highly centralized company that budgets conservatively should know whether or not a possible partner has many risk takers. And a sales organization which uses a low salary/high commission scheme needs to know how salespeople are rewarded in acquisition candidates.

When the deal is friendly and time permits, a buyer can make organizational assessment an integral part of its due diligence. Grow Group, once a small supplier of solvents and specialty thinners for automakers and now a half-billion-dollar diversified business, is an example. The company has formulated a "comprehensive checklist for an acquisition" that examines the organizational structure, business and MIS systems, and human resource management practices of promising candidates. An acquisition team reviews these criteria with possible candidates, has its management complete the checklist and prepare requested documentation; and then commissions opinions on "fit" from in-house financial groups, an environmental committee, human resources, and varied line executives.

Human Resource Involvement. Studies by David Robino and Kenneth DeMeuse confirm that executives downplay human resource factors before the combination but elevate their significance afterward.[12] Furthermore, a study of British acquisitions by Egon Zehnder International found that companies who gave combined organizational structures and systems a clear "people shape" (cited by 59% of successful acquirers) had better results than did those who confined their designs to prevailing business or theoretical parameters (cited by 61% of acquirers having problems).[13]

It makes sense, therefore, to involve human resource executives from both sides in early dealings and to gather their counsel not only on HR matters but more broadly on the human side of the combination.[14] HR's facility with interpersonal relations, where present, can also help in conflict management in an acquisition team and promote better dialogue between the two managements who may be unsure of each other's motivations and intentions.

Counsel may also be needed in specialized HR areas. Many executives in selling companies have employment contracts with parachute provisions. Expert analysis of the legal and financial implications of these arrangements can forestall later problems or, at least, limit the "surprise." Labor lawyers may be needed to review collective bargaining agreements and forewarn management about the likely impact of proposed changes. And, of course, experts in employee benefits—another area where the AMA found incompatibilities often lead to problems—have much to contribute.

The Problems with "Misfit"

"Misfits" between the buyer's and seller's organization may not make or break a deal, but they will require careful post-merger management. Return to the case of HP and Apollo: Hewlett-Packard, a $9 billion company with 90,000 employees, is a multidivision business. Its Workstation Group was only one part of a larger business sector that included personal computers, peripherals, and other product lines. That sector, in turn, was nested in the Computer Business Organization that had separate arms for manufacturing, networks, marketing and sales, and international operations. The key point: HP was a big company, complex to Apollo eyes, with diverse responsibilities and work charters parsed out among various groups, divisions, sectors, and lines of business.

HP managed all of these interdependencies through matrix management and formal planning, targeting, and measurement systems. A large corporate staff department, in turn, formulated policies and reviewed results to ensure commonality and coordination across the company.

Apollo, by comparison, with $600 million in annual sales and 4,000 employees, was organized by function. It was, however, very closely tied together as a result of its size and operation as a stand-alone business. Marketing and R&D, for example, worked as a team in product planning and development and sales and service were closely linked with the factory. Apollo defined itself as a "systems integrator" and operated through the bottom-up collaboration of people from many specialties and functions. HP seemed to be more of a "components" company in its approach to engineering. Various "entities" were assigned parts of a project and tasked through the company's infamous management-by-objectives approach.

How would the two organizations fit together? One integration model would have HP "adopt" Apollo but run it as a separate "entity." This would give the subsidiary needed cash and marketing muscle. The problem: It would cancel financial synergies and work against product integration. It would also leave Apollo sales and manufacturing as "stand alone" cost centers outside of the reach of the centralized HP manufacturing and field organizations. Too costly, said HP manufacturing and field executives. And *too different.*

Another approach would have HP "occupy" Apollo and wholly integrate it. This would make it conform to the HP structure. The problem: It would work against brand identity and customer retention. It might also cause employee turnover and risk the "crown jewels"—Apollo's R&D capability. Workstation management fought against this option. "You don't spend $500 million to buy technology and talented people," argued one group manager, and then "piss it away."

A function-to-function mapping of the two organizations shows clearly the problem of "misfit" in this case. (See Figure 3.1.)

In the end, HP decided to integrate Apollo partially— with manufacturing and sales to be absorbed and marketing and engineering to operate semiautonomously as part of the Workstation Group. Even this would be tricky because Apollo graphics and software would be matrixed into other parts of HP and only hardware R&D would develop its own programs and products.

HP's "mixed model" would break up the formerly integrated Apollo business. For the deal to achieve HP's strategic aims, the Apollo division would have to find a niche

Figure 3.1
Organization Fit—Hewlett Packard and Apollo

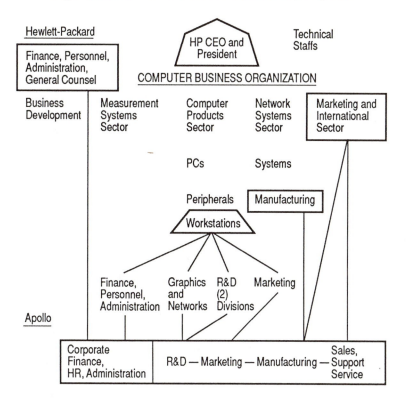

Figure 3.2
When Companies Don't Fit Together as Depicted
by Acquired Company

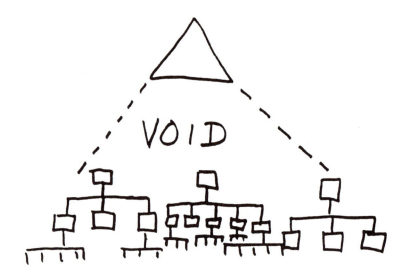

in HP's Workstation organization and learn to work through various matrix relationships in the parent company. Manufacturing and sales would have to learn to do things the "HP way." In the meantime, differences in the structures and reporting relationships between the two organizations would create a "void." (See Figure 3.2.)

CULTURAL COMPATIBILITY

There is a difference between organizational and cultural compatibility. Organizational characteristics are the visible aspects of how a company is organized and operates. Knowledge about formal structure, systems, methods, staffing ratios, and such can be obtained via organization charts, planning documents, and, when circumstances allow, presentations and briefings. It is also important to delve into the informal organization, exploring beliefs and values in the two companies, and evaluating how things really work.

The Stepford Wives versus the Hell's Angels

When HP and Apollo people first met, for example, some clear cultural differences came to the fore. HP people were very polished, professional, and company minded. Many had long tenure and had grown up in HP. By comparison, Apollo people were more entrepreneurial and accustomed to job hopping. As a consequence, some in Apollo were excited about working in a well-managed and high quality company. Others were wary of bureaucracy and began to look around for another start-up situation. This would have an impact on postcombination turnover.

These stylistic differences were evident in norms in the two companies. HPers were described as very polite and collegial at initial meetings. No one would raise his or her voice or confront directly another manager. In addition, HPers were seen as good listeners, good at summarizing points, and honestly interested in doing what was best for the company. This was their emphasis in discussions of the combined company's design.

By contrast, Apollo people seemed more politically oriented (particularly senior management) and inclined to slug it out in public forums. Heated confrontation was not only accepted, it was expected. To some Apollo engineers, "winning" meant advancing your own project whatever the true benefits to the company. This was their orientation to the combination.

Needless to say, cultural differences would complicate planning in this case. The problems were summed up by the characterization of HP people as the "Stepford wives" and Apollo people as the "Hell's Angels." That said, there were three key factors would facilitate cultural integration in this case:

1. HP and Apollo were in the same industry. Because the two companies could "talk" common technology, customers, and competitors, and because each had faced common problems, there was a natural affinity between people from both sides.

2. HP created a joint-company planning process that would allow both sides to develop a better understanding of and more respect for one another.

3. Turf struggles, confusion, and culture clashes marked early integration, but both sides recognized that Sun and DEC were forging ahead in the marketplace. An external "enemy" helped competing interests to come together.

Testing Compatibility

We have worked with several companies prior to their legal combination to assess cultural compatibility. Managers in each of the organizations are asked to identify (1) the physical and structural characteristics of their business (2) how the organization actually operates and (3) the beliefs and values behind these practices. This kind of analysis delves into the depths of an organization, moving from surface characteristics to norms and practices to the core beliefs (see Appendix C). Care needs to be taken to identify whether specific practices are to be found companywide or are unique to particular functions or divisions. It is also important to ascertain whether cultural beliefs and values are shared among members of an organization or specific to particular sub-cultures.

Once these rosters are complete for each of the companies, the two sides are brought together to describe, say, what structures and systems they have and how they really function. The intent is to reveal, for example, not only how information is collected and disseminated, but how it is used by managers and for what purposes. In one case, for example, the two companies appeared to have very compatible budgeting and control systems. However, it was learned that one company took its projections very seriously, tracked results weekly, and that group managers presented the data to senior management for regular review. In the other company, by contrast, projections were ballpark figures and revised regularly through consultation with peers and staff personnel. Senior management had confidence in group management and operated on a management-by-exception approach. These seemingly similar systems were based in different management cultures and a closer look at these differences led the two managements to revise plans for integrating planning and control systems.[15]

THE RUSH TO CLOSE

Psychologist Harry Levinson says that "When companies merge and acquire, it's a lot like falling in love. They don't want to be dissuaded. And they certainly don't want to be careful about it. They just want to jump in."[16] Why this pressure to speed up such a critical decision? Executives often come to identify with a candidate and, whether their aim is courtship or conquest, they may not consider the risks objectively or slow down their momentum once the other party is in their sights. Line managers charged with screening candidates are eager to return to their primary responsibilities. Their near-term rewards come from producing operational results, not from screening out candidates. Outside advisors, especially investment bankers, are compensated on a transaction basis, so it is in their interest to conclude the transaction quickly and get on to the next one.

There are additional forces which increase the momentum to close a deal. First, acquisition decision makers are often isolated from their organizations. They don't have access to dispassionate colleagues who can add "reality checks" to the screening process. Second, they have to maintain secrecy. This further isolates them from wide-ranging counsel. Third, prestige is on the line. Kudos go to those who complete a deal. There will be second-guessing if the transaction falls apart at the last minute.

Buyer Beware. Before completing the transaction, the consequences of the acquisition for all stakeholders must be examined—including customers, suppliers, employees, unions, communities, and stockholders. Resistance from each party should be considered as part of the basic decision to acquire and the eventual implementation plan.

To alleviate the pressure to rush through this phase, acquisition teams need to be coached and encouraged to delve into organizational and cultural fit. Incentive systems that recognize thoroughness and effort, not necessarily whether it leads to a sale, reward managers for making good buys and for resisting bad ones. Another way to reward managers for making good buys is to tie incentives to the longer-term performance of subsidiaries not just near-term results.

There is something to the adage that haste makes waste. A Peat, Marwick & Mitchell study of 22 leading companies with extensive acquisition programs faulted buying companies for failing to consider (1) whether professional and managerial talent in an acquiree was sufficient and could be retained, (2) whether the buyer could easily replace departed talent and had an executive who could lead the combination, and (3) whether there was sufficient chemistry and compatibility between the companies to make the combination work.[17] All three of these factors need careful consideration before a deal is completed.

Follow-Through

As the deal is completed, the problem of fragmentation comes full circle. Line management, for example, may adopt a "go-slow" attitude and look to get better acquainted with acquired marketing and manufacturing managers before moving ahead with any integration. By contrast, the CFO and financial staff are often revved up to begin consolidations and introduce corporate financial and planning systems.

Who is positioned to negotiate these competing models of integration? Oftentimes, no one manager or a group of managers maintains a generalist's grasp of the transaction.[18] As a result, the strategy for combining is uncoordinated and an acquisition team will send "mixed messages" on how the two companies will be combined. Then, of course, staff and line management descend on the acquiree with their own plans and priorities and a siege is underway.

To complicate matters, top management often ends its involvement with the purchased partner at this point and turns integration over to business group managers. The problem is twofold: First, group managers may not have participated in establishing the logic behind the combination, and, second, they may not had the opportunity to study for themselves the most appropriate course of action. Nonetheless, they are handed over fixed expectations from acquisition planners along with implicit urgings to do necessary dirty work from top management. In many cases, the "handoff" to a group vice president and functional heads results in a "fumble."

Caution Before Closing. Successful buyers have a clear sense of the "game plan" when they close a deal—the subject of our next chapter on strategic and psychological preparation. And successful sellers know what they have gotten themselves into. Certainly it is crucial for the two managements to have gotten better acquainted before the close, where this is possible, and for the group managers who will ultimately run the business to have had their say-so.

This is the last chance to test assumptions and understandings—otherwise, they may haunt the honeymoon. Group management needs to consider carefully whether or not target company expectations are realistic and whether promises proffered during courtship will be honored in a breach. Moreover they can also speak frankly to acquired executives about integration prerequisites: where consolidation is likely, where differences in culture will and will not be tolerated, and, frankly, where the lead company management is unwilling to negotiate. As frequent buyer Willard Rockwell states, "the more thorns we extract at the outset, the less chance of infection later on. The earlier we make our intentions known, the smaller the possibility of subsequent misunderstanding."[19]

Furthermore, it is up to the buyer to have managers at the ready to replace departing target company executives. Whether desired or not, turnover of top people is a fact of life in mergers and acquisitions today. Peter Drucker cautions:

> It is an elementary fallacy to believe one can "buy" management. The buyer has to be prepared to lose the top incumbents in companies that are bought. Top people are used to being bosses; they don't want to be "division managers."[20]

"KING BROADCASTING FOR SALE— EVERYTHING MUST GO!"

A Seattle television entertainment program had a field day with its "everything must go—cameras, lights, helicopters" spoof over the proposed sale of King Broadcasting, a 40-year-old privately owned media company in the Pacific Northwest. Other skits featured home video shopping for "one media empire" and a Nike-esque advertisement saying "just buy it." Inside King, meanwhile, there was confusion and concern.

King was founded by Dorothy Bullitt in the late 1940s who served as its "conscience and queen" until her death in June 1989. Two sisters inherited ownership of the company and in August 1990 shocked employees by announcing that they were selling the company and using the proceeds to "protect and enhance the high quality of air, water, and land throughout the Northwest."

Environmentalists hailed the message. But to King people, like reporter Julie Blacklow, it felt "like a punch to the heart." The press projected Capital Cities or General Electric as possible buyers. Both would mean "an end to King as we know it," said one employee, and the beginning of an era "where 'bean counters' run broadcasting." Industry analysts speculated that buyers would spin off King's cable systems. Meanwhile, insiders worried that King's commitment to public service would erode.

"We're not on the auction block!" countered CEO Steve Clifford. Indeed the sisters reported, "We're in no hurry to sell. The company is in good shape. We can wait until we get a good offer." With that said, they and other Board members formulated three criteria for a buyer. One who would:

1. Buy the company as a single entity—no deals for just tv, radio, or cable;

2. Have respect for King employees—and treat them right;

3. Have a track record of public service and social responsibility.

This would mean, as Harriet Bullitt said, "There are certainly people we will not sell it to." With these three criteria, management began the business of searching for a buyer and responding to overtures.[21]

The Selling Side

As the King case illustrates, selling company executives are by no means passive participants in this process. They must, for example, assemble data on their company, set their own criteria for a desirable owner, and scout for buyers.

Many times, too, they seek particular parent companies and do their part in courtship rituals. In these respects, the seller and buyer operate in parallel. Nonetheless, selling executives have somewhat different motivations in the transaction and contend with particular dilemmas when completing the sale.

Motivations to Sell. Owners of privately or closely held firms may sell for any of a number of personal reasons, ranging from restlessness, retirement, and the absence of an heir to marital, health, or financial problems. In the King case, for instance, the sister/owners reported: "We'd rather sell now at a time we choose than wait for a forced sale when we die. That happens to a lot of families and we just didn't want it to happen to King." Certainly their philanthropic aspirations were unique. And the fact that King was so healthy and profitable puts it among a select group of selling companies.

More often, reasons for selling a private or smaller public company center on management's inability to grow the business, sustain profitability, or cope with a downturn. Divestitures account for a substantial number of larger-company deals. But, in either case, there is often the connotation, warranted or not, that top management on the selling side has "failed."

This sense of failure subtly permeates the seller's motivations. For instance, it often means that owners and managers are fixated on their asking price to the exclusion of other considerations in keeping the business a going concern. King formulated strict criteria for a buyer. Other companies aren't so choosy and, in the heat of negotiations, focus their attentions primarily on the financial contours of the deal. Certainly an inflated selling price provides failing management some psychological recompense. It also gives them a handsome financial payout. It can, however, put a substantial debt burden on the acquired company and force new corporate owners into otherwise unnecessary cost cutting or asset sales.

Second, a sense of failure often puts sellers at the seeming "mercy" of buyers in the marketplace. Psychologist Lawrence Tuller notes that many selling companies, cash-poor and lacking confidence, jump at the first attractive offer without carefully considering the consequences. Oftentimes, they fail to evaluate the fit between companies or preview the eventual combination. This is not simply a matter of financial fixation and greed. Tuller suggests that sellers are afraid of not finding another buyer.[22]

This speaks directly to the seller's motivations. In a study of 200 acquired owner/CEOs, Robert Hayes and Gerald Hoag found that 87% of those who remained after the acquisition put substantial effort into investigating their potential acquirers.[23] Certainly this was the intent of King's owners who, though they planned to leave the business, felt deeply committed to management and employees.

By comparison, the vast majority of owner/CEOs who left early limited their inquiries to financial matters, in many cases simply accepting the offer of the highest bidder. Very little time was invested in getting to know the acquirer's top executives or management philosophies. The majority were unaware of why the parent company had acquired them and admitted making no effort to determine what plans, if any, the parent company had for their businesses. In many cases, the owners dealt almost entirely through intermediaries such as brokers or investment bankers.

Needless to say, this cavalier attitude has implications for managers and employees who stay with the business. It is not unusual for them to point the finger at the departing owner/CEO for "selling out" and leaving the company in shambles. This is complicated, of course, when acquired senior managers have severance arrangements that allow them to "cash in." Here, too, the sense of failure plays a part. Many executives simply prefer to "start over" rather than dedicate further effort to an enterprise where they see themselves as having failed.

Certainly these human factors make dealing difficult—for both buyer and seller. Furthermore, a good deal doesn't necessarily make a good combination. The two sides have to get better acquainted and plan the next moves. This is complicated when the integration is complex and the two cultures are not so compatible. It's even harder when people aren't psychologically prepared to join.

CHAPTER 4

Strategic and Psychological Preparation

I have seen the relationships of acquiring and acquired organizations strained terribly by inadequate preparation, lack of foresight—even outright deceit. Repeatedly, executives directly responsible for negotiations have reneged on commitments...when integrating a new company into the parent organization. One reason executives reverse themselves so frequently, and relationships disintegrate at the integration stage, is that no adequate conceptual scheme exists with which to think through and to plan the acquisition process in its entirety.
—Robert A. Howell, "Plan to Integrate Your Acquisitions," *Harvard Business Review* [1]

"There's especially a lot of emotion in it when you're under attack," says John Grady, former vice-president for finance at Garlock. *"It's as if you've just found out that someone's made a more attractive offer to your wife."*
—from "Two Tough Lawyers in the Tender-Offer Game," Stephen Brill, *New York*, June 21, 1976. [2]

At 4:00, right after the market close on Monday, May 5, 1986, word hit the street that Burroughs wanted to acquire all of Sperry's 58 million shares of outstanding stock, trading at around $50 a share, for $70 a share in cash and securities. Blumenthal was bullish when he telephoned Sperry president

Joe Kroger, talked with him about the necessity for a quick response, and steeled himself for the bidding game. Kroger and his colleagues at Sperry were "struck dead." They had analyzed their own merger and acquisition preferences and ranked Burroughs "dead last." They found there to be too many incompatibilities between the two companies' product lines and market directions and fretted over the financial implications of a merger. There was, moreover, widespread skepticism in the market and industry about the prospects of the merger. The new company's revenues were only one-fifth of those of industry leader IBM, and analysts predicted that its growth in market share would be negligible. There would be massive debt to service and some predicted that layoffs and divestitures would amount to a "blood bath." Certainly history was working against the combination. Honeywell's acquisition of GE's computer business and Sperry's purchase of RCA's had both been failures. Would this combination be "inspiration," as Blumenthal wished it, or "desperation" as many analysts projected?

Burroughs people were undaunted; they had the mind-set of winners: "Everyone was up. We were the aggressors." But behind the elation were speculation and intrigue. There were business and personal gains to be had from consolidating Sperry operations, adding new customers and markets, and filling in Burroughs' product line. However, no one had any detail on how or when this would be done.

On the Sperry side, there was as much uncertainty and plenty of dismay. "Top management told us this would be bad—disastrous" noted one midlevel manager. Another reported, "Our people are not emotionally prepared. I have one guy who is a 32-year employee. When I told him he would never have to prepare another quarterly report bearing our company name he started crying right there on the phone."

This chapter looks at the critical precombination period where the integration framework is set and people and companies prepare to join. It considers the mind-set established in the Burroughs and Sperry merger where customers might defect, and a hostile bid put the two companies at odds. Next it looks at models of integration and how companies can apply them to think through their strategies. Finally, the chapter examines the emotions associated with buying and being bought and what can be done to establish mutual expectations and some degree of comfort between combining managements.

MAKING
THE BUSINESS CASE

Two factors lay behind Burroughs' purchase of Sperry. First was the market benefit: the customer confidence to be gained by "critical mass." Second was cost savings: the promise of greater combined efficiency. Blumenthal and a team of top-level Burroughs executives had spent months gathering data from industry analysts, trade publications, and knowledgeable executives to formulate a "first-pass" strategy for consolidation and cost cutting. Financial synergies could be realized in (1) procurement systems and supply relationships, (2) product and market planning, (3) manufacturing and assembly operations, (4) capital spending, and (5) administrative overhead. The strategy in R&D would be to maintain both companies' computing architectures while promoting the cross-fertilization of technologies, and strengthening efforts in advanced system design, distributed processing, data communications, and artificial intelligence.

This was, in outline, the business case for ensuring, at minimum, the survival of the combined company through an advancing industry shake-out and, at best, its rise to become the preferred alternative to "Big Blue." Still, Sperry customers were doubtful that separate architectures would be maintained and industry analysts predicted that a substantial chunk of the Sperry user base would defect. After all, 44% of the Sperry Series 1100 users also worked with IBM. Software conversion costs would be an effective barrier to the loss of upgrade business, but there was a clear risk that, unless user fears were allayed, new applications might increasingly go to IBM.

Furthermore, there was widespread conviction that Blumenthal could never make the combination work. Wrote one analyst,

> If Mike B. gets bogged down in the potentially enormous and massively disruptive internecine product and turf squabbles, then it's a bad deal for everyone directly involved—shareholders, employees, customers—and the industry will love it. In that case, the stock is an AVOID.[3]

A MERGER OF EQUALS

Right after Sperry agreed to the sale to Burroughs, Blumenthal moved quickly to get the two companies into the merger-of-equals mind-set. He announced, for example, that Sperry president, Joe Kroger, would join Burroughs' president, Paul Stern, on a joint-company leadership team. To retain Sperry management, he also proposed new five-year employment contracts with 26 key employees, replacing severance agreements previously in effect. The new agreements were designed to allow Burroughs more flexibility in moving the executives to other jobs with "comparable" duties. But the whole emphasis was to keep Sperry leadership, which was the link to the Sperry customer base.

In addition, Blumenthal further articulated the principles that would govern the merger:

1. **Partnership**—The idea that the two sides will come together as equals. Partnership and equality, rather than takeover with winners and losers, will be the basis for combination actions.

2. **A New Identity**—Neither Sperry nor Burroughs will survive; a new company with a new identity and a new name will be created. A new identity will eliminate a sense of competition and hasten the development of common commitment to a new idea.

3. **Meritocracy**—In the new company, the jobs will go to those best qualified, regardless of which company they come from. This is the good old American principle that what counts is not where you come from or who you know, but what you can do.

The lead party in a takeover is expected to dominate and have its way with a target. Because the success of this merger depended upon partnership, and because Blumenthal had the power and conviction to insist on meritocracy and unity, a combination of co-equals was begun. Sperry head Joe Kroger recalled,

I give Mike great credit. This 'merger' idea was a big culture shock for Burroughs when they found out they were not necessarily going to be the dominant player. He made it clear that these two companies were coming together and we would pick the best people for the jobs.[4]

STRATEGIC PREPARATION

The deal is done. In the best of cases, the buyer has sound reasons for undertaking the merger or acquisition and has found a company that fits most of the desired criteria. Now the two managements establish a skeletal model for integrating and prepare for the flesh-and-blood work of bringing their creation to life.

High-level leadership on both sides is crucial at this phase. Buyers often have fragmented and self-serving images of the combination. Sellers seldom have their act together. This means top management on the buyer's side needs to take an active role in establishing the integration framework and its meaning for management. Certainly Blumenthal exercised this leadership when defining key synergies in the Burroughs and Sperry merger and setting staunch principles for putting the two businesses together.

This is the essence of strategic preparation: making sure management on both sides understand the synergies behind the combination and what it will take to realize them. The aim is to get them into the right mind-set. More detailed analyses, models, and plans for integrating through the ranks come later—after the two sides are legally combined, managers begin to work more closely with counterparts, and complicated situations can be studied in more depth.

What do managers need to think through at this stage? Thoughtful answers to the following questions establish the basic parameters for integrating two businesses:

1. Is the combination a merger of equals or an acquisition?
2. What are the "real" synergies in the combination?
3. How much integration is needed to make the combination work?

Merger or Acquisition?

As we noted in Chapter 2, the combination "script" is set by the relative size of the two companies and the friendliness of their intentions. Still, it is quite common for buying companies to misrepresent the true story line: We've heard many "parent" company executives position their friendly acquisitions as a "true marriage." This sets up false expectations of equal power and voice in integration decisions—particularly on the "adopted" company's side. (See Figure 4.1.)

Figure 4.1
Merger or Acquisition?
As Depicted by Acquired Employee

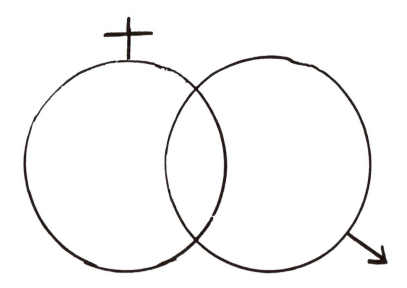

Merger: "Look those two are making love!"

Acquisition: "Look somebody's getting screwed!"

Take the case of a high-tech acquisition where the parent company promised to take "best from both" and "merge systems and people." Acquired management cheered the prospects and bathed in the "warm and fuzzy" manner of their large and successful buyer. One year later, 85 out of the top 100 acquired managers had left—"burned but not surprised," said one exiting executive, by their new owner's "clumsy and heavy-handed manuevers." "I just wish they had told us the truth at the start," said another, "maybe we could've gotten our 'mind right' and approached this thing differently."

Make Intentions Clear. Compare this buyer's waffling with the words of another CEO who made his intentions perfectly clear to acquired management:

> We did one "hands-off" acquisition and lost money. We did another like "two equals," had a hell of a lot of problems, and lost money. This one we're doing "our way". We're successful and people like working here. We think you'll like it, too. We're not "know-it-alls" and there's plenty of opportunity for good people in our company. But, if you can't deal with this, get out of the way as fast as you can, "cause we're moving ahead."

Interestingly, this straight-talking acquirer retained most of the subsidiary's senior managers, introduced change with plenty of input and no more than the usual resistance, and made money on the deal. Not warm and fuzzy, to be sure, but as one acquired executive said, the CEO was "smart, fair, and a straight shooter," adding, "and a welcome change from the usual bullshit."

Straight talk has to be complemented by hands-on leadership to keep a friendly merger friendly and maintain reasonable power parameters between a parent company and subsidiary. In the case of Burroughs and Sperry, it would taken an extra measure of evenhandedness and leadership work to turn the seeming "conquest" into a merger of equals. By contrast, it takes scarcely any effort at all to transform a friendly acquisition into an "occupation."

For example, Times Mirror executives were "honorable" toward Graphic Control's managers, but they weren't involved when corporate staff descended on the subsidiary.

"One (financial type) brought in a big book of rules and regulations and thrust it at me," GC's CEO Will Clarkson recalled, "in effect saying, 'this will bring you to heel.' We just had to do it the way they wanted it done, period. No ifs, ands, or buts. It was done thoughtlessly, territorially." Power plays by corporate finance and human resource managers wreak havoc in many acquisitions. Its up to top management to establish the integration framework and to ensure that unwarranted and unbecoming power moves are prohibited and punished. Otherwise, there is no need to think through the integration. It's an academic exercise and merely delays the bloodletting.

Sources of Synergy?

The "added value" of a combination is reflected in the potential synergies between the two companies.[5] Operational synergies, for example, come from combining and consolidating two businesses in the same industry. Many mergers and acquisitions in health care, financial services, the airlines, the oil industry, and pharmaceuticals are predicated on such synergies. In these instances, firms join to reduce costs, create barriers to competition, and win greater market share.

More specific product or marketing synergies come from the combining of manufacturing, sourcing, and distribution (in product-extension mergers) or of marketing, sales, and service (in market-extension deals). This gives the buyer more flexible manufacturing, greater market power, and certain economies of scope. In turn, the acquiree gains access to capital, more manufacturing facilities, larger distribution channels, and, in theory, more professional management.

Synergy can also come from the transfer of strategic capability between companies. Here it is imperative either to transfer resources between the two companies or to share distinct skills and know-how. HP's acquisition of Apollo was based in this motivation. GM's acquisition of Ross Perot's EDS and IBM's stakes in Rolm, MCI, and Intel all rested on the desire for technology transfer in exchange for funding.

Set Priorities. Every merger or acquisition yields a roster of *potential* synergies. It's up to top executives to identify which ones are *critical* to success. Blumenthal, for example, made continuation of both Burroughs' and Sperry's product lines a cornerstone of integration. This signaled customers that they could count on continuity from their vendors and sent a reassuring message to the two company's R&D teams that their jobs were secure. Blumenthal also pledged from the start to retain the two companies' sales forces. He reasoned that while manufacturing would put up with some confusion from "headquarters," the sales force might bolt. To preempt this, he announced that sales would be "strengthened" in the new organization.

Chemical Bank's Approach. When top executives define the key synergies and financial benefits to a combination, they also need to be aware of risks and potential problems. Counsel from planning and human resource specialists can help to inform the pace of their decision making.

When Chemical Bank acquired Texas Commerce, for example, a team of merger planners from both sides undertook a benefit-risk assessment that compared desired synergies against potential integration problems. Among the roster of human and logistical problems identified were:

- Turnover of key people
- Refusing assignments/malcontents
- Relocation costs/downtime
- Post merger performance drops
- Lost customers/capacity/synergies
- Morale problems

Figure 4.2 shows how the planners proposed the two companies approach integration decisions based upon (1) the value of synergies versus (2) the risks in integration. As a result of these analyses, the two banks preplanned their general integration under a holding company structure and postponed major decisions involving centralization and consolidation until the two managements could study the situation more fully.

Figure 4.2
Pacing of Integration in Merger

	Low Risk in Integration	High Risk in Integration
Integration: *High* Savings and Synergy	DO IT! Pre-Plan it now	WAIT! Study it together
Integration: *Low* Savings and Synergy	HOLD OFF! Post-Plan it later.	FORGET IT!

Degree of Integration?

Integration is not an "all or nothing" proposition. Options range from full integration and consolidation to near separation of the firms in a holding company model with various levels of "coupling" in between.[6] The degree of integration is typically determined by the operational and financial synergies between companies. It's up to senior management to set guidelines for conduct consistent with the appropriate degree of integration sought. (See Figure 4.3.)

Full integration is most common in cases where companies buy within their industry. Large acquirers, for example, often control operations in a smaller subsidiary and combine product lines, marketing, and sales. In the case of full-scale mergers, of course, the two companies' R&D labs, supply and distribution channels, and corporate staffs are also combined.

This kind of combination has the highest success rate among all types. But success hinges on two sets of managers learning to cooperate and work together. Certainly problems with organizational and cultural fit can work against them. Furthermore, Professors Andrew van de Ven and David Bastien make the point that full integration is the most stressful way of combining—it upsets both businesses and puts

Figure 4.3
Degree of Integration between Companies

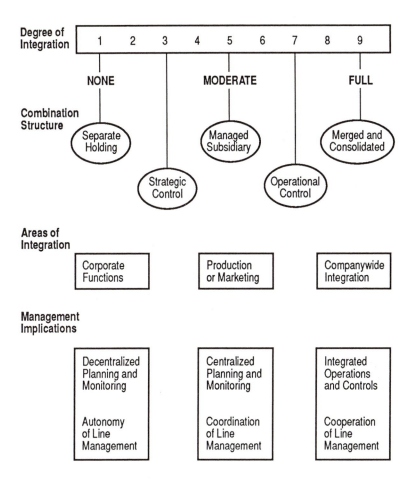

people in direct competition.[7] Pledges of meritocracy sound noble, but the real test is whether these promises are honored in a breach.

Partial integration is most likely in cases where the buying company wants to add to its product line or extend its market reach. These deals are tricky—as Apollo and HP learned. They require a balance between the buyer's needs to control products and/or markets and the subsidiary's needs for autonomy. High levels of cooperation are essential to gaining the synergies that come from the transfer of management expertise, marketing or manufacturing knowledge, as well as technology and other valuable intellectual resources.

The scorecard on these types of combinations is comparatively poor. Initial savings in corporate staff reductions can be offset by coordination costs. Partial integration also can send "mixed messages" to subsidiary management as to "who's in charge" and disrupt the operating rhythms of what was once a freestanding business. This puts the onus on managers—from the lead and acquired company—to think through integration options carefully and devise workable methods to coordinate their efforts.

Lower levels of integration are found when companies combine for the sake of financial investment. The successful scenario for a lead company in this financial arrangement is straightforward: Leave the other company's management structure in place; capitalize on modest financial synergies in banking, legal, and stockholder relationships; perhaps work together on selected projects, but otherwise keep an arm's-length distance.

As sensible as this sounds, there are plenty of horror stories where the parent company "smothers" a subsidiary with reporting requirements and controls. The problem is that the buyer's financial systems are dominated by the logic of it's core business. Its planning cycles, expectations of risk and return, and systems of measurement and evaluation, developed to suit one type of business, often don't fit the circumstances of an acquiree. Nevertheless, lead companies often impose these methodologies on companies whose very success depends upon the integrity of their homegrown systems. Merger analyst Mark Shanley notes that this "centralized" approach to integration can drive away many layers of management and lessen earnings.[8]

Furthermore, it also takes time to realize a financial payoff following modest levels of integration. In a study of 16 acquisitions by ten conglomerates, two business school professors found "acquisitions that were motivated by the parent firm's desires for immediate financial results were not found to be very successful. Even the most successful acquisitions took up to five years to meet management's expectations."[9]

Turnarounds. Naturally, the value added equation is different when a buyer acquires a troubled business. When a target is performing poorly, the lead firm has to effect a financial turnaround. This means transferring in management, bringing in new technology and systems, setting ambitious performance schedules, and often micromanaging cost-cutting activities.

However, turnarounds need not involve the usual "housecleaning." Take the approach Sanyo followed in its acquisition of Warwick. Sanyo executives found one Warwick plant so unkempt that they immediately had the facility cleaned and painted. Along with an infusion of capital, they arranged to rehire previously laid off employees to meet increased product demand.

This is the case where a business buys into a new market and supports a company lagging in its growth plans. Typically, the parent company shapes the subsidiary's long-range business directions. And shorter-range profit plans and budgets are given close scrutiny along with various exception reports. McKinsey & Co. recommend that parent companies act as a "sponsor" of subsidiaries in these kinds of deals.

UNIHEALTH AMERICA: MAKING TIME AN ASSET

The time between the seller's decision to accept the buyer's offer and the legal combination of firms is crucial for setting the combination off on the right course. This can be a substantial amount of time—over two years elapsed while regulatory bodies deliberated the proposed merger of Southern California Edison and San Diego Gas and Electric—

and it can be wasted or put to good use. The experience of UniHealth America shows how to make time an asset.

Lutheran Health Society (LHS) and HealthWest merged in the summer of 1988, creating UniHealth America, a $1-billion- plus holding company with 12 nonprofit medical centers, 2 health maintenance organizations (HMOs), and various other health care services.

Samuel Tibbitts, Lutheran's CEO, had a clear vision of the combined company: "It had to be a true integration. The whole basis for merging was to pull from the strengths of the two sides to create a strong organization to compete in the southern California market." LHS and HealthWest organized their respective HMOs differently. LHS operated a "group model" in which members chose a physician group with practitioners in various specialties. HealthWest allowed each family member to choose an individual physician as their primary care physician. Moreover, LHS's HMO was much larger (320,000 subscribers compared to 50,000 in HealthWest's HMO) and, unlike HealthWest's, federally qualified.

Tibbitts assigned the responsibility for studying organizational fit to both firms' senior corporate planners. They compared financial synergies against possible organizational problems. "First we had to know where integration made sense," Tibbetts recalled, "and only then did we begin to look at cost savings which might be achieved. So we sent off the planners. They came back and said, 'there's a good fit between the organizations, but a problem with the HMOs.'"

Their "first-pass" acquisition model was modified to leave the HMOs separate, while integrating all other business units. Then the two sides' corporate planning executives were joined by the two CEOs and both sides' chief legal counsels. "We only went forward with decisions if everyone—the board, planning group, and management—believed it was the right thing to do," emphasized Tibbitts. "This saved us when one side or the other was ready to walk. We'd have to go back to the table and work things out."

Even in such a friendly combination, there are cultural problems to contend with. In the creation of UniHealth, differences in philosophies of management control cropped up.

LHS was run in a decentralized mode, while HealthWest was strongly centralized. Finally a compromise was struck, with former LHS business units retaining their autonomy in some areas but conforming to more centralized policies and controls. "It was enough for me to be comfortable with," conceded Tibbitts.

Finally, LHS and HealthWest used the several months required for legal review and approval to set up the new company's management structure and put it to work. "Over nine months, the top team came to decisions on just about everything. By the time we merged, all policies were approved by both sides' boards, human resources programs were set, and it was determined who would stay and who would go in the first personnel cut."

Certainly time can be an asset. Still, unforeseen complications and unintended consequences await managers and employees on both sides. A sound strategic mind-set readies people for the tactical work ahead. They also need to be psychologically prepared for the human trials and trauma—many of which they have begun to experience in this precombination phase.

THE MIND-SET OF THE BUYER

To the victors go the spoils. Certainly takeovers are exhilarating for the winners. But even for executives involved in planning and executing a friendly deal, there are few moments in a career which equal the intensity and satisfaction of buying another company.

An Air of Superiority. This translates into a strong sense of superiority in the lead firm. The lead company's executives have just made a big deal. They are heady, confident, on a roll. This attitude carries over into assumptions that the winning company's procedures, policies, and systems are superior to those of the purchased firm. Being the dominant party also contributes to condescending attitudes about the other side: "They are still battling the problems we solved five years ago;" "Wait until we show them how to do things;" "Our systems will really bring them into the 1990s!" or "They are nice enough people, but they need a lesson or two on how to run a business."

A Sense of Urgency. As the combination begins, lead companies are impelled to move fast and consolidate their gains. The team which has orchestrated the deal—the CEO, outside lawyers and bankers, and, perhaps, a few senior executives—often hand off the task of integration to, say, a group vice president and functional managers, each of whom have their own agenda and plans. What they have in common is a need to gain control.

There is always some uncertainty about precisely what has been bought—who they are, what they do, and whether or not they really know how to run their business. The sense of superiority often leads acquiring managers to suspect that financial problems in a subsidiary have been hidden from them and that there are many skeletons in the closet awaiting discovery. Hence auditors and junior staffers are sent in to study the situation and in most instances aim to please the boss by unearthing all of the partner's failings.

The Taste of Power. This fuels managers' momentum in the lead company to dominate the action. They have studied the situation longer and have clearer plans and priorities. Moreover, they are rewarded for meeting budgets and producing results, not for how fairly or smoothly they manage the integration. Hence, they typically move with haste, while chomping at the bit to get the integration done and get back to "real" work. As a result, lead side managers often unilaterally dominate the action and impose their own integration plans.

The Psychology of Buying and Consolidating

There are, of course, executives whose ego and temperament lead them to advance their own interests in buying a company and consolidating their control. Furthermore, even among men and women of goodwill there are natural inclinations to favor one's own company and its customs and normal drives to gain power and approbation by coming out on top. However Harry Levinson, a counselor to many executives on both sides of a deal, notes that there are also unconscious forces that impel lead company managers to exhibit what he terms "controlling behavior."[10]

One such motive is fear, which is manifest in the belief that unless the company grows, it will be bought or destroyed. This leads acquiring managers into "empire building" with subsidiaries and is paralleled by staff managers adding to their "fiefdoms." These forceful managers may see themselves as powerful and strong. But Levinson says that, behind the facade, they are concerned about being small or weak.

Fearful executives are prone to deny their own fears and sublimate them into an obsessive desire to control and dominate their counterparts. Inside, they are concerned that the other party may be smarter, savvier, and more competent, perhaps even a threat to them. Thus, outwardly, they treat their counterparts as bumpkins who need some professional grooming.

A second unconscious motive is obsolescence. As organizations age, they become more bureaucratic, rigid, and inflexible. Their executives, too, become obsolescent. An obsolescent company tries to make up for its lack of initiative and spontaneity by buying a younger, more energetic firm. Unfortunately, its bureaucracy generally ends up strangling the younger company, too.

This sense of obsolescence leads executives to adopt a defensive posture when faced with "uppity" executives. They denigrate the new methods and outlooks of acquired management and respond sharply to ideas that challenge the lead company's prerogatives. And resistance on the acquired side, in turn, is attributed to a lack of experience and realism.

PSYCHOLOGICAL PREPARATION

What can be done to rein in the controlling behaviors of lead company executives and ease their unconscious fears? The proper outlook has to be modeled and managed at the top. Some headiness on the part of lead company executives is inevitable. It is imperative, then, that the CEO set the tone and articulate the principles under which the combination shall commence.

It is important, too, for the boss to instill what psychologist Abraham Maslow terms "psychological safety."[11] Certainly job security is desirable. But when CEOs can't guarantee this, they need to counsel their top people personally and ensure they are taken care of financially. They can also help their teams "work through" this difficult period.

One buying CEO had regular breakfasts and lunches with his management team to unburden himself and encourage them to talk about their "issues" in the first month after a merger. The meals came to be labeled "group therapy" but attendance never wavered, and one vice president called them "the best thing we ever did as a group." The boss used the meetings to review plans and tactics, assert his view of the competencies of the other company's management, and praise the to-be-combined team as the "best in the business." These meals, complemented by lots of management-by-walking-around, helped the buying company to absorb two "early retirements" on its side and to welcome three managers from the other side to the top team.

Merger Manuals at Citicorp. Acquiring managers down the ranks also need to prepare themselves for a combination. Citicorp's international consumer banking division commissioned in-house planning specialists to produce a textbook and training program for managers on how to plan and conduct acquisitions "the Citicorp way."[12]

The first volume of course materials covers all major aspects of the acquisition process beginning with the formation of an acquisition team and how to search for and select an acquisition candidate. Then it addresses the human aspects of the combination—the merger syndrome, we/they dynamics, and the clash of cultures—plus methods of integration planning. An important section covers "The Citicorp Notion of Integration"—What does integration look like? How much should we integrate? How fast should we integrate? Finally, it deals with many aspects of the postcombination phase.

Exercises in the program have managers go through a goal clarification exercise, to set their strategic priorities in integration, and a role play in which they play the part of an acquired manager. It is hoped that by empathizing with acquired management, buyers will better appreciate the need to work closely and carefully with them, albeit with the acquiree in the role of "junior partner."

Training at AT&T. Soon after AT&T announced its intentions to merge its Information Systems and Communications divisions, top management in the lead division began to prepare its managers for change. The director wanted to prevent managers from getting into a "we" versus "they" mindset and to begin thinking like "one team."

A daylong training and planning session was designed. Prior to the event, a consultant administered a written survey to all 80 affected managers and interviewed each of them, either individually or in a focus group format. This identified the full range of managers' expectations of the internal merger and their concerns about it. The off-site meeting began with the consultant reviewing the typical challenges posed by mergers and the human dynamics. Then the focus shifted to the specific issues identified in the surveys and interviews of Communications/Information Systems management in the region. Five factors emerged as central to the success of this internal merger:

Success will be determined by:

- The degree to which we manage the integration process well (i.e., communicating, providing chances for people to participate in decisions, and building ownership of the change)

- The level of energy and enthusiasm we have and develop in our people (i.e., minimizing burn-out, addressing concerns about limited growth opportunities and worries about whether "another shoe will drop")

- The quality of direction we provide (i.e., developing a sound business strategy and a workable implementation plan)

- The degree to which we educate one another about our businesses (i.e., developing knowledge regarding each side's products, the new boss's expectations, and criteria for success);

- The degree to which we address clash of cultures and create trust with our counterparts

The 80 managers were then broken into ten groups, two covering each issue, to clarify their expectations and concerns about how their division would approach the assigned issue. The groups were then asked to recommend (1) what, as individual managers, they could do to address that issue to create a successful integration and (2) what they needed from senior management in the way of leadership, structure, and support. The full group reassembled and each small group reported its recommendations. The session concluded with each manager preparing a personal action plan, selecting from the roster of recommendations how they were going to lead the transition back in their own functions. The regional director took the groups' feedback to senior management in the form of his personal action plan.

This program accomplished three important goals. First, it empowered managers with guidelines and techniques for managing integration in their own units. Second, it previewed for managers many of the pitfalls which plague typical integrations. Finally, it involved managers in the development of action steps to address and avoid the pitfalls. The managers left the session committed to personal plans of action and with much greater confidence in their ability to lead the change.

THE MIND-SET OF THE ACQUIRED

Psychological preparation is more difficult for acquired managers, one of whom likened a bid to "being hit by a truck." GC's top managers, for example, were frantic over their late-Friday takeover bid. Two top executives became sick over the weekend, and others suffered from nightmares and insomnia. There was finger-pointing over the failure of Clarkson and others to mount a more effective takeover defense. Finally, they recognized the inevitable—the only alternative to takeover was to be "bought" by Times Mirror.

Why is a takeover so debilitating to a company? From the start there is a sense of violation: It is quite common for executives to see themselves as being "raped" and to describe their buyer as an "attacker" or a "barbarian." However, even in friendly deals, acquired managers often describe themselves as being "seduced" by promises that changes will be minimal and as being "taken advantage of" once they are forced to accommodate to the new buyer's demands.

A State of Shock. "Everybody took cover," remembers one executive whose firm was caught up in a bidding war, "every day there were new bombs coming out of the sky." A state of shock permeates a company following an unfriendly acquisition. But even in some friendly deals, executives wander the halls after a combination is announced, unprepared to assume new duties and responsibilities. John Handy, president of a New York search firm, found that 90% of nearly 1,000 senior and middle managers he studied were "psychologically unprepared" for the changes in status and organizational structure they would encounter following their company's acquisition.[13]

Defensive Retreat. One way executives cope with their shock is by a defensive retreat. This allows acquired executives to regroup and formulate a "battle plan" for countering the "enemy." At GC, this led to a strategy of "noncompliance" and various tactics to resist what they perceived to be "technocratic steering." In another company, a top technical team retreated ostensibly to prepare a report on their R&D activities for perusal by their new owner. Instead, they contacted a competitor and left en masse.

A Sense of Fatalism. Finally, takeover targets and smaller acquirees often feel powerless to defend their interests or control their fate. Even when a company is "rescued," the consequences are frequently out of their control. After Clarkson had conducted all the negotiations with Times Mirror's CEO, for example, he was unilaterally assigned to report to a group vice president. Another executive said, "When GC was independent we could dream. We might not achieve but it was damn exciting to try. We can still dream but, holy shit, there are dream killers out there. Once you start dreaming, they are going to wake you up in the middle of it."

GCers were deeply troubled by the "onslaught" of Times Mirror staffers into their company and the imperious manner of their counterparts. They came to describe their parent company as an "amoeba" trying to absorb them and termed staff departments an "octopus" that was reaching out its tentacles into every functional area. Such characterizations bespeak unconscious fears that underlie the resistive behavior of acquired executives.

The Psychology of Being Bought

Many managers use Elisabeth Kubler-Ross's stages of reactions to death and loss to illustrate their personal reactions to being acquired.[14] In the case of GC, top executives repeatedly "denied" the reality of their plight. When the firm was hit by a takeover bid, for example, top management first looked for illusory legal loopholes to counter it. Then, in a bout of wishful thinking, they believed that their "loyal" stockholders would not sell. Their subsequent anger over the bid carried over into dealings with Times Mirror. The stage was set for bargaining and months and months of conflict with the "powers that be."

These reactions can occur all throughout an acquired company. Some will deny their vulnerability to job loss. Others may exaggerate it. An acquired middle manager told us he was immune from job loss because "they don't have anyone on their side who does what I do." Two months later he was gone. Another told us, "they're not keeping anybody!" and immediately took a less attractive job elsewhere. He missed out on a chance to participate in a joint-company technical venture.

Once the inevitability of impending change is accepted, anger rises. Often it is first directed at top management of the acquired firm: its members are blamed for "selling out" and "feathering their own nest." Then it is directed at new owners. And while expressions of anger allow people to vent their emotions, many become "stuck" at this stage and are never able to move to an accommodation to the new situation.

In terms of saving their own souls (and hides), individual executives will take steps to make themselves indispensable and begin politicking for their people. Failing that, they will follow *Business Week*'s advice and "make secret personal plans...discretely look for jobs...and abandon ship before it's too late."[15] Only after a time will people accept the change and be ready to work with counterparts in a genuine and committed way. For some executives, this may be a matter of weeks or months. Other times it takes years. In many cases, this stage is never reached.

Preparing the Acquiree

The best form of psychological preparation for an acquiree is frank communication from a buyer that clarifies expectations and yields common ground. Many acquirees have legitimate fears of being dominated by new owners or absorbed into their business. When the lead company wants to build partnership or grow a business, it needs to communicate this and act accordingly. At the other extreme is the case where a smaller outfit, having performance problems, is acquired by a larger parent company and has the expectation of being "saved." Citicorp encounters many acquisitions of this sort and has developed the full scenario.

Mismatched Expectations. The problem here is that buyer and seller have different expectations of the combination. On one side is management in the failing company, having operating problems, being underinvested, and faced with staff reductions. On the other is the new owner, exuding power and promising that there are better days ahead. Acquired executives relish the prospects of dipping into the "deep pockets" that will bail them out. This leads to the common "salvation" expectation that the buyer will fix up problems and pour in capital. Major organization and technological changes are anticipated, along with new product introductions and hard-hitting business plans. (See Figure 4.4.)

What happens next? At least in the case of Citicorp, the buyer uncovers deep problems and presses local management who is dismayed and resentful. Consultants may be brought in to straighten things out and, in the process, push aside local functionaries who try to protect their flanks, their reputations, and their jobs. Deep pockets prove inaccessible. Instead, cuts are mandated and budgets are trimmed. The acquiree feels dominated and betrayed. Hoped-for technology transfers are slow in coming, and new product development is sacrificed to short term cost containment.

Citicorp has had great success in rescuing failing banks and turning their operations around. Their principles and practices are straightforward: honest communication, fair dealings, strict accountability, and "tough love." Citicorp managers are trained to bring realism sensitively to acquirees.

Figure 4.4
The "Saviour" Expectation
Following a Merger or Acquisition

History of Target

- Failing performance
- Operating problems
- Under-invested
- Staff reductions

Stereotypes of Buyer

- Deep pockets
- Large and powerful
- Superior technology
- High power/goal driven
- Smarter and savvier

Leads to Expectations:

- Buyer will fix problems
- Buyer will pour in money
- Major organizations and technological changes
- Lots of new products
- Goals and business plan right away

What Often Happens:

- Buyer uncovers lots of problems
- Target dismayed and resentful
- Buyers import people to "fix" problems
- Target mistrustful and protects flanks
- Fewer dollars, not more; cutbacks and one sided changes
- Target feels dominated and betrayed
- Technology change is slow; product development takes time
- Target managers and performers jump ship

Other outfits don't prepare local management and take no prisoners in turning operations around. As one manager who lived through this scenario reported, "If this is salvation, I'd rather be in hell."

Raids and Rescues. The difficulties of arriving at mutual expectations are compounded in the case of corporate raids and rescues. Merger consultant Price Pritchett makes the point that a buyer's "raid" generates enormous resistance on the target company's side. Hence Blumenthal "bent over backwards" in his dealings with Sperry management and emphasized the theme of partnership. By comparison, Pritchett notes, rescued management may be so "grateful" to be saved from a raider that they allow the buying company to impose too much control over them.[16] There are exceptions of course. Indeed, GCers recognized themselves as "ungrateful little brothers" in dealing with Times Mirror. The upshot is that buyers have to be prepared for strong reactions from acquirees—favorable and unfavorable—in these kinds of deals.

Simulations and Training. Several universities and management education centers run merger training sessions, where executives can experience, through case studies and simulations, some of the stresses and strains combinations bring and can "rehearse" effective modes of coping.[17] The Niagara Institute near Buffalo, New York, for example, runs a merger simulation where trainees are put into the roles of buyer and seller and participate in a precombination planning exercise. The American Management Association's course on mergers and acquisitions gives participants information on the merger syndrome and clash of cultures. None of this, of course, can substitute for handling the "real thing."

RITES OF PASSAGE

Sigmund Freud makes a key distinction between mourning, the normal condition of sadness and grief, and melancholy, a neurotic condition that impairs functioning. Freud notes that most societies have grieving rituals that allow for normal mourning. In their absence, people are at risk of a protracted period of depression.[18]

Good-bye to the Good Old Days. Take the case of King Broadcasting, the Seattle-based media company that was put up for sale following the death of its founder. Many employees were grief stricken at losing the "old ways" and fearful over who might buy them. A survey of senior managers found declines in morale among top managers and those they manage. The survey also found more rumors, more tension and anxiety, and more concerns about turnover. (See Figure 4.5.)

Figure 4.5
Acquired Company's Reactions to Possible Sale
Top 40 Senior Managers

	About the same as usual	Worse or much worse than usual
My own morale and enthusiasm for the job...	46%	54%
The morale of managers who work for me...	56	44
The morale of employees in my work area...	42	58
The level of rumors...	28	72
Tension and anxiety...	23	77
Employee comments about voluntarily leaving the company...	50	50

To respond, King's top management hosted an off-site meeting where top managers could educate themselves about people's reactions to a combination and mark their passage to an uncertain fate. Each of the executives contributed personal memorabilia to a cenotaph. This marked their burial of the past. In turn, a large group of managers devised a roster of cultural values they hoped to retain which was presented to prospective buyers. The session concluded with managers drawing a "ritual mask" highlighting their fondest memories of King. Holding their masks they relived their hiring, key career moments, and events of significance, humorous and otherwise, or just cited people who meant so much to them. One attendee noted, at the end of the ritual, "Now I'm ready to move on."

A Grieving Session. GC's top executives also went through a mourning period following their sale to Times

Mirror. To help the top team work through the Kubler-Ross stages, an external consultant orchestrated a grieving meeting for GCers. The grieving meeting allowed executives to mourn the loss of the "glory days, gone forever." Clarkson and his team shared their personal losses and were comforted by their friends. It also enabled them to expiate their anger over the takeover attempt and prepare themselves to deal with Times Mirror more openly and authentically.

One executive described himself as in "Kafka's Castle"— where demons would appear and disappear, leaving him fearful and out of control. Another talked about turning over the company to "younger men" who could better adapt to working for a parent company. A third talked about the fun they might have, "not the way it used to be," but still fun trying to maintain their own ways and even "evangelize the heathens" over to their philosophy of doing business.

Still, the team was not ready to envision or contemplate any sort of "new beginning" after the grieving meeting. It would take months and months, as we shall see, to move through what one called the "twilight zone."

PART THREE

MANAGING
THE MERGER

CHAPTER 5

Stress, Uncertainty, Anxiety

There were a couple of months where we sat around and worried all day. Then we started to worry that we were worrying too much, so we went back to work for ten minutes. Then somebody would call up and say "Did you see the papers this morning? Are you getting laid off?" So we'd go back to worrying again.
— Former CBS employee, quoted by
Anne Fisher, *Fortune*, May 23, 1988[1]

Of course there were negative reactions...but it didn't feel like a takeover. We were treated with genuine respect, we were listened to and treated fairly.
— Bendix manager after takeover by Allied-
Signal, quoted by Joseph McCann and
Roderick Gilkey, *Joining Forces*[2]

Mergers and acquisitions affect almost everybody in a company. An American Management Association survey found upheavals in management structure and changes in company policies in over three-fourths of 109 acquisitions studied.[3] Pay grades and benefit levels were changed in half of the cases, and significant reductions in force were undertaken in over one-third of them. In the majority of companies, this led to significant problems in productivity, morale, and turnover. And those with problems said that management did a lousy job of communicating with people and getting them involved in the transition.

This goes to the source of the merger syndrome: People don't know what to expect and, in today's environment, generally anticipate the worst. For some, the prospects of change pose uncertainty: There may be new duties to master, a new superior and peers to adjust to, and new policies and procedures that alter established ways of going about the job. For others, there is the more palpable threat to job security and company identity. Whether real or perceived, it is the potential for change which makes people anxious as a combination is announced.

All of this becomes stress inducing when it taxes a person's ability to cope effectively. Unsure of why change is occurring and how it may affect them, and unable to voice their concerns or control their fate, people's accustomed ways of coping with stress are exaggerated. It is commonplace, for example, to see people handle stress through the familiar "fight/flight" reaction. Certainly anger and aggression are prominent in takeover targets. But they can also be found in friendly acquisitions when people perceive new owners invading their turf.

By contrast, lethargy, detachment, and other signs of escapism can be found among acquired white collar professionals whose work keeps them out of political power circuits. Engineers, accountants, and human resource personnel sometimes stick their heads in the sand while their bosses jockey for power. Underneath, however, many internalize their stress and slack off their performance.

Fight/flight reactions are normal and should be expected after the sale. But both can be costly. Angry managers cannot work for the common good: They are spoiling for a fight and will spoil the attitudes of their direct reports. Flighty professionals can also produce problems. They simply can't be counted on to contribute fully to fact-finding or decision making but will surely second-guess the resulting decisions and gripe openly when they don't meet their satisfaction.

Stress also takes its toll on people's well-being. Marked increases in sleeplessness, headaches and back pain, alcohol and drug usage, and quarrels at work and home are reported for months following announcement of a sale. More than a few who have "kicked the habit" start smoking again. Walk down the corridors in merging firms and you'll hear coughs and sneezes and see running noses and aspirin bottles. And these somatic symptoms last: At the headquarters of an acquired Fortune 500 manufacturing firm, incidents of high blood pressure among employees rose from 11% in the year preceding the merger to 22% in the year following its announcement.

Carried to the extreme, merger-related stress can unsettle people in one or both companies, put the two firms at odds, and set the combination on the wrong course.[4] This chapter looks at sources of stress and what companies can do to combat it—beginning with senior management. Later sections look at how merging and acquired companies can prepare people for change, effectively communicate with them, and offer them psychological support.

WHAT MAKES A MERGER SO STRESSFUL

Why are combinations so stressful for executives? For one, there is more work to do and less time to do it in. The sheer amount of work involved in combining two firms—digesting enormous amounts of information and making rapid-fire decisions—is overwhelming and absorbs senior executives' time and energy. Compounding this is the pressure they encounter to maintain day-to-day results in the face of their employees' discontent and dismay.

Tension filters down through an organization. Staff and lower level managers are called upon to assemble information—without knowing the whys and wherefores. Employees are urged to keep their noses to the grindstone and not worry about all the uproar around them. Meanwhile, the boss is mostly invisible and, when in sight, seems harried and circumspect.

Second, there is a great deal of uncertainty as to the future. Questions abound for which there are no given answers: How will reporting relationships be structured in the new organization? Which firm's policies and procedures will be followed? Will pay and benefits be affected? Will decision making practices change? Will previously promised promotions or job assignments be honored? How will redundancies in staffs and functions be resolved? Will people leave or be let go? No one has reliable answers to these questions.

Finally, this is a time of insecurity. The rumor mill circulates horror stories which show the buyer to be rapacious or the seller's circumstances to be dire. People congregate around coffee machines and water fountains, in lunch rooms and watering holes, to hear the latest gossip. They obsess about how the combination will affect them. A study in one acquisition found that, on average, two hours per employee per day were spent speculating about the acquisition for months after the sale.

What Exacerbates Stress in a Combination

Several factors exacerbate merger stress and erode people's ability to cope with change. To begin with, many people are surprised by news of the deal. Securities and Exchange Commission guidelines constrain what can be said before the merger or acquisition is formally announced. Furthermore, most companies negotiate in secrecy lest leaks or rumors affect stock trading and the eventual sale price.

Then, when a formal announcement is made, it often concentrates on the deal's financial and strategic parameters without saying how changes may affect employees. Pre-combination planning, where feasible, typically focuses on structural integrating. Seldom does anyone systematically think through the human implications. As a result, corporate communications and human resource specialists have to play "catch-up" with needed communiqués and support services.

Meanwhile, the press and battle-scarred veterans weigh in with sensational and unsavory stories. Who can counter people's fears? Employees want to know what changes will occur. Yet, in many instances, there is no detailed plan in place and few definitive answers to employees' questions. Middle managers and supervisors, who are themselves unclear about next steps, show their discomfort and become close-mouthed for fear of creating false expectations or saying the wrong thing.

Stress Begets More Stress

Basic research on stress highlights other factors that add to the angst:[5]

1. The amount of stress people experience is based upon their subjective perceptions, not on any objective reality. The personal preoccupations, rumor mongering, and fight/flight reactions associated with the merger syndrome all stem from people's assessments of their situation and personal patterns of coping with stress. Certainly objective events factor into subjective perceptions, but the stressfulness of a situation is in the eye of the beholder.

We've described, for example, how Graphic Control's top managers, first hit with an unfriendly takeover bid and then forced into a white knight acquisition, had grounds for upset, anger, and dismay. But top management's hostile reaction to its new owners was driven by fantasy as much as fact and stemmed from their emotional upset.

In another case, rumors of downsizing following the merger of two small Southern banks led to massive turmoil and turnover among branch banking personnel. Lenders and tellers had heard rumors of layoffs in corporate offices and concluded that they were next on the list. This was in stark contrast to management's intentions of eliminating redundant staff positions but leaving the branches intact to ensure customer service.

Stress increases people's vigilance to information and yet leads them to simplify and distort what they hear. Hence merger managers have to plan their communications, be especially attentive to what they communicate, and rely on several communication channels to reach their people.

2. The stress of an event is determined by the amount of change it implies, not necessarily whether the changes will be good or bad. Research shows that marriage and births can be just as stressful to people as divorce and deaths. Both disrupt the status quo, entangle family and friends, and require that people adapt to new circumstances. Most mergers are seen by employees, right from the start, as offering a mix of good things and bad. Some changes may be for the better—say, improvements in the benefits package or increased capital to hurry new products to the market—and some may be for the worse—lessened autonomy or a required relocation.

People are capable of coolly rationalizing these costs and benefits and sorting them out. But generally people are heated up during a combination and anything but studied and dispassionate. In one case, an acquiree gained some new product offerings and marketing support from an equivalent unit in the buying company. However sales territories had to be reorganized and product groups realigned. Key managers, expected to be charged up by the opportunities, were instead wracked by sickness and weighted down by worries. When changes were announced, moreover, sales personnel bickered over assignments and tried to freeze out their counterparts when closing their sales.

The implication is that managers have to take special steps to prepare people for change and rally them to the cause. Getting them involved in the transition process is key to gaining people's commitment.

3. The effects of stress are cumulative. A series of small, seemingly innocuous changes can add up to big headaches in a combination. In a deal involving two New England banks, modest changes were proposed in the data processing operations of the smaller bank by its new parent. An operations manager was sent out from the parent company to install new systems aimed at standardizing transaction coding formats and reducing overtime. Then came coding problems and a sharp increase in overtime.

A management trainee and clerks arrived from the parent company with a get tough attitude: "If the coding isn't done right, we won't process it."

Subsequently, a data input clerk from the subsidiary complained to her supervisor, "They won't handle our work," who, in turn, went to her supervisor contending that the "big-shot" trainee and parent company clerks were "mean and rude." This was carried up to the head of the small bank, who contacted his superior in the parent company, who sent then down the message, "Process their work and stop this nonsense." Ultimately, two sets of clerks, four managers, and two senior executives got bollixed up in this modest change. And, after six months, processing problems continued and overtime expenses, in both the subsidiary and parent company, "shot through the ceiling."

There are extraordinary demands on executives to stay on top of the combination and help people through the change. But executives are caught in a double bind: While the managerial requirements are to look out for people, their natural response is to look out for themselves.

TOP-LEVEL LEADERSHIP

How combining companies respond to people's stress, uncertainty, and anxiety is to a large extent determined by top-level leadership. The key figure is the CEO. A Federal Trade Commission panel of merger experts concluded that the character of a firm's M&A activity is "more likely to be a function of the style and personality of the CEO than of [his or her] staff's analytic and planning capability." As one panelist stated, "The [combined] company is going to become what [the boss] wants it to be. The CEO is always the driving force...."[6]

Leadership of a combination extends beyond the structural integration of companies to the joining of people. Successful change is led by CEOs who put their personal imprint on people management. This means:

- Creating a sense of human purpose and direction
- Putting together a leadership team
- Focusing management on success factors
- Winning the commitment of people

Human Purpose and Direction

This top-level work is exemplified by Mike Blumenthal in merging Burroughs and Sperry. In person, on video, and through communiqués, he defined where the combined company was going and how it would get there. He provided people a clear picture of his vision and values. And he articulated principles which would guide the combination and transition to the new organization.

A Rallying Point. Right after the sale, Blumenthal went on a two-week tour of Burroughs and Sperry facilities to deliver what came to be called "The Speech." He traveled to Düsseldorf, West Germany, then to Switzerland and around Europe to Japan, then back to the United States to Minneapolis, site of Sperry's largest manufacturing facility, then to Sperry's headquarters in Blue Bell, Pennsylvania, and finally back to Detroit, Burroughs' base. Regardless of the location the message was the same: "The spirit of the merger is partnership, bringing together two top computer companies to realize the potential greatness of their unity and to compete more effectively in the fast growing industry of information systems."

In describing his tactics in the weeks following the merger announcement, Blumenthal recalled,

> Mobs of written communication went out and good people were in charge of that. But I also personally did a lot of traveling. I went everywhere and made speeches, interviewed people, and went to dinners with groups in all places in the world where there were relatively large numbers of Sperry people. One must not underrate the importance of a personal appearance by someone who has become a symbol of the change.

Personalizing the Vision. It seems as though top executives everywhere develop "visions" to announce major changes. Glossy brochures, marching songs, and slick videotapes herald bold moves and bright possibilities. But all too often, employees toss out the pamphlets, tune out the music, and turn off the VCR. High minded missives and profligate promises of a better day can ring hollow to dubious acquirees. Glitz and glamor have their place in corporate communications. But so do credibility and a homespun manner.

In this case, Blumenthal *personalized* his vision of the new company by sharing with executives his own career history and life experiences. Early in his career, for example, he had worked in companies riddled with politics. When he came to Burroughs, therefore, he took steps to rid management of turf battles and flank protection. He replaced executives with "competent" people and, in his words, "Their competence proved out." What did he expect of executives in this merger? Speaking to top managers on both sides he gave these ground rules:

- **No politics.** Personal maneuvering and wiggling your way to the top will be the best way to *not* move forward. No putting down one another, even in subtle ways. You will *not* get ahead by saying bad things about you colleagues.

- **Show your people the same respect and professionalism we have shown you.** Let's be friends and colleagues.

- **Avoid cronyism and cliques.** Even though it is easier to staff with people you know, let's be fair.

He then added,

> It's not like building any other organization. Subordinates will be uncertain and need to be worked with and welded into a team. Communicate, communicate, communicate. . . . We will succeed. Remember to have fun and take a sense of satisfaction as things take shape.

Putting Together a Leadership Team

"You want to ease my stress," stated one Sperry executive, "tell me if I've got a job!" Blumenthal could not make extensive top management appointments at this point in the merger. His reasoning: The new organization had not been designed, and he did not yet know the full qualifications of Sperry managers. As a Burroughs executive remarked, "If Mike names top people now, he'll go with our side. Who would you appoint? Managers whose weaknesses you know or those whose flaws are still a mystery?"

The success of many mergers depends on the CEO putting together a leadership team that represents both sides. Target company executives often have vital industry and customer connections, credibility, and know-how. And a major concern of acquired employees is that their leaders stay on at least through the transition phase. At the same time, the CEO needs to hold on to top talent on the buying side—some of whom, as in this case, find themselves in unwelcome competition with acquired executives.

Blumenthal was committed to keeping most of the top Burroughs and Sperry people and melding them together as a team. In addition to forming the Merger Coordination Council and joint-company task forces, which put both groups of executives on equal footing, he also met regularly and individually with top managers. Here he would be a self-described "pocket psychologist" working from impressions and drawing upon his persuasive skills to keep executives on board. He recalls: "It was very important in the beginning to have a merger where key people were perceived and seen by everybody to be working together as a team. I worked extremely hard to bring that about."

He knew, however, that he could not expect to create a new organization built on partnership without the two company presidents of Burroughs and Sperry. And keeping them would be difficult. Paul Stern, then president of Burroughs, was quite adamant about securing the number 2 job in the combined company. Stern had been Blumenthal's "strong arm" in overseeing operations and running business reviews. He found it "ridiculous" when Blumenthal proposed the creation of combined company leadership team and was "insulted" when he was not named second in command. Joe Kroger, then president of Sperry, had led the effort to resist Burroughs' bid. He doubted that Blumenthal would even want him around and was suspicious of working alongside Stern in a joint post. How did Blumenthal keep these two on board?

> I appealed to their self-interest in two ways: First by making it financially worth their while to be seen as being cooperative. And secondly, by saying to them 'Look, this thing is wide open. There is absolutely no reason why you should not emerge from it as a possible successor to me.' And the beauty of that was that I really meant it.

Blumenthal also gave the two men clear measures for success. "I said 'You know what I am trying to do. You do it. You make everybody work together.'" Stern and Kroger stayed with the combined company for over a year after the merger—through the transition period and to the point where both could depart without undermining the spirit of partnership.

Critical Success Factors

What's important to the success of a merger? How should decisions be prioritized? To address these matters, the CEO or, as appropriate, head of a merging business unit needs to identify critical success factors. These factors define what is important and has to be accomplished.

Mike Pickett and Merisel. When computer product distributors Softsel and Microamerica merged to form Merisel Computer Products in 1990, CEO Mike Pickett offered a clear vision of the combination: a true merger leading to a new company name and structure. A series of functional task forces would study integration options and make recommendations for how to organize and staff the new company. Through speeches, videos, and meetings, Pickett told staff that the result would be "the best, biggest, and most profitable worldwide computer products distributor."

To achieve this dream, Pickett delineated a roster of critical success factors for his management team, including: increase market share worldwide; maintain a low-cost, efficient operation; secure the best brands; and be the easiest distributor to do business with. Pickett also tasked executives with achieving a timely and effective integration and communicating the proper image of the combined company and its strategies.

Take note, however, that plenty of combining companies define such success factors and then neglect them when planning integration. What distinguishes Pickett was his dogged communication of these factors and insistence that managers take them to heart. Operations managers, for example, translated the challenge to "be the easiest distributor to do business with" into a goal of same-day shipment of any order made by 5:00 P.M. Studies were then undertaken to determine, first, if this goal was realistic and, then, what procedures would be needed for achieving it.

To the work force at large, these critical success factors were an initial statement of the objectives of the postmerger organization. Through employee meetings and newsletter articles, they were clarified and discussed. This gave meaning and substance to what had otherwise been an unformed concept of the mission of the new organization. "I was afraid that all the merger planning was going to cause us to take our eye off the ball and give our competitors an opportunity to hack away at us," recalled a middle level marketing manager in Merisel. "Hearing Mike Pickett say that securing the best brands was integral to the new company, I understood, for the first time, that we were going to be aggressive in signing up new vendors. This raised my confidence in the merger in general and showed that our leaders had their priorities straight."

Pickett also gave his team "Ten Commandments" for managing through the transition. (See Figure 5.1.) The commandments served two valuable functions. First, they established crisp, authoritative guidelines for behavior. Managers understood what Pickett expected of them and how their conduct would be appraised. Second, and of equal importance, the process of reviewing them helped Pickett himself to clarify what was needed to make the merger a success.

Figure 5.1
CEO's Ten Commandments of Merger Leadership

---

1. Provide Direction

- Define your own critical success factors for the merger. What has to happen in your area if this merger is to be a success?

- Focus people on short-term objectives, deadlines and assignments—long-term strategies come later.

- Aim high and push staff hard—people are prone to introspection during a merger—challenge them and keep them busy. Turn that anxiety and stress into productive energy.

- Make history—your organization probably never needed a figurehead as much as it does right now. This is your opportunity to become a true corporate hero, part of the folklore of the organization. Be a key role model, inspire others.

2. Expect Change

- Expect a drop in productivity during the integration process, and an increase in the stress level.
- Prepare staff for change. Staff want and expect change—they want things to get better as a result of the merger.
- A certain amount of resistance to change is expected and positive; without it you have a lethargic, complacent organization. Manage it, tell staff why they are going through this process.
- Expect power struggles by the people underneath you in the organization. These may be significantly more intense than they have been in the past.

3. Be Positive

- Rise above the noise and confusion, empower yourself, be upbeat and enthusiastic.
- Develop a high tolerance for ambiguity—be flexible.
- Keep a sense of humor. Try and introduce a sense of play into the process—see the humorous side of problems as they come up.
- Keep a sense of balance. Don't let yourself get overwhelmed by merger issues.

4. Clarify and Manage Issues

- Separate urgent from important. Avoid being sidetracked by low priority issues—make sure the priorities are clear.
- Sort out issues into those that can be dealt with right away and those that can be left for awhile—get on with issues that are of high strategic importance.
- Make sure you have a clear understanding of the problems that need to be handled—don't always believe your own press releases.

5. Inform Yourself

- Take time to understand the psychological change process that the staff is going through—show understanding.

- Ask people's opinions—find out staff names, single out individuals in public, over praise positive behaviors.

- Keep in touch with the organization and its problems—get out with the sales force and into the plant.

- Invite bad news—don't shoot messengers—don't settle for people telling you what they think you want to hear.

- Learn about the culture of the other organization, its history, the way it does business, its promotional process—even its dress code may be different.

6. Inform Your Staff

- Set out to clear up the unknowns and rumors, be specific and candid.

- Give staff the good news and the bad news—don't patronize people or assume that they only want to hear the good news—level with them.

- Be available and visible to the staff—ask questions and be prepared to discuss concerns.

- Give staff a chance to ventilate, express themselves.

7. Get Your Staff On Board

- Be honest. Don't make promises you cannot keep just to take the heat off in a difficult situation. Rebuild your credibility—assume that staff are looking for reasons to distrust you.

- You are a new boss—remember that your staff have to decide if *they* want to work for *you.*

- Give staff reasons to believe that the merger is being well-managed. It is their future too.

8. Build Your Team

- Meet with each manager, make sure each knows their decision-making authority, reporting relationships and performance expectations.
- Build confidence in your team to restore momentum to the organization.

9. Let the Staff Manage Their Way Through It

- Encourage initiative and risk taking—try to shape behavior and not judge mistakes—be a good coach, not just the boss.
- Don't try to come up with all the answers. Paint broad brush strokes with your operating principles and let staff fill in the details.
- Delegate a lot or you will be spread too thinly and people will get demoralized.
- Give staff time to settle in and make things work.

10. Get On With It

- Get on with the integration process—be action-oriented.
- Take the pain, get it over with as quickly as possible and move ahead. Your staff will thank you for it.
- Create some positive improvements and high profile successes early in the game.
- Be prepared to make the tough decisions in order to minimize political behavior.

Winning People Over

Critical success factors become the "steak" of management's message. It also helps to add some "sizzle." One CEO, for example, "kicked off" his company's purchase of another with a "pep rally" in a nearby auditorium. Such events signal that a merger is different from previous organizational changes. And they remind people that this is not business as usual. Nonetheless, employees are more likely to believe that a merger makes sense when they can see that there is a need for change and when they hear how it will benefit them personally. The key is to help people understand and accept why current strategies won't work in the postmerger organization and to buy into the rationale behind new ones.

Bob Johnson and DirectoriesAmerica. When DirectoriesAmerica, the Yellow Pages publishing unit of the United Telephone system, bought a small independent publisher, acquired employees feared the worst. They liked their current familial climate, access to the owner, and lack of formal company rules. And they feared being owned by a "huge conglomerate" controlled by "MBAs."

Bob Johnson, DirectoriesAmerica's general manager, took on the job of winning over the acquired work force. In group meetings, one-on-one sessions with key managers, and written documents he spelled out the benefits of new markets, an expanded product line, and state-of-the-art production facilities. The acquired sales staff got excited by the opportunity to sell more products in growing markets, and production employees looked forward to receiving computer equipment which would "bring us into the 20th century!" People also recognized that their new owners could give them the financial and technical muscle to compete with the "big-time operators"—Ameritech and Southwest Bell—making recent inroads into their territories.

Words and Deeds. Winning people over depends on action, not words alone. It is standard procedure today for the CEO in a parent company to send out a polite letter welcoming an acquired work force to "our family" and reassuring them that "we will work together." Though a nice gesture (when honest), people are looking for more tangible signs of togetherness. Soon after acquiring Western Airlines, for instance, Delta employees visited Western's airport lounges, bringing homemade cakes and cookies and welcoming Western people into their family. Western staff made reference to this considerate treatment for months to come.

Another thing that alienates people is hearing their company referred to in stereotyped or derogatory ways. It's one thing to say that your own company is "screwed up" but it's quite another to hear new owners say so. That smacks of a putdown. This can, of course, work both ways. Case in point: When a parent company we worked with introduced its Japanese-style "Hoshin" planning it was dubbed "Oh Shit" planning by the acquiree. The implication: Find generic ways to talk over common issues. For example, rather than compare one side's management-by-objectives approach with the other's performance-planning-and-review system, talk over "performance management" in the new situation.

Company Identity and Titles. Acquirees are especially attentive to signs of new owners' real intentions. Nothing turns them off faster than symbolic signs of domination. The upshot: Place both companies' names and logos on official communiques, at least for the first few months after the sale. Hold meetings on both sides' turf or at neutral sites. And delay changes in signage and badges until people have adjusted to the situation.

This is trickier, of course, in cases where the buyer intends to conform the subsidiary to its corporate regimens and merge product lines. Hewlett Packard, for example, agonized over retaining acquired Apollo's name and brand identity. A careful assessment of Apollo customer attitudes and employee preferences led to the decision to maintain an Apollo line of computers and retain Apollo's distinct identity as an HP division. How about cases where there are differences in job titles and salary grades? In another case, new owners agreed to "grandfather" acquired managers and engineers under their old titles and to phase in pay equity between the two work forces.

There is, however, simply no point in signaling that the two sides are partners when the lead company plans to dominate the action. Nor should the theme of partnership be artificially emphasized in cases where a subsidiary will have substantial autonomy or two large companies will more or less coexist. What's important is to achieve consistency between rhetoric and reality.

HELPING EMPLOYEES MANAGE STRESS

As the sources of employees' stress are many and varied in a merger or acquisition, so also does stress management have to take different forms. Top level vision, communication, and sensitivity are important but can only do so much to ease the strains on people during this difficult time. Human resource and corporate communication specialists have responsibilities to fulfill. So also and especially do line managers and supervisors. The roster of stress sources and remedial actions in Figure 5.2 highlights how companies can help employees to manage merger stress.

Figure 5.2
Managing Merger Stress: Symptoms and Remedies

Stress Symptoms	How to Respond
Worry or Fretting, Fear, Loss, Anxiety, Anger or Withdrawal	Self-Assessment and Counseling Sensitization Seminars Realistic Previews
Uncertainty and Rumor Mongering	Regular Communication Merger "Hot Lines"
Loss of Control	Employee Involvement Employee Assistance
Loss of Focus or Commitment	Performance Planning Retention Programs

Self-Assessment. As a first step in stress management, people have to size up their own situations and "reality test" how a combination might affect them. This means a careful assessment of risk factors and opportunities:

1. **The type of combination.** Are the companies in the same industry, implying more duplication of functions and likelihood of change? Or are they in different busi-

nesses, meaning the buyer needs current management and is less likely to make many operational changes?

2. **The buyer's track record in past combinations.** How has the buyer handled other acquisitions and what has been the fallout?

3. **The likelihood of change in one's function.** How has one's business unit been contributing to overall company results? How does it fit into the acquired or merged company's future strategy?

4. **The way people have been treated.** How have previous reductions in staff or transfers been handled? What kind of assistance has the company offered to help people find new positions?

5. **The opportunities inherent in a combination.** What new business opportunities does the combination provide? What career paths open up?

Counseling. A combination provides people an opportunity to assess their situations, rethink career choices, and consider alternatives for the future. Careful self-assessment and career counseling serves two functions. First, this can help employees to distinguish the real from the imagined costs and gains of a combination. Second, this enables them to clarify their own personal and career aspirations.

As an example, "Dr. Ken," as Psychologist Ken Myers is called at Northwest Airlines, made counseling and career planning available to all Northwest and Republic employees following the merger of those two firms. David Workman, vice president of human resources at Piedmont, also included employees' family members in counseling sessions after his firm's acquisition by USAir.

Wellness. Applying principles of "wellness" programs can also minimize the physical and psychological impact of a combination. Doctors advise stressed employees and managers to build in quiet time, get exercise, eat sensibly, and ask for extra help and support at home. The health office of one parent company offered stress management courses for all merged personnel, and its nursing team led lunchtime walks and after-hours fitness sessions in service of keeping people healthy. We have also found that some people find solace and gain insight from keeping a journal or diary of their feelings and experiences during a combination. This can help them keep track of their emotions and attain some perspective on the situation at hand.

Sensitization Seminars. Company-sponsored seminars or workshops are useful for educating managers about merger dynamics and preparing them for the work ahead. Seminars we have led begin by sensitizing managers to the signs of the merger syndrome, how cross-company conflicts arise, and why cultures clash. Then guidelines for managing employees and for building positive relations with counterparts are discussed.

It is advisable, where possible, to meet separately with managers on each side of the combination. This allows them to get their feelings on the table amid peers and colleagues facing similar circumstances. Follow-up sessions then bring the two sets of managers together to describe their situations, discuss emotions, and compare their cultures. This sets a base for developing mutual understanding and finding common ground.

It is important that upper-level management be present and involved as this type of training works its way down a company. Following the merger of Molson Breweries of Canada and Carling O'Keefe, for example, senior vice presidents from both sides introduced companywide sensitization sessions and afterward responded to employees' questions.

In addition, there are a variety of useful books and articles that can be distributed to employees on the "human side" of mergers and acquisitions which provide guidelines for helping oneself and one's people through the "shock waves." It helps when managers and supervisors distribute these materials and then hold meetings to discuss the implications for their work areas.

Realistic Previews. Several research studies show that people who are given a comprehensive picture of what a combination will mean for their work area suffer less stress when the change begins and hold their company in higher esteem in the aftermath. This "realistic preview" minimizes surprises and psychologically prepares people for what they will soon face.

In one systematic study, Professor David Schweiger of the University of South Carolina researched the impact of such a realistic preview in two manufacturing plants following the merger of *Fortune* 500 firms. The same day this friendly merger was announced to the press, employees received a letter from their CEOs explaining who the merger partner was, why the merger was occurring, and how it would help both companies.[7]

Then, in order to test the benefits of communication in a merger, it was agreed that one of the two manufacturing plants would receive a full preview of the psychological and operational aspects of the merger. At this "experimental" facility, a newsletter detailing upcoming changes was sent to each employee twice a month; a telephone hot line was set up to handle questions, and the plant manager met on a weekly basis with each of eight departments to discuss plans and address concerns. By contrast, management at the "control group" site used their normal media, memos on the bulletin board and occasional meetings, to keep people informed.

What happened? Ratings of commitment and job satisfaction dropped at both plants in the first month as some layoffs were undertaken and jobs were changed. Ratings of management's trustworthiness, honesty, and concern for employees also dropped. Self-reports of stress and intentions to seek work elsewhere increased. Within a few months, however, the realistically prepared employees regained their prior ratings of job satisfaction and saw the company as being far more trustworthy, honest, and caring than those in the other plant. Eventually, performance improved over premerger levels. By contrast, at the control plant, subject to "normal" communication, attitudes grew worse in almost every area measured as time went on.

COMMUNICATING TO PEOPLE

Effective and informative communication serves to lessen employee stress in a variety of ways.[8] First, it helps people make sense out of the uncertainty surrounding them and estimate how changes will affect themselves and their work situation. Second, it enhances management's trustworthiness by establishing a climate of openness and frankness.

Finally, it signals that management has a game plan and is able to articulate it.

A regular flow of communication early on gives people the confidence that they will be in the pipeline for news of subsequent decisions. This can directly affect postannouncement performance levels. Rather than put time and energy into idle speculation and worry whether or not they will hear about changes, well-informed employees can keep more of their attention on the job at hand.

While companies may not be able to say what specific changes will occur after a combination is announced, there is pertinent information that can be communicated. For example, people can be told how the combined company plans to make decisions and introduce change and how business will be conducted during the transition period. They can also be told about general employment plans and policies, the likelihood of changes in pay and benefits, and other matters of concern. Certainly employees want to know *today* whether their jobs are going to be eliminated or changed. Letting them know that a decision will be made, say, within four months is more stress inducing than no news at all.

There is no one best way to communicate in a combination. It is advisable to use a mixture of regular channels (company newsletters, weekly staff meetings) and special forums (merger bulletins, special employee meetings) to get the word out. It is also important to establish two-way communication. Some firms use toll-free "800" telephone numbers for rumor control and to solicit anonymously employee questions and concerns. Another company relied on its electronic mail system to establish a "dialogue" between acquired employees and new owners. How the information gets out to people is less important than the fact that it does indeed get to them (Appendices D and E describe what to communicate and how to communicate during a merger or acquisition).

Why Managers Don't Communicate. As important as these formal modes of communication are, none is a substitute for face-to-face communication. Yet individual managers have many "excuses" for neglecting or altogether avoiding their communication responsibilities.

"There's nothing to say." Managers are uncomfortable communicating when they themselves don't know what changes are in the works. They figure that employees will be skeptical when told "I don't know." In most instances, by contrast, employees understand that merger decisions are complex and that answers to their questions may not be known. When leveled with, people appreciate that management is carefully considering options rather than committing hastily to decisions that might not be in anyone's best interest.

"No news is good news." Many managers like to believe that they are buffering people from merger-related stress and that a lot of talk about the situation only exacerbates concerns. In our experience, however, rumors fill the communication void. And the grapevine always thrives on the downside of developments. Company communications programs need to present the upside prospects while acknowledging the problems and pain. Closed-mouth company leaders breed suspicion and heighten fears that "there must be something they are hiding" or that "management just doesn't care about me."

"Let the communications people do it." Corporate communications staffs can be of tremendous help, but they should not serve as the primary mouthpiece of management in this case. Employees want to hear from and be heard by their leaders and managers, not substitutes. Where communications people are most effective are in getting management's message out en masse. They can also be of great assistance to individual managers by arming them with Q&A packets and by helping them to plan and schedule employee meetings.

"We've already told them that." Employees have an insatiable thirst for information about what's happened and happening. Regular updates, even if containing nothing new, are important reminders that management is still in touch with their concerns. We've also advised managers to simply hold "listening sessions" with employees where their job is to keep quiet and take notes, allowing employees to express their frustrations, hopes, and concerns. The larger point is that there is no such thing as *overcommunication* in this situation.

INVOLVING PEOPLE

There are many ways to involve people at various points in the transition process. A study of 80 firms involved in M&A by Professors David Schweiger and Yaakov Weber found that most companies (75%) encouraged their managers early on to meet and talk with their counterparts informally, and many (59%) hosted social functions so that they can get to know one another better. Fewer (44%) used formal cross-company transition teams, and only a small number (22%) cross-fertilized by exchanging managers during the transition period. Naturally, the recommended degree of individual involvement depends on how much integration is contemplated and people's position in the hierarchy.[9]

Transition Task Forces. There is a direct link between people's participation in the combination process and their support for eventual changes. Many find themselves powerless during this time and feel "out of control." By giving them some say-so in merger decisions and their implementation, companies give people the chance to control activity within their sphere of influence. There are practical reasons for gaining employee involvement in decisions: Those who are closest to the action have the most knowledge to contribute to fact finding, can best identify whether certain options are practical or imprudent, and can begin to gear up logistically for implementing change. There also are psychological reasons: By participating in the process, people put a piece of themselves into decisions and have a personal investment in seeing them through to success.

The most significant form of involvement is through participation on transition task forces charged with studying, planning, and implementing change. The work of these task forces is examined in depth in the next chapter. It is important to note here that, apart from their substantive benefits, transition task forces allow people on the two sides to learn about one another—personally and professionally. This helps reduce the "unknown" and also fosters the creation of cross-company "networks" which prove invaluable for getting things done when change is actually implemented.

Informal Exchanges. Another way to get people involved is to encourage informal exchanges between the two work forces. Many merging companies initially urge managers to stay away from their counterparts—no calls, no contact—and to act as though nothing was going to change. This just adds to uncertainty and creates artificial barriers between the two sides. Instead, have managers reach out and build rapport.

Of course, care must be taken to ensure that these are not "missionary" expeditions or opening gambits in the game of conquest. Instead, make them opportunities for both sides to "show their stuff." People are proud about what they bring to a combination and welcome the chance to show off their products, marketing savvy, and everyday business practices. They are also curious about what their new partners have to offer. Two-way exchanges can take place through formal presentations, smaller "show-and-tell" meetings, and visits by contingents from one company to the other.

Social events, receptions, or dinners through which combining managers or staffs can get to know and learn from one another on a more relaxed basis also help. Be careful, though, to intersperse people from the two sides at sit-down dinners and working sessions. It is not unusual for people from each company to band together magnifying rather than minimizing "us" and "them" feelings.

Some companies have come up with creative ways to involve employees in transitions further down the hierarchy. At Burroughs and Sperry, for example, over 32,000 entries were received in a contest to name the new company. Soon after it announced plans to acquire Western Airlines, Delta airlines asked Western employees to indicate their support for the acquisition by writing to the Department of Transportation. Grateful that they were acquired by the "Rolls Royce" of the airline industry, Western employees were eager to participate in the approval process.[10]

CARING FOR PEOPLE

Stress stemming from the merger of Carling O'Keefe and Molson Breweries in Vancouver was a contributing factor in a recent murder-suicide. . . . It may have also led to five fatal heart attacks at the two plants since January, 1989, when the merger was announced.[11]

This report from *The Vancouver Sun* highlights the darkest side of mergers and acquisitions. Said one local union official, "People were dropping like flies." Said another, "After the incident, we convinced the company to get employee assistance counselours to be more visible."

As stress increases during a combination, so do employee needs for special care. Employee assistance program staffs should be active, visible, and overly solicitous. To help them cope with the stress of combining, a growing number of firms provide counseling to employees at all levels. One company commissioned a well-known psychotherapist to conduct confidential one-on-one sessions with overwrought executives to "talk" about "merger issues" at work and the impact at home. The therapist found several cases of depression and incidents of stress-related infections and substance abuse. Fortunately, these psychosomatic problems abated with time. One counselee suffering from a temporary increase in blood pressure noted, importantly, that sessions with the therapist "helped me get a lot of things off my chest."

It is of course advisable to use trained professionals in cases of high risk or actual trauma, but in several firms we've worked with, characterized by a high degree of openness and fellow feeling, managers and employees have offered their troubled peers personal and career counseling.

Merger Raps. Certainly it helps to have the CEO and other top-level executives say publicly that they recognize people have stresses and concerns and that they will be sensitive to emotions and feelings as the integration moves forward. But real support comes from private sessions between a superior and subordinate, or from group "grieving" sessions such as the one conducted in Graphic Controls. At Western Airlines, for example, in-house psychologists and employee assistance professionals responded to signs of the merger syndrome by leading lunchtime "merger raps." These sessions let employees share their feelings about being acquired by Delta, vent their worries, and learn that they were not alone in their concerns. Mixed feelings about the change could be expressed, as one reservations clerk spoke up, "I am grateful for all that Delta has done for us, but it still hurts when I answer the phone and say 'Delta' instead of 'Western.'" The sessions also were a forum in which employees could exchange strategies for coping with change—how to respond to the questions of family members, how to deal with the loss of the Western corporate identity, and how to establish new positions in the Delta organization.

THE ROLE OF LINE MANAGEMENT

While human resource and staff specialists can be a valuable asset in minimizing employee stress during a combination, someone has to run the business. Many companies urge managers and supervisors to operate in a "business-as-usual" mode. *This is impossible.* Instead, managers need to put extra effort into performance planning and give extra attention to people.

Minimizing Postmerger Drift. Merger consultant Price Pritchett notes that most companies go through a period of postmerger drift after the sale.[12] It is crucial, therefore, for managers and supervisors to expect some declines in performance and to reestablish goals and priorities for their people. Two general guidelines serve line managers well during this period:

1. Provide people direction and set performance expectations.
   a. Review goals and assignments—what's critical?
   b. Expect some performance drops—what can slide?
   c. Psyche out the staff — who's okay? who needs help?
   d. Don't overmanage and underlead—set high expectations!

2. Remind people that they have a job to do.
   a. Identify key priorities—must dos—and let people know.
   b. Reestablish and monitor short-term performance goals.
   c. Increase feedback on job performance and results.

d. Really praise good, consistent work—show it matters.

e. Handle poor performance carefully—support and coach.

Visiting and Being Visible. However, the best means of calming stressed-out employees and keeping their focus on performance is through management by walking around. This is a familiar and reassuring sign of continuity to employees and signals that management has nothing to hide from them. Regular visits also give managers more feedback about how people see the transition and enable them to test and gauge preliminary proposals for change.

Retaining Key Talent. Finally, a common mistake made by managers is to assume that they really know and understand what their people are thinking and feeling during this period. This can be especially costly when a manager assumes that key talent is committed to staying. A merger invites top performers to rethink their career path within a company and test the market for outside opportunities. Headhunters are happy to help them in their search. Three strategies can aid a retention effort:

1. Assemble a list of top performers in an acquiree and get to them quickly with job offers and appropriate incentives. This is crucial in cases where certain "human assets" (say, the sales staff or engineering experts) are crucial to the success of the deal. It helps to listen to the counsel of acquired leaders (formal and informal) who may hold the key to retaining people.

2. Watch out for "sibling rivalry" on the buyer's side after the well publicized "signing" of acquired superstars. When warranted, buyers need to reassure their employees that their contributions are recognized and that the objective of the merger is to add to, not replace, existing talent.

3. Let managers who are obvious choices for retention know that the company is counting on them. This is a stressful time when perceptions are muddled: Do not take the risk of assuming that talented people know how highly they are valued.

In summation, remember that human stress, uncertainty, and anxiety are *inevitable* in a merger or acquisition. Our message is that a portion can be reduced by positive and proactive management.[13] Sure the natural inclination is for CEOs to move on to other matters and for executives to cope with their own stress by retreating behind closed doors, leaving employees to "tough it out" and cope as best they can. But this is another reason why so many combinations fail.

CHAPTER 6

Managing Integration

Proceed carefully. Let things take root. You're not laying down astroturf; you're planting seeds.
— Advice to Citicorp managers on the integration process[1]

The chairman brought the top 10 people from both firms together and told us that we had a lot of potential if we could merge product lines and use each other's systems. They then told us that, although there would be some start-up costs, they were confident that synergies would more than outweigh these and that we shouldn't have a performance dip. The two sides were left staring at each other wondering why we were there and how we were going to make it work.
—Manager quoted by David Jemison, "Process Constraints on Strategic Capability Transfer During Acquisition Integration"[2]

As two companies combine, there are a multitude of decisions to be made, encompassing reporting relationships, budgeting and performance requirements, operational structures, and staffing levels as well as the integration of policies and compensation, measurement, and control systems. The common scenario is for the lead company to guide these decisions through its tried-and-true integration framework. Regular acquirers have well-mapped-out models of and procedures for integrating smaller concerns. However, there is a body of evidence to suggest that past experience is not always the best guide to planning a new combination. Managers frequently oversimplify the planning process and overrely on analogies from past successes to develop and justify their stratagems in a new situation.[3]

Furthermore, "packaged" integration plans seldom take account of hard-to-get-at synergies and a partner's idiosyncracies and preferences. Typically, these issues are not addressed until a crisis forces harried executives to make ad hoc decisions driven by time and testiness rather than by careful review. Effective precombination planning, where possible, can forestall some of these crises and establish a skeletal framework for integrating the businesses. But it is after the sale that companies typically delve into the details.

Now new players join the deliberations, as staff personnel and midlevel managers become involved, and people have to contend with counterparts whom they do not know, trust, or can yet depend on. It is the need to address and resolve integration issues, complicated by a lack of knowledge and an absence of trust, that leads executives on each side into a crisis management mode.

CRISIS MANAGEMENT

Research shows that formal organizational structures and routines dissolve in the first stages of a crisis.[4] Executives go their own way in analyzing the situation and responding to it; there are high levels of tension and conflict, and turf protection and self-promotion are commonplace. Crisis management is aimed therefore at pulling executives together and focusing their brain power on the problems at hand. In the typical combination scenario, a top body of executives on each side emerges to "take charge" of the situation.

However, each management team in a merger has its own definition of the situation, its preferred methods for analyzing problems and confronting conflicts, and its own distinct interests to satisfy. In the case of Graphic Controls acquisition by Times Mirror, for example, GC's proposals for getting people together to review options and make collaborative decisions about the best form of integration were "foreign" to the parent company. It seemed a needless waste of time and energy in a routine situation where Times Mirror had a "plan" for integrating subsidiaries, and where, as a matter of course, it implemented standard procedures and strictures. Given that the parent had rescued the subsidiary, GC's complaints about these "givens" smacked of ingratitude and disrespect.

In the case of Burroughs and Sperry, the lead company had no preordained plan for integrating Sperry. On the contrary, it was up to the leaders of both companies to work together in a collective forum to figure out how to draw from the strengths of both organizations in building a new one. This high-minded idea was resisted by executives on both sides who objected that, rather than appoint task forces, managers should be appointed forthwith and be left to decide how their functions should be organized. That would, in Blumenthal's opinion, have led to Burroughs' domination. He countered that the true merging of the companies, under the principles outlined, required in-depth analysis of the best structures and careful selection of the best people to run them. Task force members should have a "free hand" in finding the best way to organize—unencumbered by personal or organizational bias. Hence task forces would be co-led by executives from both companies. This way fresh thinking would be brought forth and decisions would be made in an evenhanded manner.

Here are two distinct ways to manage the integration of two companies. In the one case, a powerful parent seeks to impose its model on a righteously rebellious child, or so it seemed to GCers. In the other case, a powerful CEO insisted on fairness and fresh thinking. Both approaches, however, would lead to conflict and consternation. The work of combining companies always does.

This chapter therefore looks at the dynamics of integration planning and transition management as a merger works its way through the two companies involved. It focuses on the challenges of integration planning through joint-company task forces and what it takes to make this kind of process succeed.

TWO APPROACHES TO INTEGRATION

The real integration issues arise when the two managements get down to planning function by function. Where will there be heat? Wherever there is friction. In the case of Times Mirror and GC, for example, the acquirer was seeking financial control, whereas GC was seeking to maintain its independence and freedom of action. Hence conflicts between the two companies centered on high level reporting relationships and financial requirements. This is typical in conglomerate acquisitions.

In cases of more complete integration, where physical assets must be combined and functions have to be integrated, conflict can be broader based and envelope many more people. Certainly the two top managements' relationship sets a tone for these dealings, but the motivations and stratagems of functional heads give business unit integration a life of its own. Decisions must be made about which company's methods and systems to adopt and which side's philosophy of marketing, service, and sales.

When the Buyer Dictates. In many mergers and acquisitions, the buyer dictates the terms of integration. Parent company financial and human resource managers come into a subsidiary, undertake extensive procedural and personnel reviews, and determine how and when the lead firm will introduce its own management systems and controls. Schedules are set whereby the acquired company will conform to new reporting relationships and regimens. Decisions come quickly in this approach. But there is a emphatic need for thorough—and accurate—planning on the part of the lead company.

Consider Alpha Electronics' (a pseudonym) integration of the corporate functions of an acquired firm, called Multi Plex (MP also a pseudonym). Alpha's overall plan was to consolidate staff functions and maintain two separate sales and marketing divisions. Accordingly, managers from both sides rolled up their sleeves and together developed plans for building on the best from each company. By contrast, Alpha's Finance and Accounting (F&A) group moved in like gangbusters. For a time their domination was limited to staff functions. Then broader conflicts erupted in the line organization from the imposition of Alpha's systems. Suddenly MPers couldn't track orders or ensure shipping dates. The separate MP sales division was in an uproar. Alpha didn't understand MP's methods of order entry and management. And its financial systems were "unplugging" the sales division. Fortunately, Alpha's senior management reined in the financial group and insisted they take a closer look at integration options. A study was commissioned, involving people from both companies, to review plans and rethink priorities. The group discovered that many a priori assumptions about the superiority of Alpha's systems were warranted but that the systems themselves did not fit MP's circumstances. Hence it was agreed that the two company's order management systems would run in parallel for a time and then be integrated gradually.

Rationality or Politics? Professor David Jemison sees this as a common strategic problem for acquirers who have what he calls a *unitary* theory of the combination and a *deterministic* philosophy about its execution.[5] Stated another way, these are buyers who accept only one model of how to do business—their own. But it also has a political dimension. We have often observed corporate staff groups impose their methods on a subsidiary with scant attention to the appropriateness or "value added." They introduce binder after binder of rules, policies, and procedures that smack of "bureaucracy" and "administrivia" to a subsidiary. It can seem like lunacy to an acquired company. But there is a method to the seeming madness. By imposing their systems, corporate staff groups *control* the integration process and often gain more resources and sway in the combined organization. One manager we interviewed had an apt political term for this process: corporate staff *hegemony*.

Professor Jemison argues that domination *can* be a successful combination strategy when a parent company wholly absorbs a subsidiary. It doesn't work, however, when the success of the combination depends on mutual synergy and the combined know-how of people. Dominated managers and employees usually leave. Or else they sabotage integration.

Adapting the work of scholars Karen Siehl and Gerald Ledford,[6] we compare and contrast integration strategies based on domination versus participation. (See Figure 6.1).

Figure 6.1
Two Styles of Integration

	One Company Dominates	Both Companies Participate
Time Frame	Short	Long
Transition Structure	Unimportant	Important
Transition Plan	High Need for Pre-Planning/ Lead Company Drives Plan	High Need for Post-Planning/ Both Companies Develop Plan
Resources	High—Lead Co. Experts and Consultants	High—Two Cos. Managements and Staff Support
Communication	One-Way	Two-Way
Influence	Unilateral	Mutual
Problem Solving	Afterward	During
Costs/Benefits	High Turnover/ More Turnaround	Lower Turnover/ Less Turnaround
	Quick but Painful	Slower but Less Painful

The Benefits of Participation. Blumenthal had a clear rationale for taking a more participative approach to integrating Sperry and Burroughs:

> First of all, we had to be substantively sure, say how you put together the field service organization, that you get the best thinking into it. Second, you want to begin to identify the best people to run things, which comes out through this process. And, third, you want people to have ownership, so that both sides feel they've had fair input...and are both architects. It wasn't just a Blu-

menthal thing. We didn't want to make unilateral decisions.

Participation takes time. Executives from both sides work on task forces and staffers at all levels contribute to fact-finding. It is likely to result in less voluntary turnover and, importantly, less turnover of top performers. And it's less painful. Still, the approach does not, of itself, put the combination on solid footing. That requires executives to lead the integration process.

CREATING "NEWCO"

Blumenthal created a Merger Coordination Council (MCC), staffed by top executives from Sperry and Burroughs, to oversee the integration of the two companies. Task forces were formed to prepare studies and recommendations on the merging and reorganization of all functions. The MCC was the focal point for senior level review and decision making. It issued cost bogeys and policy guidelines for each task force. These were the only benchmarks established. Blumenthal pointedly emphasized that although cost guidelines were sacrosanct, the task forces had free reign in formulating recommendations in support of six integration objectives:

1. Develop the new organization.

2. Integrate marketing worldwide.

3. Review noncore businesses.

4. Consolidate operations.

5. Integrate products.

6. Improve financial performance.

The task forces, cochaired by executives from each company, met continuously for six months after the sale and reported their findings over the course of several high-level review meetings. There was a risk that the task forces would favor current practices at the expense of innovative thinking. On this matter, Blumenthal noted,

> It was evident where the relative strengths and
> weaknesses (of the two companies were)....nobody goes
> into this with a blank mind...but I really wanted partic-
> ipation.... I always took a posture that, for example, we
> could set up a Line-of-Business organization or we might
> not....You guys look at it, there are pluses and minuses.

This structure was conceived of as something more than just a temporary vehicle for introducing change. It was designed, instead, as a *seed bed* in which to grow a new company culture. Early on executives began to refer to themselves as part of "NEWCO," meaning new company, and social events and ceremonies helped them to build trust and confidence in one another. Blumenthal made it a point to plant his own seeds among executives:

> I have a view and therefore a style of how I think a
> company ought to be run and how decisions ought to
> be made at the top....You try to be open and honest and
> let it all hang out with your colleagues and try to have
> team consensus....Now I tried to do that (as head of the
> MCC) with occasional lapses into arbitrariness.

MANAGING THE INTEGRATION
PROCESS

When the intent is to put companies together participatively, it is important to have a formal transition management structure. But several factors must be considered before moving ahead on this method of integration:

1. The design of a formal transition structure

2. The responsibilities of transition team

3. The orchestratation of analyses and reviews

Designing a Formal Transition Structure

In the case of Burroughs and Sperry, and several other companies we have worked with, the formal transition structure has had several elements.

Top-Level Oversight. Top managers' role is to lead integration through a coordinative body that sets guidelines, oversees analyses and findings, and fits recommendations into the big picture. In the case of NEWCO, this group was called the Merger Coordination Council and included Blumenthal, the presidents of Burroughs and Sperry, the two chief financial officers and human resource heads, plus legal counsel. This group initially met weekly and then monthly over the course of the nine-month integration effort. Each member received a briefing book updating recommendations and plans for integration throughout the two companies (see Figure 6.2).

Figure 6.2
NEWCO Transition Structure

MERGER COORDINATION COUNCIL

Staff Liaison

Chairman
Two Company Presidents
Legal Counsel
Two Financial Officers
Two Human Resources

LINE COMMITTEES
(Co-Chairs)

STAFF COMMITTEES
(Co-Chairs)

Domestic Marketing
International Marketing
Product Operations
Customer Service
Program Management
Research & Development
Federal Goverment
Defense Systems

Accounting and Finance
Legal
Human Resources
Corporate Communications
Investor Relations
MIS

Certainly there are other workable models of top-level oversight. In the case of Molson and Carling O'Keefe, for example, two top executives were taken off their regular assignments, retitled "managers of strategic redeployment," and charged with overseeing merger planning and implementation. In another case, a "kitchen cabinet" composed of the buying company CEO and his team plus three acquired managers met initially to set the integration framework and then periodically to review progress and decisions.

In the joining of Hewlett-Packard and Apollo, as a final illustration, a single project manager, Brian Moore, was tapped to coordinate the work of various task forces in HP's Workstation Group and to intersect with the deliberations of a "technology convergence" committee chartered with merging the two companies' computing architectures. Naturally, the nature of the deal (whether a true merger or acquisition), the depth of integration (full to partial to scarcely any at all), and the scope of activity (whether companywide or within a single division) influence who exercises top-level oversight and how much is needed. In our experiences, however, top executives generally do not exercise as much oversight as needed and too often delegate responsibilities to managers and groups lacking the fortitude or muscle to make tough decisions.

Functional Task Forces. Functional task forces (or transition teams), chaired and staffed by managers from both organizations, are needed to study potential areas jointly for integration and enumerate the strategic and operating implications. Task forces report and make their recommendations to the top level coordinating body.

Fourteen task forces were formed in the case of Burroughs and Sperry, representing all the major line and staff functions. Senior managers from each company cochaired the task forces, and members were drawn from both sides. Each team was given a general assignment and ground rules for going about its work. "Cronyism and empire building were taboo," recalls former Sperry president Joe Kroger. "We made it clear that people must have open minds. Those who would try to protect their turf would be 'eliminated'."

In the case of the Allied/Bendix merger, seven joint-company task forces were formed supplemented by the efforts of special subtask forces and outside consultants. Members worked 60 to 70 hours per week, meeting alternatively in Morristown, New Jersey and Southfield, Michigan, the two corporate headquarters. A corporate jet made daily shuttles between the two cities so that people could meet at each other's locations and still be home at night with their families.

David Powell, senior vice president for public affairs in the combined company, offers a summary of two key ingredients to the success of this approach: "You have to have a blend of aggression and humility. The former allows you to be decisive while the latter makes it possible for you to be sensitive and listen to people."[7]

Staff Support. Beyond these formal structures, there is also a need to provide staff assistance to the transition leadership and task forces. In the case of Burroughs and Sperry, for example, a young marketing manager, Curt Girod, kept track of data bases and documentation, prepared briefing books, coached individual managers on protocol and presentation formats, and handled the arrangements for MCC meetings. Girod was a crucial communication link between Newco executives and Blumenthal and helped all concerned to handle differences in personality and style.

In another case, an executive devoted his energies full time to the self-titled role of "merger czar." He tracked the work of joint-company task forces, brought functional heads together for informal coordination meetings, and, when warranted, "blew the whistle" on power moves and helped to reassert fairness when politics began to prevail.

Outside Consultants. Outside consultants can offer needed technical advice and lend an impartial review to task force findings. A team from Booz, Allen & Hamilton, for example, worked with marketing executives from Burroughs and Sperry to review their studies and conclusions. This was, after all, a "bet the company" decision complicated by the fact that the sales force of Burroughs was geographically organized while Sperry had a "line of business" organization.

Consultants with expertise in organizational development can also contribute to this kind of transition process. Consultant Robert Blake, for example, has teams from both companies prepare, separately, their view of the synergies obtainable and problems posed under different combination scenarios and then present them to their counterparts. Blake acts as a "process facilitator" to ensure that each side's views are heard and understood.[8] This kind of facilitation has the added benefit of breaking down some of the barriers between the two groups.

Assigning Transition Team Responsibilities

A transition team is only as good as the people who lead it. Most experts recommend that top functional managers headup task forces, as they will have ultimately to run the operations. But there are instances where a politically astute manager can fleece a more accommodating counterpart. As well, there are cases where current management is so vested in the status quo that there is little room for give and take.

Hence Blumenthal made careful selection of task force chairs a top priority. He knew that cochairs might get knotted up in infighting while representing their constituencies. Thus he personally interviewed candidates to find people with "breadth, good analytic capability, and objectivity." Some top executives were not assigned task force responsibilities. Instead their job was to run current operations. Others were assigned membership, rather than leadership, roles because, frankly, they were not "team players." Eventual selections were executives of commensurate rank from both companies.

Then, to ensure the freest range of thinking possible, transition teams were staffed by people from diverse functions. The operations task force included a manager from marketing. The customer service team had representatives from manufacturing who, incidentally, introduced some of their models for total quality improvement into the service function. Also included were some "fresh faces" drawn from the ranks who had no axes to grind or people to protect. In several cases, this careful selection of leaders and members led transition teams to abandon the past practices of both companies and propose more innovative recommendations.

It is often necessary to take some transition team leaders off their normal assignments and charge them with the task of making the integration work. Certainly there are risks that this will lead to problems back in each organization where "nobody is minding the store." One solution is to have outside consultants gather data and prepare recommendations. Another is to involve recently retired or near-retirement executives. Of course, it helps to have junior executives do much of the legwork. For transition teams to be effective, however, they must be staffed by multitalented and highly credible figures. Short-term operational losses are worth the long run benefits of putting the companies together right.

Guidelines. Blumenthal kicked off his first meeting of the MCC and transition team cochairs with an energizing speech about his hopes for the combination. Then came financial realities. Not including divestitures, $150 million in savings would have to be found in the first year with another $200 million in savings the second year. His aim was to double earnings per share. Achieving this "fast start" would be essential to building confidence in the new company, Blumenthal noted. It was also imperative to reducing debt and improving the combined company's credit rating.

Earnings like this were far beyond financial analysts' expectations and the premerger performance of both companies. Skepticism ran high, exceeded only by the wonderment of how it could be achieved and worries about where the cuts would come from. Blumenthal specified "a six- or seven month decision horizon" and charged executives with coming up with the necessary financial, operational, technical, product, and marketing changes needed to make the new company "something we'll all be proud of."

An MCC member recalled his reaction: "No one had ever been through a merger of equality before. Everyone realized that they had to simultaneously come up with innovative plans for the new company, keep the business running at peak levels, and all under a time constraint. It was really challenging!" Others were not so upbeat.

Executives on Trial. Many managers from both sides were "on trial" during this transition process. Merger experts advise lead companies to get management swiftly into place before beginning any integration. This recommendation is sound and workable in cases of modest integration, where few managers are in direct competition or when many acquired senior managers are leaving. In this case, however, Blumenthal had not yet sized up managers in Sperry and decided to use the transition process to gain perspective on their capabilities. He made it known he wanted to appoint executives who could work together.

Some could not countenance this delay and pressed Blumenthal to make management appointments—and quickly. One Burroughs manager lobbied him repeatedly and threatened to resign unless he was named to head a combined business. Blumenthal finally told him, in no uncertain terms, that unless he could respect the "we" proposition, he would have no place in the new company.

Another top executive commented, "You can't have business heads 'sit on the sidelines' as a new organization is being designed." But Blumenthal was adamant about giving task forces free rein to design the best organization possible without concern for the person who might eventually run it. In the GE-RCA deal, as a counterpoint, line executives were named first and then directed studies to plan implementation.

Certainly the NEWCO, transition teams could have floundered with leaders lacking formal rank and title. In most cases, however, skill, persistence, and personal credibility enabled task force cochairs to exercise influence without formal authority. Of course, the chairman's imprimatur behind their task force leadership gave them added weight.

Orchestrating the Process

All the work involved in tracking decisions, coordinating interrelated plans, and ensuring a smooth flow of communication can be mind boggling. Hence there is need for procedures to ensure that information gets to and from the right people, that different teams implicated in a decision meet and agree on a course of action, and that recommendations point in a compatible and coherent direction.

In the case of NEWCO, for example, several task force heads complained that they were either ahead of or lagging behind other groups. One manager noted that he could not contemplate plant closings until he knew the product profile. Another said he could not estimate staffing requirements until the severance arrangements were clarified. A complex process like this *segments* the work of task forces. Thus there is a risk that task forces will formulate recommendations based upon their own idiosyncratic assumptions and criteria. They may also fail to digest fully the ramifications of their recommendations for other areas. How can segmentation be countered? It is essential for task force cochairs to act as *integrators*. In this case, for example, the cochairs of interdependent teams held several offsite "skulling sessions" to compare progress and discuss common problems. Curt Girod and his staff ensured that recommendations from different groups were compatible. Furthermore, the MCC reviewed the assumptions and methodologies used by task forces and insisted that teams crosscommunicate.

Reviews. To ensure coordination of the transition teams, the Merger Coordination Council met frequently to obtain updates and issue needed directions. During one meeting, for example, it was discovered that sales representatives from each company were continuing to "clobber" one another in bidding for customer contracts. Accordingly, guidelines were issued to prevent new colleagues from undercutting one another. In addition, several off site meetings were held where task force cochairs would meet, en masse, with the MCC. This kept everybody abreast of problems and publicly highlighted requirements for further coordination.

Nourishing the Transition. There was also some fun at Newco. We've mentioned the red baseball caps bearing the Sperry and Burroughs logos. At another executive review, caps with "NEWCO" across the front were distributed and Blumenthal spelled out for his colleagues what the future would mean for them if they met financial targets: more fun and more money! And, in a simple gesture, spouses of task force heads were sent a crisp bill of sufficient amount to enjoy a lavish night on the town with their hardworking honeys.

TRANSITION MANAGEMENT TASKS

The transition period sets the terms of the combination—it is hoped by design rather than by default. Is it truly a merger or more like an acquisition? Are functions going to be consolidated, partially integrated, coordinated, or left to run their own way? Completion of combination plans answers these kinds of questions. They also signal whether the combined company or an acquiree will expand in scope and staff or contract and reduce ranks.

Top executives and combined company task forces have three interrelated transition management tasks to accomplish. The first is *knowledge building*. Each side needs to teach the other how it goes about doing business. This can be crucial: A study by Egon Zehnder International found that the number one problem cited by 25% of combining companies was a lack of understanding of their partners.[9]

The second task involves *relationship building* and conflict management. Every integration is marked by some degree of mistrust and conflict at the point of integration. Reporting and power relationships are realigned. Functions have to be integrated or, at minimum, coordinated and placed under new types of control. New interpersonal relationships have to be formed. All this produces tension and backbiting.

If the conflicts are not managed, companies suffer through bureaucratic infighting, parochial politics, and destructive power struggles. The usual result is lost efficiency, higher costs, less innovation, and frustrated and frazzled people. If, however, the conflicts are handled well, then the parties can bring original thinking to the combination, come up with creative solutions to problems, and develop more innovative products, services, and ways of doing business.

The third task concerns *implementation*. Integration can be strategically planned and then subverted by turf-grabbing managers on the lead company side, turf-protecting managers on the acquired side, or simply by unexpected developments that necessitate a change in direction and put new parties into conflict. Transition teams have to lay the groundwork for implementing their plans and bring supervisors and employees into the loop.

Knowledge Building

To make sound decisions, managers on both sides need to draw on each other's knowledge to define the combined company's structure, strategy, and business identity. Naturally, this requires a close look at the financials and staffing patterns in each company, whatever the type of combination, and a closer look at products, marketing, corporate staff, organizational structure, and business systems as warranted. The key task is to identify the problems and prospects of making the combined business model work.

Apple-to-Apple Comparisons. In the Burroughs and Sperry case, common procedures were established to compare the companies:

1. **Functional analyses.** The two companies were organized differently, so a first step in making "apple-to-apple" comparisons was to compare the two sides' functions. Each task force identified core common functions to be analyzed and then noncore functions which would be handled separately.

2. **Baselines.** Next, baseline figures of costs and headcount were summarized for core areas.

3. **Organization structure.** Each task force recommended an operating structure for its area of the business. The guidelines were to design a structure that would make things happen quickly, keep staff close to essential business and customers, develop broad spans of control, encourage a "hands-on" approach to the business, and balance the supervision of staff groups against the need to service line units.

4. **Staffing plan.** Lists of qualified candidates were prepared for each position below the function head, down to first-line supervisors. This involved preparing position descriptions, analyzing staffing requirements (e.g., education, previous experience, functional expertise, etc.), and listing candidates along with their years of service, time in current position, Burroughs versus Sperry affiliation, rating of readiness, and other pertinent information.

5. **Management process and support systems.** Management policies, decision-making processes, and support systems that related directly to organization, staffing, or cost reductions were identified, and recommendations were made for their partial or complete integration across the two companies.

6. **Cost reductions**. Finally, each task force developed a specific cost-reduction plan. Savings could be identified from various sources: redundant or superfluous activities, productivity improvement, reduced service level, make versus buy decisions, or choosing a more efficient way of doing things, whether based on the using the "best" of one company's existing practice or finding an altogether new way of operating.

Analyses and recommendations in these six areas were then forwarded to the MCC for review and approval. To build knowledge further, task force cochairs from other areas would sit in on these reviews, make comments, and answer questions as to the implications for their areas.

"**Open Kimono**." Eyes can really be opened when knowledge building reaches what one manager described as the "open kimono" phase. In the HP and Apollo case, for example, engineers from the two companies played "nicey-nicey" until it came time to decide whose approach to hardware and product development would prevail. HP had standard procedures for hardware design and product delivery that were executed under a formal phase review process. Specialized teams would work on "components" of a computer system and engineers relied on a "test-correct-retest" model of product certification. By comparison, Apollo created cross-functional teams to build computer systems and executed product delivery through its program management organization. Its engineers operated under a philosophy of "simulate-verify-ship" with faster time to market but, oftentimes, more quality problems (see Figure 6.3).

Once these differences were aired, argued through, and understood, a task force of engineers from both sides listed the many pros and cons of each approach. HP's model was less flexible, but Apollo's was more costly. HP's made better use of capital and got manufacturing involved early on. Apollo's promoted more teamwork and stimulated more entrepreneurial energy. As the engineers "got naked" they began to see ways of drawing on each other's methods. In the end, it was agreed that HP would retain some of its design and delivery systems and Apollo would retain some of its ways as well. Practices of common interest and applicability were, in turn, introduced to relevant work areas by their author—either an HP or an Apollo engineer.

Figure 6.3
Hardware Product Development:
Hewlett Packard versus Apollo

	ADVANTAGES	DISADVANTAGES
HP MODEL		
• Process driven	Shared resources	Less flexibility
• High quality	Plant involvement	R&D not in cost/product specs
• Internal vendors	Better capital utilization	
• Complex infra-structure		
APOLLO MODEL		
• People driven	Program manage-ment	More overhead
• Time to market	Entreprenurial spirit	Lab-and-manufac-turing overlap responsibilities
• R&D retains prod-uct responsibility		

New Methods. This illustrates how there is often a need to reexamine and restate the strategy behind the combination in light of these analyses. Many times new business opportunities emerge as the partners get to know one another. In other instances, they discover that hoped for synergies can't be realized. This means rethinking, say, the integration of product lines or the coordination of marketing plans—or, in the case of HP/Apollo, the full merger of product development programs.

What happens in cases where neither company's approach is optimal? Again, in the case of Burroughs and

Sperry, each side had a "half-ass" benefits program. "Put them together," noted one manager, and "we'll make a complete ass of ourselves." Accordingly, Mike Losey and a team of human resource people scrapped both benefits plans and devised a new flexible spending benefits account. They actually saved money with the new plan and won the approval of most employees.

Relationship Building

To truly combine companies requires the development of a unified mind-set, rapport, and confidence between the two managements and a sense of common purpose. Combination principles establish the basis of a relationship between companies. But they don't guarantee that managers and task forces will work together effectively or find common points of integration.

There are at least three different kinds of conflict that hamper the relationship between combining companies:

Power-Based Conflicts. These emanate from differences in the size of the two parties and their relative degree of influence over integration decisions. In principle, two big companies can merge their operations harmoniously and large companies can influence smaller ones without acrimony. In practice, however, power moves by a buyer and resistance by subsidiary managers often lead to open hostility.

Substantive Conflicts. These stem from the competing perspectives and priorities of the two functional heads—in staff areas, manufacturing, marketing, sales, distribution, and so on—about how their units should be integrated. The squabbles over the different engineering practices of HP and Apollo are an example.

Symbolic Conflicts. Surface conflicts over the integration of financial systems or coordination of marketing plans may represent deeper-seated battles over cultural superiority versus inferiority. In the case of HP and Apollo, for example, the real battle was not over engineering methods per se; rather it was over the standardization of a very entrepreneurial technology-driven business.

All three types of conflicts are played out in the integration phase. Hence managers have to contend with them in task forces when it comes to studying options and making integration decisions. This means that conflicts have to be anticipated in advance and managed online.

Transition Team Building. Transition teams reap real benefits from some form of team building to clarify their communication and develop better working relationships. A member of a Newco transition team recalled his first team meeting:

> It reminded me of a high school dance, all the girls on one side and all the boys on the other. We really didn't know what to do or say. It was awkward for the Burroughs side because we had instructions not to appear as if you wanted to "rape-and-pillage". It was awkward for the Sperry side for obvious reasons.

To move beyond this awkwardness, some transition teams participated in off-site workshops to learn more about merger dynamics and clarify team members' expectations and roles. These groups moved through the stage of what one observer called "ballroom dancing" to the point where issues were openly addressed and resolved. By contrast, the less well-managed groups became bogged down in "religious wars." Said one cochair, "Several of the task forces became polarized, setting the stage for establishing enemies and bad feelings between the two sides."

From our vantage, groups that went through team building got off to a faster start and made more progress. Teams that neglected to set ground rules and build fraternity tended to put off tough decisions and reached more impasses.

Problem Solving and Conflict Resolution. Because of time pressures and anxieties, there is a tendency for transition task forces to rely on horse trading and compromise rather than problem solving and conflict resolution when it comes to integration decisions. There simply isn't enough time to gather and digest all the needed facts or to review and challenge fully the assumptions used in developing recommendations. Once a course of action is chosen, in turn, commitment escalates because the costs of going back to ground zero are simply too great.

It has been recommended that to prevent escalating commitments and to reduce "groupthink," time be set aside by policy groups to reevaluate previously abandoned courses of action and recalibrate the costs, risks, and benefits of chosen courses of action. Task force cochairs are advised to conduct such investigations before committing themselves to integration plans. Otherwise, the boss may do it!

In the case of Newco, as an example, Blumenthal was the final arbiter of task force recommendations. He repeatedly queried task force cochairs on the matter of horsetrading or compromises by asking them to review their rationale for decisions, by looking at the options they rejected, and, in some instances, by aggressively challenging their conclusions. Pretty soon other executives picked up the gauntlet, and "sloppy work" earned task force chairs a collective rebuke from peers.

In another case, teams appointed a "devil's advocate" to criticize their recommendations and speak in favor of abandoned alternatives. In still another case, a team undertook a "role reversal" wherein the buying company argued in favor of the acquired company's methods and vice versa. This unlocked the conflict and led to a resolution of differences.

Finally, there can be problems in having too little conflict. At Newco, again, some task forces seemed to be ducking tough issues and "going along to get along." Here Blumenthal instituted a new merger principle: "When in doubt, do it now." This forced teams to bring conflicts to a head and get them resolved lest the chairman intervene.

Implementation Plans

In many mergers, the work of transition task forces begins and ends with recommendations. In other cases, by comparison, task forces are chartered with developing implementation plans. In the case of Hewlett-Packard and Apollo, for example, Brian Moore's transition team developed a step-by-step implementation plan specifying integration activities and responsible managers. Careful tracking systems enabled the transition team to coordinate schedules and make necessary adjustments in timing and sequencing. It was found, for example, that plans to introduce HP's order entry systems into Apollo were unrealistic. Accordingly, HP backed off its aggressive timetable and used the added time to train sales personnel in new methods and perfect a computer program for transferring Apollo records to HP systems. In another merger, a senior manager maintained plans and timetables covering seven major integration areas ranging from functional consolidations, to product coordination, to the layoff and outplacement of personnel. He would update his charts weekly and review them with top managers. An illustration of his work, tracking the consolidation of international customer service, along with responsible executives, shows how invaluable such tracking can be (see Figure 6.4).

There can be a "human side" to implementation planning as well. At one merged company, for example, transition teams hosted events where managers and employees could socialize together and exchange personal experiences and professional expertise. On a broader scale, companies can hold "product fairs" to educate people about one another's products; arrange for regular cross-fertilization of people; and, where warranted, stage special celebratory events to help people let go of the past and get excited about the future.

Communicating Developments. As transition teams continue their studies, there is a continuing need to keep the two organizations abreast of transition team developments. In the case of the integration between Alpha and Multi Plex, for example, communications people issued daily updates of merger-related news and published a special newsletter that addressed, over the course of the transition:

- **Issue 1.** Strategic rationale for merger. Vision of combined company. Profile of the CEO and an interview on the principles to be followed in putting companies together.

- **Issue 2.** Graphic presentation of combination model with implications. Task force charters and membership. Key strategic issues to be considered. Profiles on top

Legend:
- ✕ Under Review
- ✳ Plan Completed
- ○ Scheduled for Implementation
- ◐ Implementation in Process
- ● Activity Completed

ACTIVITY	Resp.	April	May	June	July	Aug.	Sept.	4Q88	1Q89	Comment
Organization, Mission, Charter	K.T.		●●							Major Subs in Europe
Conduct Reviews	K.T./J.M.			●●						Announced 6/15 - 6/20
Picked Country Service Managers	K.T.			✕✕✕✕	✕✕✕	○○	○○	○	○	Week of 6/20
Conduct Worldwide Service Mtg.	K.T./J.S.			✳						Country structures in place by 6/30
Org. Intergration at Country Level	K.T./W.F.		✕							Assuming CV installed base
Finnish Dist. Negot'n	K.T./F.F.				○✕○	✕○	✕○	○	○	Revised escalation proc. for tech. probs.
Tech Support	K.T./W.F.									Comb. groups, standize on ISIS, SIMS
MIS	K.T./R.M./D.M.									Transfer to Mktg.
User Groups	K.T./J.P.									Consolidate planning and reporting
Financial Mgmt Reporting	K.T./E.J.									Numerous Differences
Integrate Service Offering	K.T./E.W.									Major Effort
Cross Training	J.S.									

Figure 6.4
Merger Implementation Plan
Customer Service

executives. General timetable as to what will happen and when.

- **Issue 3.** Description of benefits to follow from integration of technologies. International developments. Proposed layoffs and percentage of work force to be affected. Statement by CEO on need for reductions and regret over loss of "treasured tradition" of no layoffs.

- **Issue 4.** Description of role and operations of newly formed placement center. Highlights of severance plan. Needs for better face-to-face communication and more cross-functional coordination. Reports on task force findings and implementation in key operating areas.

- **Issue 5.** Newly combined benefit plan. Articles on integrated electronic mail services and employee award clubs. Updates on business moves.

- **Issue 6.** Domestic customer service management appointments and reorganization plans. Reorganization of human resources and plans for sales/marketing kickoffs. Placement center update with employee interviews and comments.

SPEED OF THE TRANSITION

Frederick Wright Searby has identified a series of competing "pressures" executives face in deciding how fast or slow to move on postcombination changes.[10] Pressures to make changes quickly include (1) the climate for change is better, (2) the momentum of the business must be maintained, and (3) it will be costly to delay making the change. Pressures to make changes slowly or put them off till later are (1) the cost of making a decision is too high, (2) more facts are needed to make a decision, and (3) any decision made now may have to be revised later on.

Searby advises that most changes should be made *quickly*—particularly when the facts are in—as this demonstrates leadership, gets people thinking about change, and reduces the apprehension of people who are waiting for the other shoe to drop. He also notes that the changes can help to "exemplify the management philosophy" of the new company. Certainly this appeals to the bias for action of most executives. Many executives have noted that there is a "window of opportunity" of, say, 100 days following an acquisition where people expect change. Blumenthal, had his own reasons for pushing ahead fast:

> We could have moved slowly, gradually, deliberatively, step by step, and taken two years. We made the decision that if you go step by step, people are waiting for the next shoe to drop. By setting the goal of finishing the merger, in terms of name, people, and product by year end, I wanted the goal to be so ambitious that no one would have the time to question it.

Searby also counsels that "special care" be given to personnel matters since the "manner in which they are resolved will tell much about the new management's style." We would broaden this to apply to all instances where cultural clashes mark the integration. Basically, this means that a lot of attention, concentrated fact-finding, and front-end planning need to be devoted to these areas.

Searby is very straightforward about the handling of executives who resist postmerger change. "Those who cannot be reoriented to new organizational relationships rather quickly must be eliminated." He cautions that this be done fairly and tactfully. On this matter, however, we urge caution. It takes time for some executives to get back on their game. We'll see this in the case of Will Clarkson and his team.

CHAPTER 7

The Clash of Cultures

I have thought of (our parent company) up to this point as an amoeba that absorbs any foreign object in its midst. But that's only one concept of integration. We haven't really explored other models of integration that might be possible.
    —Division general manager, whose company was acquired by a conglomerate[1]

I never knew how strong our culture was until we were acquired.[2]
    —Middle manager

The merger of defense contractor McDonnell Corporation and commercial airplane manufacturer Douglas Aircraft blended two firms with complementary business strengths. It also brought together two work forces, proud of their respective companies' past contributions to the aircraft industry, each set to one-up their merger partner half a continent away. Soon after the merger became legal, pencils were printed with the new "McDonnell-Douglas" name. In St. Louis, pencils were stamped with "McDonnell" next to the eraser; in California, "Douglas" was nearer the eraser end. Both sides wanted their name to last longer as pencils were used.

Companies involved in a merger have unique histories, folklore, and leaders as well as products, markets, and ways of running the business. People are generally proud of their company traditions and cultures. It is part of who they are and what they know succeeds. When a merger brings together two companies, a natural reaction is for people to compare their own group—say, a division or department—with the other and make distinctions between them. Often this precipitates a clash of cultures. This chapter looks at why cultures clash in a corporate combination and how companies manage it.

WHAT IS CULTURE?

The concept of culture draws from anthropology and interprets how peoples live and organize themselves. It links surface characteristics of a society, such as language, appearance, and dress, with their roots in the knowledge, beliefs, and values of the native population. As such, it is often represented as a system where behavior—such as rituals and interactions—are based in people's assumptions about the natural world, society, human nature, and the self. These deep truths about the world come from how people are socialized, which is culturally determined, and are reinforced in the cultural institutions of the homeland.

Scholars of formal organizations have made the point that how a company goes about doing business is indicative of its culture. Professor Edgar Schein of MIT, for example, contends that company cultures provide "answers" to people about how their organization adapts to its environment and provides for their material and psychological needs.[3] Expressed another way, Professor Andrew Pettigrew defines culture as the "glue" that holds the human organization together.[4] As such, culture connects the formal organization, including company policy, strategy, and structure with the informal organization—taken-for-granted ways people interact, think, and go about their everyday behavior.

Corporate culture has been likened to breathing: You don't really think about it until it is threatened. People frequently take their company cultures for granted until a change, like a merger, creates fears that desired aspects of their way of life may be lost. Managers come to revalue key aspects of their company culture as they contemplate a combination. Implicit knowledge of how their company works, and how policies and systems sustain the firm, come to be explicit as they compare their ways with the other side's and reflect on what might be lost. This often leads people to defend their own culture during a merger or acquisition and attack the other one.

CULTURE CLASH— GRAPHIC CONTROLS

To illustrate how cultures are perceived in a combination, consider how managers in Graphic Controls saw their company and the culture of Times Mirror several months after their acquisition. These findings come from interviews with GCers conducted by the authors and Dr. Amy Sales, a cross-cultural psychologist and colleague on this project.[5]

Right from the start, it was apparent that GC and Times Mirror had different expectations about this "business deal" and how it should unfold after the sale. GCers, for example, expected that they would be an active party to all integration decisions. Further, they anticipated that the two sides would study each company's ways of doing business and choose the best systems. Times Mirror, by contrast, had long-established methods for integrating subsidiaries and expected its recommendations would be implemented as a matter of course.

This reflected a cultural difference between the two companies—at least in GCers' eyes. GC people believed in making decisions based on what they called the "authority of knowledge" (rather than power) and through a participative (rather than autocratic) process. This belief system was "Greek" to Times Mirror executives. Times Mirror operated through the "power of aristocrats," in GCers' eyes, who "never heard of participative management." GCers' first contact with their counterparts was, accordingly, "like going to another planet" (see Figure 7.1).

Figure 7.1
Times Mirror/GC Cultural Differences

	Times Mirror	GC
Business-Related Behavior	Monthly reports Two planning meetings Realistic targets "Broadway" presentations	Quarterly reports One planning meeting per year "Stretch" targets Theater-in-the-round
Interpersonal Behavior	Product oriented Command "Chop-chop" Problem solving fast when routine, slow when complex No confrontations "Close to the chest"	Process oriented Request Courteous Problem solving slow but implementation fast "Everything on the table" Open disclosure
Values	Financial, numbers people Power of the aristocrats Third party communication Low levels of responsibility "Protect your ass"	Operations people Authority of knowledge Face-to-face communication High levels of responsibility "Fail forward"
Philosophy	Political Benevolent, authoritarian Control and performance	Familial Participative management "Extraordinary results from ordinary people"

Business-Related Behaviors. GCers noted, first, business-related differences between the companies that were a matter of policy, practice, or custom. These became the focus of early postacquisition conflicts between the two parties. Times Mirror expected detailed monthly reports from all of its subsidiaries and hosted two in-depth planning meetings per year to review results and develop business projections. Times Mirror's systems put a premium on setting realistic financial targets and reaching them. The reviews were normally conducted in a "Broadway-style" boardroom where presentations were to be crisp and polished.

By contrast, GC executives had a different approach to running their company. Managers were given liberal capital expenditure budgets and met quarterly to review targets and results in a freewheeling atmosphere. Annual planning meetings focused on products and markets, much more so than finance, and "stretch" budget projections were revised regularly in line with changing business conditions. Periodic meetings were held with supervisors to review progress and revise targets in a "theater-in-the round" type of meeting.

Interpersonal Behaviors. Business relations between the two companies were complicated by differences in norms and behavior. GCers described Times Mirror executives as very "businesslike, crisp, decisive . . . chop-chop," particularly when demanding information or proposing changes in GC. This represented a strong "product" orientation to human relations. Still, they would keep things "close to the chest" when GCers asked questions and were unable or unwilling to respond quickly to GC's initiatives.

GC people, by comparison, spent more time in the "process" of decision making and would openly put "everything on the table." Both sides agreed that decision making in the subsidiary was as "slow as molasses." But GCers countered that implementation was swift because everybody would "buy in."

Differences in style begot misunderstandings and miscommunications throughout the combination period. Not only were there differences on how to integrate, there were conflicts over how to resolve these differences. At GC, the norm was to air differences openly with the parties involved. Often this involved talking about trust and working relationships—taboo subjects in the parent company. At Times Mirror, personal confrontation was avoided. Instead, third parties—typically other executives—were used to convey concerns.

Values. Differences in the business-related and interpersonal behaviors between the companies led to deeper inferences about the values of the two companies. GCers came to believe that Times Mirror was singularly "profit oriented" and populated by "numbers" people who didn't care about GC's operations or people orientation. Their intent was to "find faults" in GC's financial systems. Staff executives were followed by "lackeys" who were not empowered to make decisions and who were unwilling to make "waves" in the parent company. All of this meant that Times Mirror managers operated with low levels of responsibility and a high "protect your ass orientation." At GC, by comparison, managers had high levels of responsibility and were encouraged to "fail forward" by taking on challenging assignments and bucking the system.

Times Mirror people would call to say "I'll be there next Wednesday at 9:00 A.M." without indicating the intent of the meeting, its objectives, or "checking whether it was a convenient time," GCers complained. They seemed to expect a "yes, sir" attitude which, GCers inferred, meant people were expected to "knuckle under." By comparison, GC's commitment to making knowledge-based decisions was seen as "Swahili" to Times Mirror.

Philosophy. These differences in behavior and values were encapsulated in shorthand depictions of the philosophies of each company. Times Mirror was a "benevolent-authoritarian" kind of organization in contrast to the "family-oriented" GC. Interestingly, GCers acknowledged that because of its size, structure, and founding traditions, it was understandable that Times Mirror would have such a managerial philosophy and be wracked by politics. However, this was denigrated as characteristic of "technocracies."

GC, as a result of its makeup and traditions had a different management philosophy and believed strongly in achieving "extraordinary results from ordinary people." What GCers also recognized, however, was that "the value system of Times Mirror will find its way into GC unless we work very hard to prevent it."

Throughout our interviews, GCers referred to three realms of culture: philosophy, values, and behavior. Although we can differentiate these realms, cultures are unified and internally consistent: philosophy is expressed in values, values are evident in behaviors, and behaviors, in turn, give meaning to a people's underlying philosophy. This means that changes in the way things are done in a company (behavior) also can change, over time, fundamental values and beliefs. This is what GCers were resisting.

STAGES OF THE CULTURE CLASH

People generally expect that hostile takeovers will result in the destruction of their way of life. This was apparent, for example, in the ill-fated attempt of TWA flight attendants to "Stop Icahn." But company cultures are also threatened in more benign situations, as the case of GC and Times Mirror illustrates. Although a chivalrous "white knight"—for saving GC from a takeover attempt—the new owner was anthropomorphized into a wolf, "slavering over our profits." Times Mirror's size, many times larger than GC, could have been equated with security. Instead, the parent company was characterized as "Big Brother," always "looking over the shoulder" of the people at GC.

However ominous the circumstances, the culture clash between combining companies unfolds in four stages:

Perceiving Differences. People focus first on discernable differences between the two companies' leaders, such as their style and demeanor, as well as their respective products and reputation, the kinds of people that work there, and practically all aspects of how the two companies operate and do business. Even the most mundane differences come to people's attention: When Avery executives arrived from California to visit acquired Dennison in New England, their sport coats and slacks became "leisure suits" and their friendly manner was declared "laid back" by their less outgoing counterparts.[6]

Magnifying Differences. Perceived differences between two companies become sharper and more polarized over time. People often start to draw conclusions that differences in, say, business systems reflect deeper differences in values and philosophy. When, for example, A. C. Nielsen was merged with Dun & Bradstreet, it was described as a "marriage made in heaven." Initially, ACN managers were struck by the heavy financial emphasis and reporting requirements of D&B, the dominant partner. Then, when profits fell short of forecasts, the message became clear: behind this financial front was the requirement that you "meet projections or die." Thereafter, D&B managers were transfigured into "tyrants" who ran everything through "numerical models" without a shred of understanding of or compassion for people.[7]

Stereotyping. Next, people begin to typecast those from the other side—noting that their kind *look* the same, *act* the same, indeed *are* all alike. In another computer deal, lead company managers were typecast as "IBMers" because of their starched shirts and blue suits. What was overlooked is that only two of the eight executives had ever worked for IBM (and had both left with the label of "mavericks"). On the other side, acquired managers were described as "hot tempered" and "bad mannered." Why? They yelled at meetings and "talked with their hands"! Then it was discovered that half of the top acquired team were from Italian backgrounds: "That explains it," commented one lead company manager.

Stereotyping is intensified when organizations from different countries combine and even when firms from different parts of the same country come together. Stories abound about "carpetbagging Yankees" who impose themselves on Southerners, "buttoned-down" Easterners who are too "uptight" for West Coasters, and "country bumpkins" who need a lesson or two from city folk. Differences in the religious affiliations and racial makeup of top executive teams can also beget widespread denigration and discord.

Putdowns. This epitomizes the final stage of the culture clash: when the other company is put down as having a less desirable culture. "We" is superior, and "they" is deemed inferior. Northwest flight attendants, for example, regarded their Republic counterparts as "prima donnas" because they did not have to clean airplanes or share hotel rooms on overnight flights. In turn, flight attendants at Northwest were referred to as the "Stepford wives," with reference to the movie about docile, brainwashed clones in a small town. Remember that Hewlett-Packard managers were referred to in the same way by Apollo people. But putdowns come from acquirers, too. Apollo was called "Appalling Computer" in HP!

A sense of superiority has consequences beyond attitudes and perceptions. USAir, for example, not only exuded superiority over acquired Piedmont and PSA, it also forced its acquirees to follow a "mirror image" strategy whereby all would conform to the same policies and procedures. And rather than search for the "best practice," USAir simply imposed its methods. PSA flight attendants, normally spontaneous and witty during safety briefings of passengers, were required to follow a corporate-mandated script. Piedmont's more sophisticated ticket-pricing system was scrapped in favor of the one used by USAir. What's behind this? Industry analysts suggest that the company's years of insulation from major competition gave USAir executives an "inflated opinion of their operating style."[8] In May 1991, USAir finally abandoned service to eight west coast airports brought into its system with the PSA acquisition. Similarly, and around the same time, American Airlines all but negated its acquisition of AirCal when it pulled out of the Los Angeles-San Francisco corridor. Here, too, the lead company's sense of superiority alienated AirCal's "laid back" employees and customers.

MANAGING THE CLASH OF CULTURES

What can be done to sensitize managers to the clash of cultures and prepare them to manage its consequences? Cases like GC and Times Mirror are problematic because the parent company was so unsympathetic and unresponsive to cultural differences and GC employees themselves were too threatened to look objectively at the parent company's culture and their own. In less volatile and more mutual situations, however, the following steps can be taken to awaken managers to and minimize the problems of a culture clash:

1. Create cultural awareness
2. Clarify company cultures
3. Promote mutual respect

Creating Cultural Awareness

A concerted effort to ease a culture clash begins with the recognition that the two sides enter a combination with distinct histories, styles, and reputations. David Roderick, chairman of USX, made it a point to play up the family-oriented culture of Marathon in a speech to both managements and promised that the steel company would not force its more bureaucratic culture on the oil producer. Similarly, HP general manager, Lew Platt, acknowledged that Apollo computer had a more customer-oriented focus than did the parent company and made sure that Apollo's engineering and marketing people kept control over product development in their areas.

These executives explicitly acknowledged cultural differences between combining companies rather than ignoring or denying them. But recognition of differences does not, of itself, forestall a culture clash. Members of both companies need to be educated about natural tendencies to stereotype and put down their counterparts. One method is to educate them about the culture clash through articles in company newsletters and joint-company meetings. Integration planning in the merger of a U.S. business bank with a Japanese-owned retail bank, for example, was kicked off with a presentation of what causes cultures to clash followed by an exercise to diagnose the two sides' national cultures. This helped executives to learn about each other's homeland and minimized stereotypic references in subsequent planning sessions.

To ease groups into a discussion of these subjects, we often have managers and employees "draw" their company cultures or illustrate how the culture clash is affecting them. This provides a visual starting point for subsequent cultural analysis and clarification (see Figure 7.2).

Cross-cultural Understanding

Promoting a good flow of information and contact between combination partners can help to clear up misperceptions. This gives people a thorough understanding about the other side—its history and heroes, people and products, style and systems—and fills a void otherwise defined by rumors and hearsay. There are many methods for learning about the two sides ranging from basic show-and-tell meetings to more in-depth cross-company cultural analyses.

Professional consultants can be useful in offering a dispassionate analysis of the character of both the lead and

Figure 7.2

Manager in Midst of Culture Clash

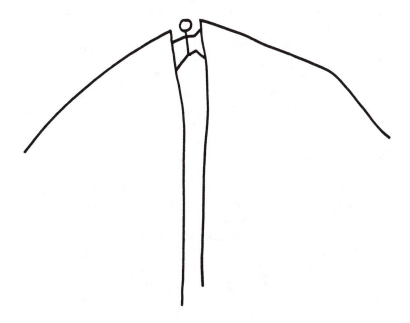

target company. The Novations Group, for example, interviewed some 275 people from Imperial Oil of Canada and Texaco to highlight similarities and differences between the two merging companies. They found a good "fit" between the two cultures. There were, however, some sharp differences between the more bureaucratic Imperial and Texaco's bias toward action. Hence the consultants diagnosed high levels of frustration on Texaco's side, which spurred Imperial to "speed up" the integration and gain more input from their partner's management.

Clarifying Cultures at Time/Warner. A more hands-on forum for cross-cultural analyses is a workshop attended by to-be-combined function managers and their teams. In the human resource areas of Time, Inc., and Warner, for example, top HR executives from each side developed: (1) a roster of the characteristics of their own culture; (2) a complementary roster of their perceptions of the other company; and (3) a roster of how they expected the other company would see them. The two sides then compared lists, noting stereotypes (both accurate and inaccurate), and points of similarity and difference which were then discussed by the two HR teams (see Figure 7.3). Time people, for example, saw themselves as "smart, polite, and professional," driven by "projects and problems" that lent themselves to "quantitative" analysis. To Warner people, they seemed "extremely competent" but very much like "MBAs." Warner people, by contrast, saw themselves as "service oriented," motivated by immediate issues which they would address "on the fly." Time people found them "sensitive and hardworking" but not nearly as well staffed. It was quickly recognized by the two teams that Time people would be the "planners" and Warner people the "reactors."

In addition, the two teams sought to find a middle ground. Time suffered from "too many meetings" and Warner from "too little communication." Time tended to do "too much at corporate" whereas Warner got "too much flak from the field." The two sides then set about finding ways to improve human resource communications without additional meetings and to push more responsibilities to line organizations without creating a new "program."

In this case, Warner's human resource function was brought into Time's corporate office and the merged company's benefit program was administered by Time experts and advanced computer system. As a result, Time brought its strong technical skills and corporate programs to the merger. What Warner added was more entrepreneurial energy and creativity.

Promoting Cross-fertilization. Culture clarification exercises between combining teams can be augmented by companywide efforts to teach the two sides about one another. Company newsletters, special brochures, and videos can all be used to describe the two partners. Efforts to talk up respective product lines and innovative management systems build mutual understanding and respect. As an example, two merged companies, sensitive to differences between their engineering- versus marketing-oriented cultures arranged for

How Time Sees Time	How Warner Sees Time	How Warner Sees Warner	How Time Sees Warner
Be fair to people Competitive benefits	*Benevolent*	Meet basic needs Meet business needs	*Low budgets*
Business partner	*Bureaucratic*	Quick and responsive	*Thinly staffed*
Broad coverage	*Strength in numbers*	Lean and mean	*No role models of best practice*
Information based— Technical/quantitive	*MBA's*	Prioritize issues— Service oriented	*Good instincts*
Project and problem Driven—figure it out	*Professional*	Task oriented— Do it on the fly	*Entreprenurial*
Consensus style Facts and analysis	*Too many meetings*	Negotiate and argue Push it forward	*Too little communication*
Smart and Polite Collegial Motivated and flip	*Open and honest*	Knowledgeable Accountable Caring and fun-loving	*Hard working*

Figure 7.3
How Time Sees Warner/How Warner Sees Time

teams of engineers and marketeers to visit each other's facilities. A lunchroom exhibit showed off the one side's technologies and the other's marketing flair. Managers also invited one another to their homes for dinners so that they could get better acquainted away from the turmoil of integration decision making.

Mutual Respect

The increasing number of international mergers adds another layer to the clash of cultures and increases the importance of understanding and respecting cultural "taboos." Matters of title and salutation, expectations as to dress and demeanor, and even how one shakes hands and enters a room have a different meaning in different national cultures. Protocols exist and combining managers can be put off when their customs are, inadvertently or not, disregarded.

These cultural slights can also cause seemingly sensible integration decisions to backfire. This was the case in the integration of European operations following the merger of two multinational firms. The plan was to centralize marketing and sales in the lead company's U.S.-based headquarters. To keep country managers in the target company on board, the new owners offered them higher-paying, but lesser-ranking, positions that conformed to the buyer's personnel grades. These appointments were turned down by executives in countries like France, where it is considered an embarrassment to play "second fiddle" after heading an operation.

The U.S. executives of the lead company were shunned by those country managers who stayed on. The new owners, in turn, concluded that members of the acquired teams were "ingrates" unwilling to "play ball." Relations deteriorated even more when the U.S. headquarters mandated a top management reorganization in the European operations, prompting the further exodus of acquired executives.

How could this scenario have been avoided? First, by considering closely the merits behind country manager appointments and titles. In several mergers we've worked with, where country managers from both sides were vying for the top job, the most qualified country manager was appointed— irrespective of company affiliation—in service of fairness. In another case, where U.S. marketing executives were clearly defined as "line superiors," the lead company took steps to enhance the country manager's responsibilities and paychecks, and the CEO personally visited each of them to demonstrate his respect for their country eminence.

Plainly it is important to be aware of the relative importance of perks, status, and titles in foreign countries as well as differences in manners and mores. Had the U.S. executives been sensitive to country customs in the case just cited, they might have more personally wooed country managers and, perhaps, offered them titles less indicative of their subordinate status.

Anthropologists subsume all of this under the rubric of "acculturation." Interestingly, they point out that the conflicts and upheaval that come from the modernization of a culture, or as a result of voluntary migrations, are far less pronounced than are those that follow forced occupations and the imposition of the dominant culture's way of life. To translate this to the case at hand, it is to be expected that different kinds of combinations will mean more or less change for the culture of one or both companies.[9]

LEVELS OF ACCULTURATION

There are many possible levels of cultural change following a merger or acquisition.[10] The most prominent are:

1. **Cultural assimilation**: where the lead company absorbs the target

2. **Cultural integration**: where the two companies blend together

3. **Cultural pluralism**: where the two companies simply coexist

In the first type of acculturation, the lead firm imposes itself and its culture on the target. As a result, the acquired company is fully assimilated into the dominant concern. In the most dramatic instances, the lead company dictates integration decisions and deposes and replaces the top leadership in the target company. Researchers Karen Siehl and Gerald Ledford, of the Center for Effective Organizations of the University of Southern California, call this a "pillage and plunder" model of integration.[11]

Assimilation need not, however, involve overt cultural conquest. As history teaches, although the ancient Romans sacked their conquerees and installed their own gods, the ancient Chinese were far more subtle and less monolithic. They merely "civilized" their conquered peoples by showing them how to eat, dress, and trade like other peoples in the empire.

Many big companies have well thought through plans for socializing smaller company executives into their ways. This means subsidiary managers have to accommodate to new practices and systems, to be sure, but it also affords them brighter opportunities and bigger paychecks.

Cultural blending, by contrast, involves the mutual integration of the two combining companies. This requires two-way influence in integration decisions and usually produces benefits and sacrifices for both sides. The Allied/Bendix combination is often cited as a case where the two companies integrated the "best of both." Bendix executives, for example, secured 33% of the top management posts in the combined company, and a surprising postmerger survey found that Bendix people had a more favorable view of the integration than did Allied employees.

Cultural blending can, however, have unforeseen consequences. A bank merger studied by Professors Anthony Buono and James Bowditch seemed to yield the "worst of both." After the end of one year of trauma in both companies, surveys found the majority of people in both banks felt "a lingering resentment toward their merger partners." The combined company's values, according to one employee, were "people are our least important asset."[12]

Cultural pluralism defines combinations wherein the companies establish a relationship based on mutual coexistence, as with USX and Marathon, or where the parent company grants a subsidiary full sovereignty. Gould, Inc., a midwestern automotive supplier that has become a high-technology company follows this strategy. Notes Gould's chief financial officer, "It would be silly for us to impose a different management style on (our acquirees) and run the risk of screwing up their success."[13]

An interesting form of acculturation involves the fundamental change of both company cultures. The "remaking" of General Electric with the acquisition and divestiture of several companies exemplifies the case of a multibusiness company undergoing a massive cultural upheaval. GE Chairman Jack Welch, dubbed "Neutron Jack" because when he visits a subsidiary, the buildings are left standing but all the people are gone, has overseen a restructuring in GE that has, even critics concede, improved the company's strategic profile and profitability. Welch has put GE managers through a "workout" program to redesign structures and processes in operating units and the overall culture of the company. Many leading academicians and consultants have assisted in this effort. Admirers of Welch also point to his innovative use of GE's Tarrytown management development facility to inculcate a new culture among managers.

STRATEGY VERSUS CULTURE

Surveys show that most executives do not take explicit account of cultural differences in making decisions about merging with or acquiring another company. They also show, however, that with hindsight most would put more weight on the chemistry between combining executives, the compatibility of business philosophies and management styles, and generally the degree of fit between the two companies' cultures.[14]

Factoring in "Fit." Alex Mandell of the corporate development function at CSX Corporation led his managers through a disciplined evaluation of possible ways that CSX might link up with acquired SeaLand. Their study addressed several questions:

1. What kind of combination is it? The CSX-SeaLand combination was both a horizontal and vertical merger—joining sea and land transportation companies. The pre-combination planners prepared five different integration options for management, ranging from simply coordinating sales and

marketing between the companies, to their partial integration, to the complete integration of the two company's transport, equipment, and distribution groups. Mandell and his team looked at both the business and financial implications of each of these options.

2. Where are there synergies? There were four potential integration areas in the CSX/SeaLand merger: operations, marketing and sales, information systems, and corporate offices. For each area, the combination planners studied the organizational structures, financial contours, and management practices of the two companies. They then made "apple-to-apple" comparisons between, say, the MIS functions of the two sides to further hone in on the potential for integrating them.

3. How will the organizations "fit" together? Finally, for each of the primary integration areas, the planners compared the organizational and cultural "fit" of the companies and the consequences of different degrees of integration. In the case of full integration, for example, there was the "potential loss of SeaLand identity" to ponder. In specific areas, there would be "conflicts with joint positions" and problems with the "diffusion" of accountability. These kind of qualitative considerations were, in Mandell's view, essential to informed integration decision making (see Figure 7.4).

This planning process highlighted several potential ways to put the companies together function by function. Ten cross-company task forces then fleshed out the data base; added their own experience, perspective, and ideas; and prepared final recommendations for top management.

Degree and Pacing of Integration. A study by the Management Analysis Center of Cambridge, Massachusetts, took this thinking another step by proposing levels of integration based on (1) the importance to strategy, savings, and synergy of integrating functions versus (2) the integration problems associated with cultural clashes (see Figure 7.5). This model draws from the research of corporate strategist Stanley Davis who shows how corporate strategy is confounded by cultural factors.[15] In the present case, the model recommends that companies combine quickly those functions that yield real

Area	Potential for Integration	Primary Integration Benefits	Level of Integration Benefits	
			Cost Savings ($ millions)	Strategic Benefits
Two-Cos. Operations	High	• Reduced costs	***	Low
Information Systems	Medium to high	• Enhanced systems • Reduced development time • Reduced costs		Medium to high
Marketing and Sales	Medium to high	• Enhanced • Enhanced distribution services transition • Reduced costs		Medium to high
Corporate Overhead – Finance – Planning – Law – Human Resources – Purchasing	Low to medium High Low N.A. High Medium	• Reduced costs • Reduced costs • Coordination of planning efforts • Reduced costs • Reduced costs • Purchasing economies of scale		Low Low Low Low Low Low

***proprietary information

Figure 7.4
Combination Planning Protocol:
Savings versus Organization Fit

Figure 7.5
Integration: Benefits versus Ease

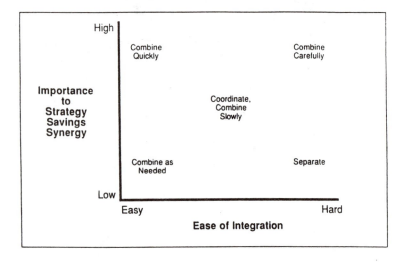

synergy wherever cultural differences are either minimal or unimportant. At the other extreme, where synergies are low and the costs of integrating are high, why bother to integrate? Keep the functions separate.

The difficult cases are when synergies are significant but so are the problems of putting functions together. In many instances, it is recommended that companies coordinate these functions, as is so often the case in product or market extension mergers. Otherwise, combine very carefully when full integration is needed but the culture collision will prove costly. This was the problem facing Blumenthal in achieving the "Power of 2."

CREATING A UNISYS CULTURE

"Am I kidding myself, or has this gone as well as could have been expected?" Mike Blumenthal was contrasting his experiences several months into the Burroughs/Sperry combination with what we had told him could occur and had at other companies. The discussion turned to the competitive strengths of the two companies:

Burroughs	Sperry
Operations and finance	Customers and markets
Bottom line	Customer satisfaction

Burroughs' strength was its operations and finance, reflected most vividly in the backgrounds of its two leaders: President Paul Stern, an engineer, and Blumenthal, an economist. Sperry was more of a marketing company, evidenced by the recent ascent of Joe Kroger from the sales organization to company presidency and as heir apparent to the CEO position. Could it be that Burroughs would dominate on product side and Sperry on marketing side? Blumenthal, lighting a cigar, asked "What's wrong with that?"

Cultural transformation in this case got off to a difficult start. Blumenthal scoffed at our first suggestions of differences between the two firms—"A foolish thought. We speak the same language because we've faced the same competition...and had to jump over the same hurdles." But we were talking about putting people and their ways of life together, not just two business organizations. There was, for example, a perception in both companies that Sperry executives were smoother and more polished than their counterparts in Burroughs. Some of this had to do with their dress, manner, and image as marketeers. At the same time, it led to the stereotype that, at Sperry, style dominated substance.

To Burroughs people, this also meant that nobody was minding the store. During one early briefing, a Sperry executive could not fully explain why his sales were $50 million off target, leading Blumenthal to conclude he was either suppressing the facts or didn't have command of them. Reports from a Sperry engineering site suggested that planned developments in a product line were seriously off schedule and that no one could explain exactly why or seemingly take the steps necessary to get things "cleaned up." Blumenthal couldn't understand why Sperry had no top down oversight over the operations of the business. When we countered that

Sperry had bigger customers and was more decentralized, he just harrumphed.

Burroughs	Sperry
Top-down controls	Lateral networks
Very aggressive	Very polished
Run by the numbers	Run by the people

As we discussed the problems of getting two groups of executives to work together in the Merger Coordination Council and task forces, however, an idea began to germinate. This would be the place to develop not only new structures and staffing plans but also a medium through which to "transform" the two companies' cultures.

People "read" a company through the lens of their own experience and culture. Cronyism had been rampant at Burroughs in the pre-Blumenthal days. Hence when Burroughs people observed their Sperry counterparts as having worked together for 20-plus years and as old friends, the imputation was that the organization was run by "an old boys' network." Carrying the scenario further, it was expected that they would look out for one another, stick together, and foil attempts to build the "best organization" staffed by the "best people."

In truth, Sperry people saw longevity and friendship among top managers as one strength of their culture. It was a mark of loyalty and commitment. Furthermore, old friends trusted one another and knew each other's moves. Hence, managers were given greater autonomy and could run their own shows without a lot of bureaucratic oversight and control.

Blumenthal was surprised to learn how many managers from Sperry perceived his management team. Paul Stern and several others were relative newcomers brought in by Blumenthal to effect a turnaround of Burroughs. He saw them as hard hitting. In Sperry's eyes, by contrast, they were gunslingers. That they had left IBM was a mark of personal ambitiousness rather than corporate loyalty. Sperry managers were suspicious that their counterparts where eager for a "quick killing" and then would leave as soon as they could find "greener pastures."

Burroughs	Sperry
Individual players	Old boys' network
Newcomers cum gunslingers	Inbred and entrenched

To address matters of management style, Blumenthal spoke about his expectations of top managers. Burroughs had become a team with Stern, Unruh, and he functioning well, he told MCC members and task force heads. Now Newco, with Kroger on board, would be run by a team. But teamwork was only one desired characteristic of the new company culture. During one conversation with us, Blumenthal stated, "I have two plaques on my wall behind you." We turned and couldn't see them. He said that the plaques were imprinted in his mind. The first one, he went on, says "Tell the Truth." He then told us how he went to the movies as a lad and hadn't told his mother. When she asked where he'd been, he lied. Further probing had led to more lies and trouble. "It's not just a matter of morality," he said, there are "just too many complications with lying."

The second plaque contained the simple message "Know Your Brief." In the Crown Cork International Corporation, Blumenthal had once worked for a lawyer/accountant who would grill him over the details of operations, travel schedules, and so on. Later, in his tenure at the State Department, he had insisted that subordinates master the details much as he had been expected to master them. Hence he now wanted his executives to study operations in detail when designing the new company.

In an address to senior management on both sides, Blumenthal summed up his life lessons in a series of challenges:

- Tell the good and the bad when you know it. The worst sin is sweeping the bad news under the rug.

- Know your brief. You are expected to know the facts of interest and call it as you see it, not as your boss wants to know it.

- Have ambitious realism in forecasting—and know your numbers all the time, not just once a year.

- Take your commitments seriously. Business reviews are important, and top executives will scrutinize them.

- It is assumed you are high-quality professionals until you prove otherwise.

Blumenthal's personal history—fleeing from Nazi Germany with his family at age 13, serving as Jimmy Carter's Treasury Secretary, and effecting a turnaround at Burroughs—was both intriguing and energizing to Sperry people, who were in need of a vigorous leader following the announced departure of their more taciturn CEO, Gerald Probst. And by exercising strong hands-on leadership, Blumenthal filled an important symbolic and substantive role as a "keeper" of the to-be-formed combined company culture.

CULTURE-BUILDING CEREMONIES

The work of Newco was culminated with ritual and ceremony. At the final meeting of the MCC, it was announced that a new name had been selected for the company from employee suggestions. The winner was Unisys—United Information Systems. MCC members were given new hats and promotional paraphernalia with the new company logo.

The creation of Unisys meant the end of Burroughs and Sperry. To celebrate the histories of the two companies, a slide show was presented at the final MCC meeting that celebrated major developments in the life of each of the companies. As pictures of early Burroughs adding machines and a Sperry gyroscope flashed on the screen, reminiscences gave way to pride as the architects of computing technology saw their products celebrated.

A member of the corporate communications staff assumed the title of CAO—chief anthropological officer—to lead a culture-building ceremony. The CAO asked eight executives each with over 20 years of service—four from Sperry and four from Burroughs—to look back at their careers and select an artifact of personal significance which represented a milestone in their careers. After dinner at an executive retreat, the CAO called each of the eight to present their artifact which was then placed in the newly established Unisys archives.

Among the contributions were a reel of steel tape from the original Univac One, serial number 001, which was used by the U.S. Bureau of the Census in 1951. A former Burroughs executive recounted his days as a sales rep in Chicago where, interestingly, his chief competition came from a Sperry district managed by Joe Kroger, later president of Sperry and now vice chairman of Unisys. Having four scrapbooks of career mementos to choose from, he selected a letter written by a customer who left IBM in selecting Burroughs. The letter, which highlighted the current challenge facing Unisys, concluded, "I am sure you have heard many times how difficult it is for management to venture away from the company which has been leader in the field and which still dominates the field from a volume standpoint. I believe it is a great compliment to you that we were able to reach this decision."

After the presentations, the CAO asked all in attendance to sign a ledger, to be placed in the archive boxes along with the artifacts. This marked their commitment and became Unisys artifact number 001.

CULTURAL RESISTANCE

In the case of GC and Times Mirror, the parent company sought to integrate its acquisition financially. This is standard practice. However, here the parent's authoritarian manner and seeming denigration of their own cultural mores, smacked to GCers of subjugation. This led them to act, in their own words, like "rebellious children." This is what is meant by cultural resistance.

Times Mirror was perceived as putting GCers "through the wringer" to feed its "profit hungry" machinery. It was also essential for GC to "change the way we do things" in order to comply with parent company policies and prerogatives. To an extent, this is a mild form of acculturation. GC's executives were able, to this point, to maintain their culture as an "ethnic minority" in Times Mirror. They had to adapt to the dominant culture's requirements (more profits) and language (money not products) and take on a subsidiary's demeanor (acquiescence), at least in formal dealings and when particular policies and rules were enforced.

However, they were successful in maintaining key aspects of their compensation plan and preserved their rights to prepare their own budgets, fully disclose financial data to supervisors, and handle contracts with outside parties without Times Mirror oversight. More important, perhaps, the top management group remained unified in its commitment to preserve GC's independent identity and to represent GC's interest openly to Times Mirror officials.

The problems of retaining a culture are more complicated when top executives in an acquired company initially negotiate and develop some rapport with parent company top executives and then must suddenly deal with a group vice president to whom they are "assigned." In this case, Times Mirror top executives were seen as "honorable men." However, the relationship between Clarkson and Chuck Schneider, the group vice president to whom he reported, got off to a bad start. Tension spread through the GC management team. The new boss was described as Theory X–oriented, a slander in GC where a Theory Y people-orientation was held sacrosanct.

In turn, GC's top management, preoccupied with the combination, let operational and personnel matters slide. When performance slumped, the acquirer began to question and second-guess business decisions, and GC's top management became even more obsessed with profit improvement. Middle and first-line managers reported pressures to increase sales and improve production, but were uncertain whether demands stemmed from the acquirer or from leaders of their own firm. Many employees talked of growing impersonality during the transition period.

Prior to the acquisition, GC's top managers regularly visited production areas and lunched with employees at all levels. Middle managers were consulted actively for input into company decisions. After the deal, top management members ate lunch in a private dining area and spent little time on the shop floor. Middle managers were not consulted on decisions about integration and were not made privy to relevant data. Employees came to see their leaders as clannish, fixated on the acquisition, and inattentive to their own organization. Many felt that the company's familial and participative atmosphere was being lost.

There is a theorem among cultural anthropologists that differences in power *plus* differences in culture *equal* oppression. GC's leaders never could convince Times Mirror of the need to get key integration managers together in issue-airing and problem-solving forums. They continued to fight over proposed changes that ran counter to their culture and would seemingly turn them into cautious and faceless "technocrats." Performance steadied, however, and then climbed.

As top management began to climb out of its shell, we were commissioned to conduct a study of reactions to the acquisition and the current outlook in the work force. Over the next several months, we interviewed 30 or so managers closely connected to the merger and conducted a survey of all GC people. The results opened eyes. GC's top leaders were dismayed over declines in people's trust and confidence in them. Morale had dropped considerably. Ratings of communication and openness were all lower than ever recorded in the company. Interviewees reported that top management's negativism was influencing the next echelon and farther down in the company.

Regrouping

An off-site meeting was held to digest these data and come to grips with continuing evidence of merger stress among top management. One manager likened himself to Robert E. Lee who "knew the South was going to lose the war" but felt honor-bound to defend it. The meeting began with a review of all the "wars" between the two companies. It was agreed that top management had looked at every conflict with the parent company from a "self-righteous perspective." "Without detachment from that," Clarkson argued, GC would "fight Times Mirror tooth-and-nail."

After spirited debate, GC's leaders concluded that they had been "their own worst enemy." They had developed a "black-and-white" picture of their company's culture versus Times Mirror's and saw GC as "good" and Times Mirror as "bad." There had been a tendency to stereotype Times Mirror managers, seeing them all as political or flank protectors, based upon single encounters or even reputations.

From this off-site meeting emerged a new attitude—more openness to Times Mirror's priorities and more readiness to respond to managers as individuals rather than as members of the "other side." Meetings were held with the next level of management to acknowledge past errors and encourage a change in attitude.

Thereafter, Clarkson exercised financial oversight and learned to "wow" his superiors at parent company review meetings. As a result, Times Mirror became less "picky," and GCers were able to incorporate increased financial pressures without "losing our integrity and sense of purpose."

Subsequent attitudes surveys showed the benefits. High ratings of trust and confidence were restored and morale began to climb. Management got good marks for openness and communication again. Relations between Times Mirror and GC showed some improvement as well. GC accepted some hitherto resisted changes in policy. These were seen as "stupid" but no longer as threats to the GC "way of life." They were also able to influence Times Mirror about selected policies and began a new era of "give and take" between the two companies.

Certainly there were Times Mirror managers who argued that Clarkson should be replaced as GC profits dropped. But rather than eliminate Clarkson, Times Mirror waited to see if he could assert his leadership. Clarkson depended on his team for straight talk and honest feedback. At one meeting, he was challenged for being an "impediment" to developing better relationships with Times Mirror. After a heavy and heartfelt meeting, he acknowledged the "need to recognize and accept the fact that changes are and will continue to be necessary." It was the first time he publicly acknowledged GC's status as *subsidiary* of Times Mirror. It empowered his team to make the combination work.

PART FOUR

THE POSTCOMBINATION PERIOD

CHAPTER 8

Winners, Losers, Survivors

Christmas Massacre
> —Announcement of layoffs in two merging
> banks that had adopted a "no-layoff" policy

Murderer's Row
> —Executive offices of bank that announced
> layoffs[1]

*In my head, I know that I am grateful that someone like Frank
Lorenzo didn't acquire us. I know I am grateful that we are
now associated with a class act like American Airlines. In my
heart and in my stomach, though, I am saddened and upset.
It hurts not being a part of AirCal anymore. We may not
have been the biggest or the most profitable airline, but I miss
what we had. It is confusing trying to learn new ways and
new faces. I don't see anyone from American understanding
that.*
> —AirCal flight attendant after acquisition by
> American Airlines[2]

Integration plans are complete. The new organization is designed. In the postcombination phase, these plans are implemented, and skeletal structures are fleshed out with people,
processes, and policies. At this point, many senior managers
are worn out and wishfully think that the combination is

"over." But middle managers and employees are still shell shocked and are just beginning to face up to the herculean tasks ahead. Care is needed, not only in building the new organization, but especially in managing the *human side* of change. The responsibility for leading change moves from corporate leaders to divisional and departmental heads during this period. But as change moves down the hierarchy, so also does the merger syndrome. Midmanagers and supervisors from the two sides may fight over staffing and turf. Efforts to integrate production facilities, coordinate regional sales groups, or align international service sectors can go awry. Functional subcultures often clash, and conflicts emerge. Stress rises and commitment wanes as people hold on to their old allegiances and have a hard time making new ones.

Success in the postcombination period hinges on the handling of people. New management assignments must be made intelligently and people on one or both sides must be moved into jobs with new responsibilities to work with new superiors, subordinates, or co-workers. There may be layoffs and reductions in force. Even in cases where most people are unaffected by change, keeping them on track is chancy. It requires managers to understand the postcombination psyches of employees and to handle them with dignity and grace.

This chapter looks at the dynamics of winning, losing, or surviving in a merger or acquisition and what determines people's fate. It considers, in order, the appointment of new management; retention issues; the handling of layoffs, reductions, and relocations; and the recommitment of people.

POSTCOMBINATION STATUS

As the new organization takes shape, people undertake a self-assessment of how they have fared in the combination. Personal status is determined not just by an objective assessment but also by a subjective appraisal:

- **Am I a winner?** All combinations have objective winners—people who realize tangible gains in status and authority, in job challenge and responsibilities, in salary or budget increases, or simply in personal recognition.

Others feel like winners because of brighter career prospects, better benefits, or increased job security in a
larger, more stable company.

• **Am I a loser?** The real losers in a combination are those
  who lose their jobs. However, people may label themselves losers because they are passed over for promotions or because they lose key projects, levels of
  authority, or connections to powerful people. Subjective
  losers feel their careers are sidetracked or stymied by
  the combination.

• **Am I a survivor?** For some employees, the impact of a
  merger proves to be insignificant. Hence they survive
  unscathed. By comparison, other survivors have been
  under threat, seen coworkers laid off, or faced stressful
  change in their departments or work. Though otherwise
  unmarked by a combination, they are angry, bitter, worried, or simply demotivated.

Who Is Affected and Why

Many situational factors determine people's objective
status as winners, losers, or survivors following a combination, some of which are rational and defensible and others
plainly political and objectionable.

Strategic Factors. Certainly the lead company's integration strategy affects people's status in the postcombination
period.[3] In an acquisition, for example, it is not unusual for
the parent company to centralize corporate staff functions,
such as the legal department, public relations, tax accounting,
and, sometimes, personnel and other "back office" financial
departments. These areas will perforce be reduced in size
and scope in a subsidiary. Many department heads who see
their jobs and stature reduced naturally choose to exit voluntarily. In other instances, their compensation proves too
costly versus their lessened responsibilities and the parent
company insists that they leave.

There are cases, by contrast, when a subsidiary gains
strength in these areas following an acquisition. When a
small manufacturer was acquired by a large conglomerate,
for instance, the smaller outfit added to its accounting staff.

New owners required more detailed financial reporting and funded the development of a new cost accounting system for the subsidiary.

Manufacturing, marketing, sales, and other line functions are typically affected by acquisitions and mergers involving businesses in the same industry. In Hewlett-Packard's partial integration of Apollo, top managers in Apollo's line units saw their job responsibilities diminished and few career opportunities in HP. Most chose to leave. Several R&D managers, by comparison, had their charters expanded and career prospects brightened by the acquisition. This illustrates how the strategy behind a deal dictated who would win, lose, or survive.

Who Bought Whom. However strategy can be subordinate to power politics in decisions about winners and losers. Take the case of a small Boston-area manufacturer acquired by a larger Pennsylvania-based concern. Here the parent company announced its intentions to absorb staff functions but to have line management operate as though it were "business as usual." Within two years, however, 9 of 12 upper managers in the subsidiary were replaced by executives from the larger company.

Was this a turnaround? No, the smaller company was outperforming the parent. Did local management "cash in"? No, none of the top executives in the subsidiary had golden parachutes, and their eventual severance packages were described as "meager." Was this part of a larger corporate makeover? No, the parent made no other changes in the operations of other subsidiaries. An acquired manager (since departed) had a straightforward explanation for managements' replacement: "They only wanted to deal with 'homegrown' people. We looked, talked, and acted differently. We also challenged them—said they operated from a '1911 Steel Mill' model. They wanted 'us' out."

Dr. Robert Bell, a specialist on takeovers, makes the point that buyers who plan to effect wholesale management changes need to be bluntly clear about their intentions.[4] As an example, Carl Icahn made no bones about his intention when conquering TWA: "We basically replaced all of top management...the whole 42nd floor. And not because they're all bad guys and not because they are all incapable. But where there's a bureaucracy, there is a problem."[5] When they understand these intentions, Bell notes, fired managers don't take it so personally and are better able to get on with their careers.

Age. Finally, there is the matter of age—and age discrimination. New York outplacement specialist Jay Bushell describes his office as a "sea of gray hair." The Connecticut General and INA merger in the mid-1980s is a stark example of why.[6] This merger was sailing along smoothly until John Cox, a top INA executive, was quoted in a trade publication saying the combined company would rather keep "up-and-comers" than "someone over 50." When pressed on this, Cox replied that he was misquoted: "My comment was that I would rather hang on to the person over 50 and let the 30-year-old go in hopes of getting him back in a few years."

The truth? CIGNA got rid of a disproportionate number of older employees through what employees derisively referred to as its RAPE (Retire Aged Personnel Early) program. This program included a personal review which employees dubbed the SCREW (Survey of Capabilities of Retired Early Workers). Certainly this is the seamy side of "downsizing." Older workers are more vulnerable than younger ones—because of higher salaries and because of the perception that many are "deadwood." An irate stockholder described the larger meaning of such discriminatory practices in a letter to the editor of The Hartford Courant: "It is sad that a company with a once-proud name and reputation has sunk so low."

MANAGEMENT APPOINTMENTS

Following a merger or acquisition, it is only sensible to get senior managers in command as soon as possible. Merger consultants Charles Leighton and Robert Tod recommend, for example, that the buyer have new top and middle management in place well before integration commences. And consultant Robert Hayes urges acquired executives to make their decision to stay or go early on as well. When they put it off, he contends, the business suffers, their people are in limbo, and it takes its toll on their own emotional well-being.[7]

In some instances, however, the appointment of management is complicated. When two businesses in the same industry merge, for example, there are many redundancies in management ranks. Who decides who runs which divisions or functions? When the lead company drives an early appointment process, its own managers are typically named to top posts. This is not just a function of who bought whom: Managers on the other side are "unknowns" and have a hard time credentialing themselves to new owners who often have better known and trusted managers hungry for bigger jobs.

This was the risk in the Burroughs and Sperry merger. To counter it, the management appointment process was rolled out over several months. Meanwhile, Blumenthal studied the résumés and accomplishments of Sperry senior managers, met with each of them personally, and observed their work on task forces. He also consulted with Joe Kroger on the qualifications of Sperry people and reconsidered the merits of managers on the Burroughs side.

Making Appointments on Line:
The Case of Unisys

The selection process at Unisys began at the top. Three months after the sale, Blumenthal announced that he, Paul Stern, Kroger, and Chief Financial Officer James Unruh would operate together in an "Executive Office." They would thereupon share responsibility for naming the next layer of management.

Criteria for Selection. Meritocracy was the stated criteria in making appointments. But this had many connotations beyond qualifications and current job performance. After all, Unisys was creating new structures which required executives to have far-reaching talents. The new head of defense businesses, for example, would have a $2.5 billion operation to manage. The European and Asian sales organizations would qualify for the *Fortune* 500. Naturally, a proven track record, command of facts and figures, and experience in a line of business were essential criteria for appointment to top posts. However several other less tangible criteria were also important in the selection of managers.

For example, executives who had a strong organizational sponsor ended up getting top jobs in the combined company. Paul Stern recalls that "those Sperry people who had formed close alliances with Joe Kroger and had been part of Sperry's inner circle were in good shape. Joe took care of them; many got key jobs and were able to recommend others for second-rank positions." In the same way, executives who were part of Stern's team got top jobs in operations, engineering, and corporate offices.

Having the "right attitude" was also critical. Executives from both sides were matched against one another in the race to run businesses. Candidates were evaluated not only on the basis of their accomplishments and know-how but, crucially, on how they presented themselves to Blumenthal and other members of the Executive Office. Their dress and manner, their ability to conceptualize and communicate, and their style of presentation made a lasting impression on Unisys's top team. "None of us admitted to ourselves that these were criteria," noted Paul Stern, "but they were." Stern also recalled:

> Winners made it a point to understand the mind-set of the Executive Office. They discerned the nature of the chairman's dream—an acquisition billed as a merger— and that the unification was to be paid by expense- and cost-cutting. They exuded the positive, rah-rah fervor. . . . They talked about how they would cut expenses, but equally, about how they would soothe hurt feelings and make things . . . go smoothly."[8]

Finally, Blumenthal was committed to having visible representation from both Burroughs and Sperry in top management positions. Three of four members of the executive office were from Burroughs. But, as top-level appointments were rolled out, the balance was more like 60/40 with the majority of operational and corporate jobs going to Burroughs' managers and Sperry people gaining more marketing and sales management posts.

A Player Draft. These executives, in turn, created selection teams to continue the appointment process through the layers of management. Marketing executives conducted a "player draft" wherein the credentials of all potential re-

gional managers were reviewed, and qualified candidates
had their names put on placards. As the draft began, business
heads shouted out their selections. The selection process, by
all accounts boisterous, was marked by controversy when
outstanding managers were sought by several business heads.
In these instances, the candidates could choose among attractive alternatives.

Certainly this process had its detractors. Managers on
both sides resented being held "under the microscope." There
was also some second guessing of appointments down the
line and charges of cronyism in particular functions. Commented one marketing executive;

> We are moving so quickly we cannot do a good job of
> evaluating who the players are. We probably make the
> right call 90% of the time. I am fearful, though, that as
> one moves down the hierarchy, favoritism will prevail
> more and more.

Business heads monitored the appointments, of course, and,
importantly, called all of the winners and losers and visited
almost every plant and district to introduce new managers
and explain the rationale behind their appointment. Still Unisys lost some talented performers whose needs couldn't be
satisfied. It is worth noting, too, that Blumenthal maintained
color-coded organization charts to scrutinize whether one
side or the other was obtaining the best spots. He also created
several staff posts for longer service executives who otherwise did not fit into the plans and priorities of the former
functions. In so doing, he showed that he was willing to
recognize and reward loyalty and past accomplishments but
unwilling to name someone to a responsible position when
they weren't the best qualified for the job.

Given the several advantages and disadvantages of the
"front-end" versus "on-line" approach to management appointments, there are no firm ground rules on when one or
the other process is most appropriate. Obviously there are
cases where acquired management bails out and the lead
company should move swiftly to replace them. And there
are many cases when the best counsel is to leave acquired
management in place, particularly when they have the skills
and desire to continue leading a subsidiary.

It is clear, however, that meritorious appointments are valued by people on both sides of a combination and that such an appointment process takes time and is fraught with problems. Blumenthal himself was somewhat cavalier about the anguish executives experienced during their "trial by fire." But, then again, he was an early winner and secured his valued assignment. To compensate, he did spend countless hours meeting with managers to demonstrate his respect for their feelings and what they had accomplished over their careers.

RETAINING TOP TALENT

"Don't impact revenue generators," came the message from one high tech acquirer. "Be certain to retain the best electrical engineers." Top sales, engineering, and manufacturing personnel from the acquired outfit were personally wooed by parent company senior management and welcomed to recognition clubs for premier performers. All of this was part of a vigorous retention effort to counteract headhunters who were making frequent calls to top talent. To further thwart them, the combined company's chairman called, too.

One reason top people leave after a merger: "The most common mistake is to assume people already know how much top management values them," asserts Richard Belous, a labor economist for the Conference Board. "The fact is, they often don't know."[9] The case of Arco illustrates the consequences of neglecting top people. When the oil company cut its work force by 6000, several star performers—never notified of their importance or reassured of their bright prospects—took their severance packages and left. *Fortune* author Anne Fisher advises: "money helps....along with bonuses, raises, stock options, and added perks. But money won't do it alone: the competition can offer that too. What stars really want to be told is that, yes, the company has a fantastic future and, if they stick around, their own futures will be fabulous too."

Retention Bonuses. When it comes to keeping valuable but more everyday employees, another strategy is the payment of a retention bonus. Even a modest bonus, in the range of $1,000 per employee in one acquired software company, kept accounting staff on hand through the difficult task of converting accounts to the parent company's computing systems. Here management made it a point to link payment of the bonus to good performance rather than for showing up to work. In another case, employees stayed on to earn a $500 bonus in full realization that their work was being phased out. Still, many groused about "selling their souls" and performed ineffectively. The upshot is that bonuses can help in the retention of people who might otherwise look for other employment. As a contractual device to keep them on for an interim period, however, there can be side effects.

DOWNSIZING AFTER THE DEAL: LETTING PEOPLE GO

Downsizings are among the most dreaded events in organizational life—for those doing it and those getting done in.[10] For decision makers, there is the agony of having to "play God." For managers taxed with breaking the news to employees, including personal friends and longtime loyal subordinates, there are upset, doubt, and identification with displaced employees. Finally, for employees parting from the company as well as for those remaining, there are confusion and depression, a sense of victimization and fatalism. Affected employees wonder "Why me?" Retained employees worry "When me?"

Downsizings or reductions in force are often viewed as unjust acts carried out by unjust people for unjust reasons. Employees can understand terminations in the case of performance problems or a breach of legal or ethical standards. There the terminated employee is responsible. They cannot, however, so easily justify the termination of employees who have performed well on the job—just because their "position" has been eliminated. The injustice mounts when people see senior executives continuing to enjoy large salaries and investment bankers and lawyers reaping huge fees.

How the downsizing is handled has as much effect on morale as why it is occurring. At Tenneco, 1,200 employees were brutally laid off over a six-week period. Many learned of their fates when they were confronted by armed guards carrying boxes for them to use in clearing out their desks.[11] At Allied Bank of Texas, department heads called meetings and then read off the casualty list in front of those to be laid off and their coworkers. Said an employee at Tenneco, "An outrageous and unnecessary slaughter of human self-respect and dignity."

By contrast, when Donald P. Kelly, then chief executive of Esmark, Inc., personally met with the corporate staff of newly acquired Norton Simon, Inc., he was able to justify staff reductions by fully explicating the financial status of the combined company. Kelly explained the number of redundancies between Norton Simon and Esmark employees and the personnel costs. He went on to describe the attractive severance packages that those asked to leave could expect. Kelly then asked for, and received, people's help in managing the cutbacks.

Memories of how "victims" of reductions are treated stick in the minds of surviving employees for a long time to come. If it is observed that affected employees are treated poorly—given short notice, a piddling severance package, and nothing in the way of personal or career counseling— then "surviving" employees are bound to fear that they are next in line for arbitrary and insensitive treatment. If, on the other hand, unaffected employees see that those who are to be laid off are treated fairly, with proper notice, decent severance pay, and outplacement assistance, then those who are retained will perceive less threat and have a better opinion of their employer. This may also lessen their "survivor's guilt." The implication: A downsizing or divestiture must constantly be managed with an eye toward those who remain with the company.

LAYOFFS IN HIGH TECH

Following its acquisition of Multi Plex, Alpha Electronics did an exemplary job of handling layoffs—the first in its history. To begin with, the lead company announced that both companies would have to reduce ranks because of job redundancies. This came as a shock to many Alpa managers who expected that most, if not all, reductions would come out of MP's "hide." In turn, acquired managers, who had been through reductions in the past, saw this as a gesture of fairness and agreed to work with their counterparts to plan and manage the reduction process.

Alpha established a reduction task force, staffed by managers from both sides; and outplacement offices were set up at Alpha headquarters and affected facilities in both companies. A consulting firm was called in to provide managers with training on the legal and operational aspects of managing a downsizing and provided valuable counseling on handling the human dimensions. Managers participated in training and simulations to practice their public announcements and to learn how to counsel distraught employees. Seasoned MP managers were assigned as coaches to inexperienced Alpha counterparts.

Once begun, reductions were tracked carefully by the task force to ensure that performance-based criteria were being applied evenly and fairly and that schedules were being maintained. A grievance board was established so that employees who felt unjustly treated could air their complaints. Full information about layoff procedures, severance packages, and other pertinent information was made public to all employees through newsletters and information packets.

Outplacement services included résumé development and interview training, career guidance and counseling, and use of company facilities (e.g., word processors, copy machines, telephones, office space, secretarial service). Alpha also notified other companies of the impending layoff, created networks of employees in particular skill areas, and hosted job fairs. A central placement center was established where affected employees received outplacement assistance and personal counseling.

Significantly, Alpha also suspended its external hiring process for several months during the layoff, in order to relocate as many employees as possible within the company. Central placement received all open requisitions and compared needs against the profiles of displaced employees. If no match could be found, an external search was permitted, but, before an offer was made, central placement again checked the opening against the current employee profile. (See Figure 8.1.)

Figure 8.1
Redeployment Strategy Following a Merger

REQUISITION APPROVAL/EXTERNAL HIRING PROCESS

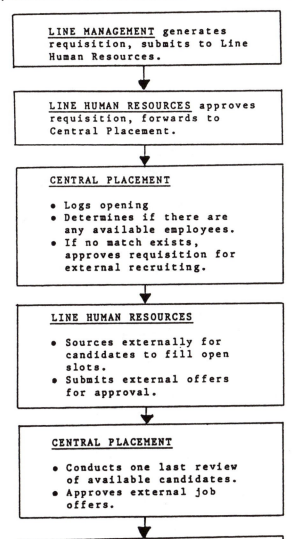

LINE MANAGEMENT generates requisition, submits to Line Human Resources.

LINE HUMAN RESOURCES approves requisition, forwards to Central Placement.

CENTRAL PLACEMENT

- Logs opening
- Determines if there are any available employees.
- If no match exists, approves requisition for external recruiting.

LINE HUMAN RESOURCES

- Sources externally for candidates to fill open slots.
- Submits external offers for approval.

CENTRAL PLACEMENT

- Conducts one last review of available candidates.
- Approves external job offers.

LINE HR

- Extends external offer

Alpha employees were nearly unanimous in their praise of the central placement service. It helped that the then healthy local economy could absorb so many displaced employees. But the signal sent to those remaining was loud and clear: Alpha still "cared about its people."

LESSONS ON MANAGING A DOWNSIZING

Alpha illustrates how companies today are improving their methods of managing a staff reduction. An American Management Association found that 36% of over 1,200 companies sampled reduced staff in 1990.[12] This compares with over 40% in years past, but the cuts were deeper and more extensive in 1990 than in past years. And the annual AMA study also shows that companies are doing a good job of assisting and supporting people who are being let go: Nearly 90% of the companies surveyed gave employees advance notice of a cutback, 80% continued their health benefits, and 50% provided outplacement services. Still, as one management writer observed, "For every company that shows genuine concern, two show insensitivity in laying people off."[13]

Certainly there is a need to manage all the stress-related symptoms associated with cutbacks. Here executives have a twofold problem: (1) how to ease some employees off the payroll as humanely as possible and (2) how to motivate the employees that remain to assume more responsibilities in a leaner organization.

Voluntary Separation Programs. Getting people to leave of their own accord through voluntary separation plans is one tactic for avoiding the full fallout of a postmerger staff reduction. The AMA study found early retirement plans for older workers and lump sum payments for younger employees to be the most popular alternatives to forced reductions. In today's market, the more generous voluntary severance plans are "5-5-4" packages. These add five years to the employee's age and five to years of service in calculating early retirement benefits. They also add four weeks of pay per year of work as a lump sum. So-called "3-3-1" programs are, however, more commonplace.

Severance packages help soften the landing of exiting employees. But companies can run into trouble with severance arrangements when they either penny-pinch or pay "conscience money." The solution recommended by the AMA: Survey other firms in the community or industry, and design a package which can be described as "above average." Also, it is recommended that employers provide exit options whenever possible: Either give employees a longer retirement "window" or an immediate cash settlement. This gives people more control over their own departure, and, because many of these plans allow employees to opt out by voluntary measures, they can minimize hard feelings.

Define the Principles. Robert Tomasko's study of downsizing practices makes it plain that top management has the responsibility to define and enforce the principles behind any reductions in force.[14] In the case of Unisys, for example, two principles predominated. First, it was agreed that cuts would be deep and fast. On the business side, this was essential to meeting financial objectives. Second, there was a commitment to be generous with severance packages in the belief that it was better to "pay now" with healthy packages rather than "pay later" with spoiled morale.

This may seem cold and calculating. There are, however, companies who err by being too cautious when cutbacks are essential and speed is of the essence. As an example, there are many instances where companies have offered "early retirement" packages only to see the most valued performers opt to leave. Some companies drag out layoffs and plant closings at great cost to productivity and even human welfare. In these operations, people are constantly waiting for the "other shoe to drop" and would prefer simply to be told the truth and be done with it. At least that was the reasoning at Unisys.

Make Cutback Criteria Clear. A study of 80 merged or acquired companies undertaking reductions in force found a strong preference for using performance-based criteria in making cutbacks in the managerial and technical work force.[15] By comparison, there was an even split between companies who used performance- versus seniority-based criteria in reductions among hourly employees. Certainly there are advantages to using seniority criteria: They can be fairly applied and justified to a work force. When using performance-based criteria, extra care must be taken in using performance appraisal ratings: There may be vastly different instruments and rating practices in the two companies. Moreover, performance ratings measure people's work in the "old" company; the knowledge, skills, and abilities needed in the new company may be different.

Prepare Management. Lawsuits from laid-off employees emanate from discrimination and recrimination. Alpha was well advised to train its managers in their legal requirements in laying off employees. It is also notable that Alpha made an explicit and legal commitment to retaining women and minorities when their qualifications but not seniority were equal to other employees.

On the matter of recrimination,[16] the precepts of a good management apply here: Prepare people for change, tell them what is happening, and give them the reasons why. Alpha managers were empowered with guidelines for "what to say" and "what to do" to comfort their people. On this point, it is worth noting that most laid-off employees find comparable employment in six months or less. That, as much as anything else, reduces the long-term impact of a layoff on their personal outlook and well-being.

Manage the Politics. Criteria for cutbacks have to be used religiously and sensitively. People's faith in fairness is shaken when cronyism or connections seem to matter more than performance and future potential when reductions are undertaken. A task force at Alpha, for example, reviewed the roster of proposed reductions against assigned criteria. This ensured that nobody was being let go because of a personal or political vendetta. In several instances, moreover, the team scrutinized the roster with regard to the race, sex, and age of proposed departures. Here, of course, the aim was to protect the company's commitment to equal employment opportunities and affirmative action.

Tell the Truth. Advice to tell employees the truth about reductions, as soon as known, is most often resisted by managers who haven't had the chance to plan and prepare for reductions. Besides, many managers concede, news of reductions leads to performance slumps, sometimes sabotage, and other problems that are best delayed to the last moment. However, this kind of deception haunts a company when layoffs are begun as the recipe for "integration stew" at one company illustrates (see Figure 8.2).

Figure 8.2
Recipe for Integration Stew
During a Downsizing
(circulated through acquired company)

1000 Canned Employees	700 Jammed Interviews
800 Instant Résumés	2 Tbsp. Stale Rumors
4 Sour Grapes	1 Tbsp. Thyme, running out
1 Pkg. Cream Cheese, softened	2 Cups Lettuce exist, please

Gather ingredients slowly while chanting about integration. Be sure to repeat certain phrases incessantly: job security, maintain identity, individual growth, opportunity. This will let optimism rise and keep morale from falling. Beat continually. Pour into an unprepared placement center for interim storage. Fry departments one at a time until finished. If schedule allows, pilfer any accessible valuables. Drain on outplacement procedures for 30 days. Serve on a bed of blind trust.

Tough truths were resisted in an entertainment firm that acquired a competitor. Plans called for common functions to be integrated six months later with a reduction in force of 20% of the acquired work force. Management was, however, persuaded to tell people the truth, and a task force was charged with preparing communiqués to the work force. Employees whose positions were to be eliminated were given four months notice and provided outplacement counseling and job hunting assistance. To keep them productive during this period, an incentive program was established to reward those who stayed on the four months and performed at or near precombination levels. Finally, and importantly, the

CEO pledged that this would be the one and only layoff associated with the acquisition. She personally pledged that, absent a major business downturn, no "other shoe" would drop. Of course, there was some worry among retained employees, but seeing how the current wave of cutbacks was handled helped to minimize their fear.

Retraining and Redeployment. Retraining and redeployment are sometimes options for lessening reductions among nonexempt employees. Alpha's redeployment effort placed over 100 people in new jobs in the firm. On a broader scale, the American Management Association finds retraining programs take four to six months to prepare people to move into more marketable employment segments in their own firm or elsewhere.[17] Some 37% of the companies sampled by the AMA also used job sharing and part-time work to keep employees on the payroll while still reducing costs.

SURVIVORS

The Kubler-Ross stages of reactions to death and loss apply as well to those who "survive" a company downsizing. They, too, may initially deny the threat of layoffs and, when they learn of their inevitability, will distance themselves emotionally from the "victims." This leads to anger as well as to what is commonly known as *survivor's guilt.* Bargaining takes the form of self-survival along with pleas to do "something more" for affected employees. Depression is attributable to people's loss of old comrades and alienation in staying on to work for such a callous employer. Eventually, survivors, too, come to accept the situation, but, as studies show, they also lose their "innocence" and become more distant and protective of themselves on the job. People are never the "same" after their company undertakes a major reduction in force.[18]

All Change Is Loss. Psychologist Harry Levinson suggests that all change is loss.[19] As he puts it, "despite the fact that change is necessary and often for the better, the new always replaces the old and, at some level of consciousness, loss is experienced." In this sense, merger survivors have to cope with the painful sense of loss inherent in change. Levinson identifies four types of loss experienced in a corporate upheaval. First is the loss of *love* experienced when people are removed from former friends and colleagues or from an organization which provided important sources of regard and validation. This type of loss is experienced when an employee is reassigned to a new superior or separated from displaced colleagues. It is keenly felt when a 50-year-old with 25 years of service to the company is told that his services are no longer needed.

Second is the loss of *support*. This is experienced when people have to establish new ties or relationships, find new coworkers to depend upon, and adopt new ways of doing things. Loss of support also occurs when a person no longer is able to apply once-valued knowledge or skills or draw upon them from trusted coworkers and mentors.

Third is the loss of *sensory input*. This occurs when people have difficulty getting the data they need to orient themselves. Familiar routines, second nature to experienced employees, are disrupted in a combination or reorganization. New ways of doing things, and new norms of behavior, have to be learned.

Finally, there is the loss of *personal agency*. People are more dependent on others and less able to solve their own problems following massive change. They may feel incomplete, incompetent, and, without assistance and orientation, eventually frustrated and depressed. This often is experienced by acquired senior executives who must adapt to the new owner's control systems and report to group management with little direct industry experience. The implication is that merger managers have to empathize with and be prepared to respond to the sense of loss suffered by their people—and themselves.

HELPING SURVIVORS COPE

Perhaps the biggest problem faced by firms after a reduction in force is the demoralization of those who remain. Some are waiting for the next wave of pink slips and others wonder what fortune lies ahead for those crewing a sinking ship. Managers can pull people out of the postdownsizing doldrums by revving them up with better prospects. This requires managers to communicate an upbeat, but not sugarcoated, message about the future and to remind people that they have both a stake and role in the company's future success.

Employees also need to be empowered by the opportunity to participate in rebuilding their company. In one food products company, hundreds were involved in studies to identify where other cost savings could be realized in lieu of further cutbacks. In a financial institution which closed several branches, employees at surviving branches participated in a proactive program to cut costs. In an electronics firm, groups of employees were assembled after a downsizing to answer the question: "What can individuals do to improve the work environment and performance to reduce the likelihood of further layoffs?"

Certainly people need space and the opportunity for grieving. Losing coworkers is like losing members of the family. Remaining employees are grateful that they survived but experience grief and guilt when walking by empty workstations. Let those who want to talk about it do so—either in group sessions or privately with employee assistance counselors.

Parting Ceremonies. Studies by Stanley Harris and Robert Sutton show that "parting ceremonies" serve an important function for the departing and the survivors.[20] They compared several groups that held ceremonies—A "Last Supper" in a hospital, "The Last Hurrah" in an auto plant, "The Wake" in an academic setting—with groups that had no formal or informal parting. In all instances, those who had shared in a parting ceremony felt better about their company, their colleagues, and themselves.

Assistance for Relocated Employees. Employees who are placed in new functions have a job but lack friends and often feel distanced from their new surroundings. The answer to "Will I have a job?" seems only to generate new and worrisome questions: "What does my boss expect of me now? How will I know if I am meeting those expectations? How do I move up? Do people get away with 'bending' the rules around here? What is the culture of my new work team?" These are the kinds of questions manufacturing employees at a merged company posed as they commenced relocating to new facilities. A consulting team, of an in-house training specialist and an external consultant, worked with manufacturing managers to help them address their people's concerns. The two specialists counseled managers and prepared a guide to "welcoming relocated employees" that covered employee concerns, the basic needs underlying them, and what managers can do to help (see Figure 8.3).

There are also relocations from one part of the country or world to another. The aforementioned study of 80 acquirers found that most employers pay for pretransfer visits and moving expenses for managers, and many assist in house purchase and mortgage buydowns. The best ones give relocating employees a thorough preview of the cost of living, climate, housing situation, school systems, churches, opportunities for dual career employment, and child care facilities in their new location. And when moves involve several people, they set up a welcoming committee at the new site and designate a "big brother/sister" to help the newcomer settle in.[21]

Divestitures: A Special Case. Executives face a dilemma communicating in a timely and open fashion with divestiture candidates: how to let people know they are on the block without risking a downturn in performance which could affect the sales price. Timing is the key here—some divestitures take months or even years to consummate, and keeping people on hold for that long is difficult. The worst scenario is having employees find out about their fate through trade publications or news reports. Laying things on the line is the most sensible strategy. Level with managers and employees that a buyer is less likely to tinker with a successful, well-running operation than with a poor producer. That motivates them to continue their hard work. If possible, give executives an additional financial incentive for staying on and maintaining operations to fetch the best price possible. Finally, sold off employees may also need help to cope with change.

Figure 8.3
Welcoming Relocated Employees

Employee Concern	Basic Need	What a Manager Can Do to Help...
How do I fit in?	Belonging	Introduce newcomer to members of the work team and major contacts through out the department.
What's my boss like?		Have lunch or coffee with newcomer on the first day. Review your own career history. Why you are here.
How about co-workers?		Assign a "buddy."
What are my manager's immediate and long range objectives?	Orientation	Introduce Performance Planning Systems. Review departmental goals, priorities, and performance plans.
How are things done around here?		Review organizational chart and workflow. Key players.
How do people communicate?	Comfort	Show departmental newsletters, recent memos; Orient to tele-communications.
How do people interact?		Discuss own communication style, formality or informality; how you work with your staff; expectations about presentations and proposals.
How can I increase visibility?	Recognition	Discuss job and performance expectations. Career paths.
How will I know if I'm successful?		Describe appraisal and measurement systems. Show forms and procedures.
How will my efforts be rewarded?	Success	Explain merit and bonus pay systems; Special recognition programs.
How can I further my skills?		Training programs; educational develop assistance; special seminars or study groups.

STAGES OF PERSONAL ADAPTATION
TO CHANGE

Psychologist William Bridges highlights the problems people encounter in "hanging on/letting go" following a merger or acquisition.[22] He sees adjustment as a three-part psychological process that extends over a long period of time.

First, people must let go of the old situation and of the old identity that went with it. A great deal of what is called resistance to change is played out in this first phase of transition. Human beings cannot move into new roles with a clear sense of purpose and energy unless they let go of the way things were and the self-image that fits the old situation.

Second, people have to go through what Bridges calls the "neutral zone" —a transition stage between their old situation and a new one that may still be unclear. In this no-man's-land in time, everything feels unreal. The stage is marked by loss and confusion, a time when hope alternates with despair and new ideas alternate with a sense of meaninglessness. Many people seemingly go through the motions during this period as a reorientation in their thinking and outlook takes place.

The third phase of transition is a new beginning. This may involve developing new competencies, establishing new relationships, becoming comfortable with new policies and procedures, constructing new plans for the future, and learning to think in accordance with new purposes and priorities. This is not simply a matter of adapting to change—it is embracing the new as a member of a new organization and team.

This stage commences for employees when they see the new organization taking shape. To this point, the transition has disrupted their sense of order and control and heightened their insecurity and experience of loss. But people are resilient. As they learn of their new assignments they begin to rebound. Now they are ready to become part of new work teams.

FACTORS AFFECTING POSTMERGER MORALE

The transition from survivor status to full functioning as a member of the postmerger team is influenced by many personal and situational factors. In an effort to identify broad classes of factors affecting postmerger morale, we tracked employee attitudes in Graphic Controls one and three years after their company's acquisition by Times Mirror. This research showed there to be a significant companywide drop in attitudes one year after the acquisition (compared to preacquisition measurements) and then a recovery in morale three years later. A more detailed analysis unearthed the factors differentiating between higher- and lower-morale employees:

1. How the Combination Was Managed. The primary predictor of postacquisition morale in GC was employee perceptions of how GC's top management handled the process. Employees who felt they were kept informed about the acquisition, understood why it happened, and saw top management dealing with new demands effectively had significantly higher morale three years after the sale than those who had a less favorable opinion of management's response.

2. Past Confidence in Company Change Management. Clearly GC had a tradition of effective and caring management that influenced postcombination morale. Specifically, the many who said GC generally did a good job of informing people, explaining business objectives, and involving people in decisions had higher levels of morale three years after the sale than the few who doubted management's effectiveness.

3. Organizational Involvement. The next most important predictor of postmerger morale was employees' identification with the company. Those who trusted management, identified with company goals and policies, and saw working at GC as something more than a job suffered smaller declines in morale one year after the sale and recouped to preacquisition ratings three years afterwards. Their commitment to the company was bowed but not broken by the acquisition. By contrast, people less identified with the company had lower postacquisition morale and were more likely to express a desire to leave GC.

4. Proximity to Change: Level and Department. Here we discovered an interesting finding: Those who were *most* affected by change had *higher* postacquisition ratings than did those who were less affected. This seemingly paradoxical finding can be best explained by the motivating effects of involvement in the transition process. Our data showed that senior and middle managers were under far more stress in the postacquisition period than, say, supervisors and employees. Staff groups in finance and human resources also reported higher levels of strain. But these managers and departments were also more involved in the process—fighting for their culture and actively participating in the planning and implementation of change. It was this direct involvement that contributed to understanding and esprit de corps. Although the combination was more stressful to those more proximal to change, it was the chance to influence decisions that, in our view, led to higher morale ratings in this group three years after the sale.

By contrast, supervisors and lower-level employees were affected more by *indirect* changes—some of which were imposed by Times Mirror. Changes in GC's compensation package, limits on the disclosure of business information, and other impositions were interpreted by many in the work force as a threat to GC's autonomy and to its way of life. Management's clannish attitude, understandable to those close to the change, was as a sign to those in the ranks that the company was being bowled over by new owners.

5. Social Support and Employment Options. People who said they received social support from supervisors and peers during the transition period had higher levels of morale than those who saw less support. People who believed that they could find commensurate work in other companies also had somewhat more positive ratings than those who felt themselves "locked in" to employment at GC.

6. Age, Tenure, Gender, and Education Level. Interestingly, none of these demographic factors was a significant predictor of postacquisition morale. Naturally, they might have been significant had there been any downsizing in GC. It is worth noting, however, that employees hired during the tumultuous transition period had lower ratings of the company than those hired during more "typical" years and never reported the same levels of motivation and commitment of other GC workers. This group has been referred to as the "lost generation" in GC.

Overall, these findings stress the importance of managing the human side of change following a merger or acquisition. Certainly GC managers had a reservoir of trust and confidence to draw from in keeping survivors motivated and satisfied after the initial shakiness in its combination with Times Mirror. But the prime predictor of postcombination morale was employees' perceptions of how management treated them and handled the changes wrought by the acquisition. Hence we cannot stress enough the importance of effectively and sensitively managing the human side of change.

CHAPTER 9

Rebuilding the Business: Teamwork

Team member #1: "For Christ's sake we're at it again. Backwards and forwards, forwards and backwards, and on and bloody on . . . here we have people, powerful people, influential people, asking us what we want. Asking us about stuff we have been fighting for for months . . . We are just farting around . . . let's get on with it!"
 Member #2: "I'm not objecting, Eric, just raising doubts."
 Member #3: "Eric, you don't expect me to agree with that. The group is being steamrolled into agreeing with your solution, your decision."
 —Dialogue reported by I. L. Mangham, "Facilitating Interorganizational Dialogue in a Merger Situation," *Interpersonal Development* [1]

Letting Go of We and They
Making Merger Fears Passé
Moving Forward with a Common Dream
Combining into a Successful Team
 —Hopes of a acquired manager heading the manufacturing team of combined company [2]

Rebuilding the business involves people. Before people commit to and work effectively as a team, they must come to grips with their new situation: What is the new boss's style? What will be expected of me? Can I count on my coworkers?

Am I committed to staying around? Members of teams left intact question whether or not established performance standards and the old and comfortable climate will be affected by new methods and systems or by changes in internal funding and the business mix.

From the executive suite to the shop floor to sales offices, people look to their immediate superiors to set direction and the new tone. This chapter examines approaches to organization and team building following a combination and the crucial work of managers in implementing change. It considers people's postmerger mind-sets and the challenges and dilemmas of team building. It also looks at two case studies: training for team building in AT&T and team building on-line in Alpha Electronics.

UNDERSTANDING POSTMERGER MIND-SETS

In order to implement integration plans and rebuild the organization, managers and supervisors leading teams have to deal with employees having different postmerger mind-sets. Some team members willingly let go of the old, adapt to new demands, and are ready to get on with the work at hand. Others are left wanting for more support and more reasons to be part of a team. Still others feel wrung out and resist efforts to move forward (see Figure 9.1).

Employees who are ready for change usually have the job they wanted or expected in the postcombination organization. They may also be "charged up" by new organizational challenges and opportunities. After their acquisition by Delta Airlines, for example, Western's data processing people were genuinely excited about the chance to learn Delta's more sophisticated computer systems. These employees are the mainstays of a new team. Their positive attitudes can be infectious and spread to others. However, too great a gung ho outlook can also alienate less spirited employees who still need time to adapt to change. We've seen instances where employees were labeled "traitors" or "sellouts" for embracing new practices of a parent company with too much enthusiasm. In Apollo Computer, for instance, the joke went around that those who were excited about Hewlett-Packard had gained their "HP-ness."

Figure 9.1
Recognizing People's Postmerger
Emotional States

THE READY

Their Situation:	Have been promoted or retained the job they want. See greater opportunity to produce and advance.
What to Hope for:	Energy and excitement. Charged up.
What to Watch for:	Overly aggressive. Acting superior.

THE WANTING

Their Situation:	Did not receive the job they wanted or were demoted. Miss former mentors, projects, and status.
What to Hope for:	Working through loss. Adjusting to new realities.
What to Watch for:	Depression. Anger and vindictiveness.

THE WRUNG OUT

Their Situation:	Have the same job, but things have changed... ...more distant from leadership ...more competition for advancement ...feel jerked around by the process
What to Hope for:	Working through frustration. Regaining footing.
What to Watch for:	Demotivation. Lack of direction and purpose.

Many other employees are found wanting: They did not get their desired job title or responsibilities, their mentor and friends have departed, or maybe their budgets or own projects were slashed. These employees can become preoccupied with their less than expected status and wonder whether it is a harbinger of a dead-end career. Their self-esteem suffers.

These employees were called "spoilers" in one acquired company because of their proclivities to spoil an entire work group's morale. They can set a combined team off on a contrary course by bad mouthing new management and subverting team performance. They need counseling to accommodate to new realities and some space to sort things out.

Despite all the stress and uncertainty, and sleepless nights worrying, most people retain their same positions and responsibilities following a merger or acquisition. Still, some feel as though they survived an ordeal and have become wrung out in the process. These may be employees who believe the situation around them has changed for the worse. For example, technical and professional talent often complain that merged organizations create added layers between them and the uppermost levels of management. Those in functions previously housed "close to the action" at headquarters may find themselves far removed from the center of power in a parent company. And upwardly mobile employees bemoan the increased competition for advancement.

There are also employees who, for one reason or another, feel they have been "jerked around" by the transition process. Cynicism grows as these employees conclude that their managers are incompetent and insensitive, or they conclude that something is going on behind their backs. They may go about their work aimlessly without a sense of direction or purpose. Naturally, it is imperative for managers to reenlist them as members of a new team.

However, gaining an understanding of people's current emotional states is more difficult than it may initially seem. Team members who are not close to their managers may put on a poker face and hide their true feelings. Some may not be able to verbalize the reasons for their discontent. And some who seem ready for change may turn out to be resistant.

Straightforward one-on-one talks between managers and team member are essential to uncovering people's emotional states. In addition, a human resources professional, a trained counselor, or even a trusted peer can sometimes open up reticent types and help a supervisor to work with hard-to-read employees.

THE CHALLENGES OF TEAM BUILDING

The challenges facing team leaders in a combination are to reenlist team members and to rebuild their teams. After tracking 14 senior executives taking over new management teams, Harvard Business School Professor John Gabarro found it took up to two and a half years for U.S. managers to establish team leadership and even longer for European managers to win people over.[3] Gabarro also found that the first three to six months of an executive's tenure set the tone for the rest of the team development process. This underscores the need for managers to move swiftly and assuredly in understanding and reaching their people.

However, postmerger team building is complicated when there are changes in the leadership and makeup of a team. Any one of the following factors enhance the likelihood of tension in newly formed teams:

- **A new boss.** The appointment of a new boss creates tension in a team as subordinates naturally do some jockeying for influence and visibility. Conflict is especially high whenever a subordinate expected to have the new boss' job or when the new boss comes from the "other" company.

- **New peers.** When combinations mix people from the two sides, they naturally divide into coalitions and exchange confidences with former peers. This can continue the we/they feelings and force managers to "take sides" in resolving conflicts.

- **New ways of doing things.** Members of an acquired team not only have to adapt to job-related changes, they also have to learn the politics and protocol of operating with a new parent company. Predictably there is a tendency to "stick with what (and who) you know." This means that people may have trouble gaining access to the informal social and communication networks of the other side and will likely encounter untold problems in simply getting the job done through normal channels.

- **New power bases.** Team leaders have to establish or reestablish their authority and clout with their people.

Sure it is difficult for a new executive to win over people
when he or she comes from the dominant company.
But it can also be difficult for an acquired manager to
retain people's loyalty when he or she is seen to be
weaker as a result of the merger. People are looking
for leaders who are well connected to new owners and
this may or may not be their current boss.

TRAINING FOR TEAM BUILDING AT AT&T

Rhea Serpan was excited to learn of his appointment as
head of the Western Region of AT&T's Network Operating
Group, a newly formed unit created by the internal merger
of the company's Communications and Information Systems (IS) divisions. He also understood the necessity for
change. Strategically, the combination would give AT&T
customers "one-stop shopping" for their computer and
communication needs; financially, savings could be realized from resulting economies of scale. Serpan was less
confident, though, about making one team out of people who
"grew up" in two very different business climates.

The Communications group, composed of veterans of
telephone companies in the pre-divestiture Bell System days,
enjoyed years of market leadership, customer loyalty, and a
track record of high quality products and service. Its management, however, was somewhat complacent and, at least
in the eyes of some executives, was not responding quickly
or appropriately to competitors. By contrast, the Information
Systems group was a new venture for the company which
had yet to achieve profitability. IS managers were seen as
risk takers but had a reputation for being insensitive to both
people and bottom-line concerns.

Serpan anticipated roadblocks to a successful integration. First, there were strong we/they dynamics between the
two sides: Each group felt that the other's management style
was inadequate to the needs of combined operations. Second,
executives had little or no experience in managing change
of this sort. They needed direction—and more than a little
self-confidence—to mold new teams. Finally, there was
a strong orientation toward holding onto past identities

and practices rather than building something new. With the considerable changes following the divestiture of the Bell operating companies, managers were inclined to retain familiar people and practices rather than look to make further change.

Serpan knew that his only hope of developing a team orientation through the ranks was to build one at the top. Consequently, he worked with specialists to develop a training program that would prepare his top three layers of managers for their new positions and, especially, for building their own new teams.

As a first step, each of the 80 managers in the combined division was interviewed, individually or in a focus group, and completed a questionnaire assessing their feelings about the ensuing change. It did not take much prodding in interviews to get managers to talk about differences between the two sides. Communications people regarded themselves as the winners in the internal merger and their counterparts as losers based on the two sides' financial performance. Communications people also believed that they were led by "professionals" while Information Systems executives were "mavericks." By comparison, managers from the IS side felt that they were performing as well as could be expected given their relatively recent entry into the market. Moreover, they attributed the success of the Communications group to traditional customer loyalty and not to the ability of its management.

Both sides acknowledged an upside to the combination, including increased benefits to customers and more opportunities to advance in the company. Yet, they also saw the downside: Nearly two-thirds of the surveyed managers expected that the combination would lead to a substantial downsizing; one-half reported less job security; and only one-third felt that people from the two sides would have equal opportunities to advance in the newly merged unit.

Still, most managers expressed a "wait and see" attitude in response to questions about whether the integration would capitalize on the strengths of both organizations. The survey also revealed a major deterrent to team building: Only 23% of the Communications managers said they trusted IS people, and just 17% of IS managers trusted their counterparts.

Given the mistrust between managers from the two sides, along with their pessimistic expectations, Serpan felt that education and a "reorientation" of attitudes was needed before setting managers off to build their own postmerger teams. A three-day retreat was scheduled with the first day devoted to a series of show-and-tell exercises in which functional leaders from the two sides educated each other on their way of doing business. On the second day, managers were prepared for action planning and the work of team building.

The day began with a general discussion of we/they dynamics followed by some "how tos" on building rapport with people from the other side, leading new teams, and establishing one's own position. Then key findings from the survey and interviews were presented. After putting the issues on the table, problem solving teams were formed to "brainstorm" tactics for reducing the barriers to team building.

The highlight of the day was a "graduation" ceremony. After the managers discussed their ideas for successful integration in small groups, they were brought back together as a large group, and each manager was asked to write down "the three *worst* ways in which the integration could affect me personally." Each also received a sheet of stationery with his or her preintegration letterhead and an old business card. Managers were then asked to stand and led outside where a wooden coffin awaited. Off to the side, a marching band sounded a somber funeral march.

One by one, each of the 80 managers stepped up to the coffin, crumpled his or her worst case lists, letterhead, and business card and tossed them in. As the last manager stepped back from the coffin, the group was startled to hear a low, grumbling noise. Slowly, a 100-ton paver rolled around the corner and headed straight for the group. At first, the managers stood paralyzed, unsure of what was to transpire. But then the band broke into a rousing rendition of "On Wisconsin," and the paver veered toward the wooden casket, flattening it and its contents of managers' worst case fears. Spontaneous cheering broke out among the executives as the paver rolled back and forth on top of the coffin.

Abuzz with excitement, the managers were asked to return inside. As they entered the building, they were handed academic caps and gowns and instructed to put them on. Ushers assembled the managers into two orderly lines and marched them into an auditorium where banners proclaiming "Congratulations, Graduates!" awaited them. Once all were seated, their regional director welcomed them and embarked on the classic graduation speech: "The day has come for which we have all worked so hard to prepare you. It is now your turn: Our destiny lies in your generation's hands!" The managers sat quietly, absorbed in the speech, understanding the meaning of these words for them. Then, the ushers brought one row of "graduates" at a time to their feet and marched them up to the stage. There, Rhea Serpan presented each one with a diploma, a "Masters of Merger Management," and a graduation gift, a share of company stock. After all proceeded across the stage and back to their seats, the group turned the tassels on their caps from left to right and proclaimed that they had graduated into their positions as leaders of new teams. (See Figure 9.2.)

TEAM-BUILDING TASKS

Group dynamics specialists contend that all groups go through a series of stages as they develop into teams. (See Figure 9.3.)[4] The role of management in guiding this progression is to transform individual players into an effectively functioning unit through:

1. **Psychological enlistment.** People need to feel wanted and to gain an emotional tie-in to the mission of their new team.

2. **Role development.** People need to be excited about their new jobs and about the potential of their team.

3. **Trust and confidence.** People need to develop trust and confidence in their colleagues and supervisors.

Psychological Enlistment: Forming the Team

Managers begin the team-building process by forming teams and setting expectations. In the initial stages, members

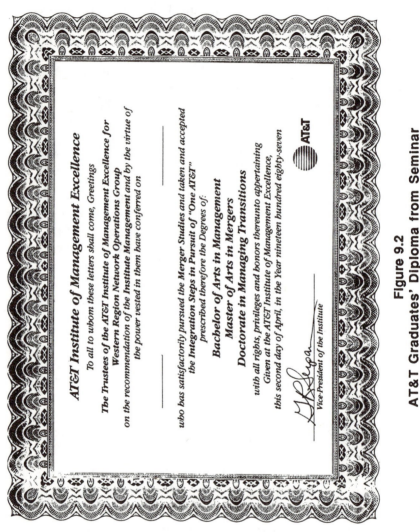

AT&T Institute of Management Excellence

To all to whom these letters shall come, Greetings

The Trustees of the AT&T Institute of Management Excellence for
Western Region Network Operations Group
on the recommendation of the Institute Management and by the virtue of
the power vested in them have conferred on

_____

who has satisfactorily pursued the Merger Studies and taken and accepted
the Integration Steps in Pursuit of "One AT&T"
prescribed therefore the Degrees of:

Bachelor of Arts in Management
Master of Arts in Mergers
Doctorate in Managing Transitions

with all rights, privileges and honors thereunto appertaining
Given at the AT&T Institute of Management Excellence,
this second day of April, in the Year nineteen hundred eighty-seven

Vice-President of the Institute

AT&T

Figure 9.2
AT&T Graduates' Diploma from Seminar
on Managing Transitions

234

are developing first impressions of new peers and superiors and the new situation around them. At issue is their own degree of *inclusion* in the new group. Employees reporting to new bosses or working with new peers go through some self-examination: "Do I really want to be part of this team or not?"

Several factors impinge on their decision. First, there is a lack of clarity regarding the group's mission as well as members' roles in making the group succeed. Before committing to a new team, employees need to know its purpose and objectives, how it contributes in the overall corporate scheme, and what is expected of them. Second, employees wonder if they are "on trial"—and whether or not they have to prove themselves. If so, there may be heated competition or, alternatively, withdrawal and apathy. Egos can be easily bruised. In turn, employees may be putting their supervisors on trial as they sort out their career options. People need to know where they stand before committing to a team.

Finally, some people suffer from personal distress as postmerger trauma lingers. This can be expressed through passive or active aggression that might turn off the boss and peers and lead to isolation. New managers, too, are forming first impressions, and many employees sabotage their futures simply because they cannot yet cope with change. Still, several steps can be take to lessen these sources of resistance to enlistment in a team:

Re-recruit Employees. Team leaders can begin to overcome resistance by acting like college recruiters courting top athletes. Here they have to re-recruit people by selling them on the near-term merits and long-term advantages of being part of their team. This involves thoughtfully assessing people's goals and aspirations, carefully considering what might motivate or turn them off, and then formally signing them up to the team. Needs for inclusion are met by reminding people of their importance and by showing them their value to the team.

Massage Egos. Many employees need extra reassurance of their worth when they haven't gained what they hoped for following a merger. Some stroking and ego massaging by the team leader is needed. For those who are on trial because of job or departmental changes, there is a need to

Leaders' Roles:	Form the team Set expectations	Establish norms Set ground rules	Build teamwork Motivate performance
Members' Issues:	Psychological enlistment "Do I want to be part of this?"	Role development "Who's in charge of this team?"	Trust and confidence "Do we trust one another?"
Sources of Resistance:	Unclear sense of team purpose, mission, role People "on trial" Personal distress	Holding onto old allegiances and alliances Internal conflict Peer pressures	Conflicts between old and new ways of doing things Different standards of performance Different attitudes about diversity
How to counter resistance:	Rerecruit people Massage egos Lay it on the line	Negotiate roles/responsibilities Clarify reporting relationships Establish ground rules	Model desired behaviors Incentives and performance management Value diversity

Figure 9.3
Stages In Building a New Team

clarify performance standards. It is, of course, important to acknowledge people's past contributions and to remind them that they are still needed and appreciated.

Lay It On the Line. Over time, however, individuals and the team have got to get on with the work at hand. Employees who continue to mope around the office, bad mouth the new arrangement, or perform well below expected levels may need a "shape-up-or-ship-out" message from the boss. The leader's objective is to lay things on the line, but this can be best accomplished with frankness rather than finger pointing.

Role Development: Team Organization

After positions are set, team members and leaders often "test" one another—struggling to determine relative degrees of influence and *control*. At issue is "who's really in charge here?" Group dynamics experts refer to this as the "storming" phase of group development. Leaders have to help their teams weather this storm by clarifying people's roles and setting ground rules. In this phase, a group's modus operandi and pecking order are established and recognized.

Again, three factors can interfere with team leaders' efforts to manage these dynamics. First, managers leading well established groups often find people holding on to their old allegiances and ways of doing things. This, for example, hampered team building between two merged sales forces. Despite being reassigned to new teams at new locations, sales representatives would travel back to their old offices to use demo equipment and their former secretaries. Some even teamed up with former service technicians who, although no longer part of their team, were bribed by "six packs" to join in customer calls.

Second, internal conflict can wrack team development. Some employees will brownnose the boss and backstab their peers in an effort to gain power. Others will be out to frustrate or harass the new boss. The storming phase can put managers in a "no-win" situation. If they assert their authority pre-emptively, conflict goes underground. But if they let conflict get out of control, the bad feelings developed may not be assuaged by later intervention.

Finally, work groups have their own informal rules and norms. One group of engineers in a high-tech company had a traditional "dress-down" day where employees wore jeans or slacks and sportswear. When a new boss first suggested that they abandon this practice, he was ostracized. Everything turned around, however, when he began to wear a cowboy hat on the appointed day. At stake in these situations is the degree to which the team leader is able to develop esprit de corps rather than mindless obedience. Actions that help team leaders at this stage include the following:

Role Negotiation. Positions and players may be set, but new job duties and responsibilities require clarification and elaboration. Role negotiation, a technique devised by management consultant Roger Harrison, has a team leader and subordinates discuss expectations of roles, identify areas of conflict or ambiguity, and engage in the give and take of negotiating a realistic role definition acceptable to both parties.[5]

To formalize these negotiations, a "contract" between the boss and team specifies role expectations and, importantly, commits them to evaluate and revise the agreement at a future date. Formal agreements like this are resisted by some managers who regard them as too "legalistic." But this distorts their intent and spirit: Role contracts are living documents which outline common understandings and start a working relationship off on a mutually agreed course.

Reporting Relationships. Employees regularly complain about ambiguous reporting relationships following a combination. To counter this, managers have to bring the organizational chart to life and delineate who reports to whom and with what authority and responsibilities. This may seem foreign to companies accustomed to fluid structures and hesitant to put on to paper the extant chain of command. It is useful, however, to overstructure in the early stages of team building when areas of responsibility are contested and everything seems up for grabs. When possible, it helps to keep reporting relationship in place for at least a while. This adds to the sense of stability and offsets wariness that management is coming up with "another change."

Ground Rules. Finally, there is a need to establish both formal procedures (regarding budgetary authority, communication formats, and so on) as well as informal norms (concerning dress, timeliness, protocol, and so forth) in a team. Team leaders are, of course, entitled to set up ground rules congruent with their personal values and the interests of the company. But effective team builders are also sensitive to the existing traditions of team members and try to respect them.

Still, sometimes change is mandated. In such instances, team builders need to provide a clear and straightforward reason why policies and procedures have to change, even when the reason is because "corporate says we have to." The rule "Sell people on change, don't just tell them about it" remains valid here.

Trust and Confidence: Getting Down to Work

After questions of membership and control are settled, the team is ready to get to work. Here questions of *trust* and *confidence* come to the fore. At issue is, "Can we do the job?" Business writer Desmond Graves points out that precombination loyalties and alliances dominate until the parties engage in a common task. Then, energy is channeled into productive work, and doubts and frustration give way.[6]

There are several reasons why teams have trouble moving into a fully productive mode. First, postmerger teams need time to sort out new methods and procedures and to learn how to work new systems. In the case of two merging manufacturing groups, for example, one team used Deming's methods of quality improvement and another used the Crosby model. This led to "religious wars" between the two sides. It took months for each to teach the other their approach to quality and to develop a hybrid approach that satisfied both sides.

Second, there may be different expectations of performance in a merged work group. Consider the case of a manager who was historically the first to work and last to leave and expected herculean effort from his people. When his work area was combined with another manager's, who had a more laid-back style, trouble ensued. By all accounts the easygoing manager's group was every bit as successful as his hard-driving counterpart's, but there was no way to divvy up their responsibilities. The hard driver secured the top post and forced his ways on the laid-back manager and employees who thereupon left in droves.

This speaks to a final problem in achieving high performance: how teams handle diversity. We've seen cases where a male manager, taking over an acquired firm's accounts receivable department, never established the rapport or performance level of the female manager he replaced; where black employees, relocated in a largely white production department of a merger partner, never felt part of the combined team and were never welcomed in; and where female executives, in a merged media company, encountered a "glass ceiling" far thicker than their previous one. Organizations have different philosophies and approaches to responding to diversity in gender, race, ethnicity, and age. It takes time for managers and employees to figure out the "rules" in each company and more time still should they try to change them. It is advisable to address trust and confidence directly in the following ways.

Modeling New Behaviors. The most subtle tactic a new team leader has in influencing people is to model desired behaviors. In one case, a senior vice president publicly heralded how much top management of an acquired firm "brought to the party" but regularly ridiculed them in closed door sessions. His team picked up the cue and began to disparage subsidiary management. The result was the gradual exodus of acquired managers, sales representatives, and technical experts, coupled with a 30% drop in revenues in one year.

In another case, by comparison, a general manager drew on the ideas and talents of both sides through regular meetings and technical exchanges. He was committed to finding "best practice" in building the service philosophy and systems of a combined function. Team leaders down the ranks emulated their superiors' evenhanded behavior, and a newly developed suggestion system yielded over 500 recommendations for improvements in service delivery.

Performance Management. Directly rewarding desired performance is the most effective technique managers have for clarifying what they expect from people. Basic principles of effective incentive programs apply here: Find out what rewards, financial and otherwise, people want and clearly link them with desired behaviors. Oftentimes it helps to reward people's contribution to integration in addition to their operations-oriented results. To encourage the cross-fertilization of personnel following the merger of two engineering firms, for example, project managers were rewarded for staffing their teams with talent from both companies.

Incentives can also be applied to people management activity. For example, after a painful reduction in force, managers in a financial services firm were given the objective of raising employee morale in their departments, and were measured through employee attitude surveys and records of absenteeism and turnover in their departments. Of course, superior and subordinate need to meet to determine performance objectives, how they will be measured, when they will be evaluated, and what rewards can be attained. This kind of performance discussion is especially important when new performance criteria are established and when a new type of appraisal system is introduced.

Managing Diversity. One parent company introduced its own "valuing diversity" program in an acquired partner in anticipation of difficulties in putting departments together. The training program focused on prejudice and stereotypes and had participants undertake role plays where they were alternatively members of "majority" and "minority" groups. According to one participant, the session was an "eye-opener" and revealed considerable discontent within the acquiree over its inattention to affirmative action and diversity. The training session was heated. But many said it helped to build trust and understanding among members of merged teams.

TEAM BUILDING TOP DOWN

"Team building" wasn't the term used by Ned Franklin, vice president of manufacturing and service for Alpha Electronics when he met with his managers and those from newly acquired Multi Plex. "Let's not be naive," he reminded people, "we've got a lot of rebuilding to do. We've got to combine our corporate cultures, where necessary rebuild morale, and grow at a greater rate than the sum of the two companies."

Franklin explained how fundamental changes in the computer industry—applications moving from minicomputers to workstations, more demanding industry standards in communication, data management, and so forth, and the emergence of multivendor environments—were forcing a change in company strategy. "We must be careful not to use past pattern as a reference point for future strategy," Franklin warned his people, "to go with the 'devil you know' rather than the 'devil you don't' is not appropriate any longer." He also told his people "we value input and will solicit it," but reminded "we also have a business to run."

With that said, Franklin outlined key goals for the combination of the manufacturing and service organizations: higher utilization of fixed assets, lower material costs, elimination of duplication in support and management infrastructure, and, importantly, improved processes and ways of doing things. That would require merging most functions, their management, and their people.

The rebuilding of the manufacturing and service organization in Alpha mirrored the process followed in the Unisys case but at the divisional level. Franklin commissioned seven task forces, in manufacturing, customer service, procurement, new product introduction, human resources, finance, and information systems and brought team heads together in an overall steering committee. A key staffer served the vital tracking and liaison functions. And each team was given aggressive cost savings targets and broad strategic guidelines and then given the running room to design their functions.

New Leadership. In this instance, however, Franklin was obliged, early on, to make management appointments. Blumenthal could use the transition period to get to know managers personally and had the resources to keep people on board through the transition period. Here, several top MP executives pulled their parachutes once the sale was completed. Franklin's counterpart announced his intentions to resign, and the rest of MP manufacturing management was ready to follow suit. Hence his first challenge was to settle on his own direct reports and get them ready to begin integration.

The decisions were agonizing. On the one hand, MP senior manufacturing managers were seasoned and successful. On the other, Franklin had bright, energetic, and able people already reporting to him. He pored over the credentials of potential direct reports, obtained the counsel of his CEO and Alpha's HR head, and discussed the candidates confidentially with experienced employees. How could he size up the strengths and weaknesses of MP managers? He met with each of them, one on one, of course, and talked over their career interests, qualifications, and comfort in working for him. Then he cautiously contacted his counterpart and gained his confidence.

In an emotional meeting, the former head of MP manufacturing laid bare his assessments of his former direct reports. Franklin subsequently met with another significant MP veteran to compare notes and correct any biases his counterpart might have had. Then came the announcement. Franklin would flatten his staff—and have three Alpha and three MP line executives reporting to him along with existing finance, human resources, and MIS personnel. The news hit with a bang. On the Alpha side, Franklin had "betrayed" three of his people. On the MP side, by contrast, there was puzzlement and optimism. Word got around that Friedman would honor meritocracy and was committed to equality.

New Functional Structures. Franklin's direct reports were given simple guidelines for developing their structures: a maximum of five layers; spans of control between five to seven direct reports; and a division of work that would maximize value-added potential, whether in technology, product lines, or service to customers. Each of the managers then formed his or her own study teams, spanning several layers of management, to conduct detailed analyses and develop plans for his or her own organizations.

Determining plant configuration was the first order of business for the manufacturing team. After a thorough cost analysis, examining shipments, labor hours, and production processes, it was decided to truly merge the two companies' manufacturing operations and reconfigure all departments. This would mean closing down an Alpha plant nearby its headquarters, closing down an outdated MP facility, and merging the rest of the work force in a state-of-the-art MP facility. Consolidations and relocations would save Alpha $45 million in manufacturing expense. It would also focus manufacturing capability on key product lines under one roof in a world-class facility.

But there were logistical and human factors to consider. Both of the companies' manufacturing facilities would have to be reorganized, unfamiliar managers and employees would have to bond together, workers would have to be outplaced, and, importantly, special steps would have to be taken to ensure that top performers agreed to transfer to new facilities rather than take attractive jobs in other companies nearer to their homes.

New Managers and Supervisors. As the plans for organization structure took shape, it was time for divisional managers to flesh out their own teams. Each one revised managerial and supervisory job descriptions in line with the new structure and prepared profiles of top candidates for review by Franklin and the steering committee. In many instances, the selection choice was obvious—where a top-flight manager was already leading a group or where one manager had far more experience than his counterpart. There were, however, some tough calls. Alpha, for example, had a corporate policy of "valuing differences" and had promoted many more women and minorities to managerial positions than had MP. On paper, the MPers had more experience and depth. In practice, however, many had "peaked" in their career growth, and Alpha people were bright, energetic, and savvy. Who should be appointed to the job?

Decisions varied from case to case. The preeminent criterion was, of course, ability to do the job. The steering committee made sure, however, that factors of energy level, flexibility, interpersonal skills, and a knack for juggling many balls at once entered into the deliberations. Furthermore, if a woman or black candidate was as qualified as a more senior white manager, then the call went to the "different" employee—in keeping with Alpha's tradition. This initially caused a backlash in heretofore white and male-dominated MP. However, when people observed that talented people from both sides gained managerial and supervisory appointments, it was generally agreed that the selection process had been diligent and fair.

Setting a New Tone. Katy Stone was appointed as vice president in charge of operations. She would oversee the consolidation of manufacturing facilities, "sign up" managers and employees, and direct the plant closings and layoffs of the largest proportion of people in the entire organization. Some in Alpha and many more in MP had their doubts: She had been with Alpha for only a few years, was only just made a vice president and officer of the company, and was, after all, a woman. But Stone had been through this before: She was the first female manufacturing executive in her former employer's firm and had to streamline operations and make cuts when sales declined in that company. All of this prepared her for the job ahead: signing up her team and rebuilding the manufacturing function along "world-class" lines.

TEAM BUILDING THROUGH
THE RANKS

Following her appointment, Stone held regular meetings with employee groups at Alpha and MultiPlexto explain the logic behind current thinking and solicit further input. Stone began to send out special "Manufacturing Alerts" to update people on plans and progress. She then orchestrated a series of meetings with her team to define a "vision" for manufacturing and adopted her own sort of transformational tactics to develop priorities for change.

Articulating a Philosophy. During one off-site meeting with her team Stone spelled out her aspirations to make Alpha the "Manufacturer of Choice" in value-added hardware, software, and manufacturing services. This was based in a philosophy of *continuous improvement* in five areas: customer satisfaction, asset productivity, quality, management development, and people involvement. Manufacturing would have to become more of a "partner" with the sales and marketing divisions as well as R&D. And this would require a change in reporting relationships and planning methodologies—which Stone meant to effect. Finally, she wanted her manufacturing team to become a leader in open communication, teamwork, leadership effectiveness, and valuing differences. This led to a spirited discussion among team members of "hard" versus "soft" objectives and whether or not Stone's philosophy was going to be forced down managers' throats. In the end, her team supported Stone's vision and began to formulate realistic action plans and criteria for measuring their success.

Reaching Out to People. Then Stone carried the vision down into the manufacturing organization. At one meeting, she had supervisors list out their hopes and fears for the combination. The fears:

Starting over

Going from known to unknown

Loss of good people

Loss of control over my personal situation

What plant stays?

Relocating

Becoming a number, losing visibility/credit

New responsibilities

Pain of layoff

Readjusting and reorganizing

Leaving familiar culture

Letting go of old boss and old friends

Transferring to an unknown area

Mortgage payment

And on and on. The hopes included:

That the scars of the merger will heal

Trust, rapport, teamwork

Becoming number one in manufacturing

Integrating different functions/cultures into one

Maintain or exceed goals

Opportunity to improve processes

More togetherness; less competitiveness

Master new job assignment

World class manufacturing organization
Growth and new possibilities
Transition ends—back to business

In ceremonial fashion, Stone collected the listed fears of the managers and supervisors, put them into a brass urn, and burned them in front of the group. This represented her belief that the fears would be transformed into hope as the fire turned the paper to ash. Then she asked the group to draw pictures expressing their images of the combining operations. One picture represented the combination in three windows: (1) two separate ant hills, staffed by Alpha and MP "ants," (2) the hills splattered by the "big foot" of the merger, and (3) then rebuilt as one colony by the ants working together on a grander scale. Another picture (see Figure 9.4) depicted the walking wounded, resuscitated in hospitals and emerging stronger than before. The poem introducing this chapter summed up the feelings of most attendees.

Figure 9.4
One Manager's Picture of Team Building

MANAGING YOUR OWN TRANSITION

> Perhaps the single most salient difference between the successful and the failed transitions was the quality of the new manager's working relationships at the end of his first year. Three of four managers in the failed successions had poor working relationships with two or more of their key subordinates and with two or more peers, and all had poor working relationships with their superiors. Among the reasons given for interpersonal problems: rivalry issues, disagreement about goals, different beliefs about what comprised effective performance, and conflicts in management style. The underlying common problem, however, was the new managers' failure to develop a set of shared expectations with their key subordinates or their bosses.[7]

This quote from Professor John Gabarro highlights how managers who put off the work of team building are headed toward failure. Still, there are some specific issues that team leaders themselves must contend with in managing their own transition.

Dilemmas in Delegation. Take the case of an acquisition. Here parent company managers taking charge of an acquired team face a *dilemma of delegation*: They can't do everything, but there are real risks in passing responsibilities to direct reports who aren't familiar with new methods or procedures and who may not yet be trusted. The new boss is likely under some pressure to speed ahead with integration and begin achieving business results. This argues for centralized authority and hands-on management. At the same time, direct reports are looking for autonomy and the chance to prove themselves. This argues for delegating responsibilities and management by exception.

Dilemmas in Innovation. Second, there is a strong tendency for parent company executives to draw on what has worked for them in the past when coping with new demands. Sticking to the parent company's "way" pleases superiors and is comfortable to those seeking continuity. But this can put off subordinates who practice the "other way," and it may not be appropriate to the tasks in question.

This sets up competing pressures between the two sides and puts the executive in the *dilemma of innovation:* Managers will be damned if they impose the parent company's less effective methods, but they'll also be damned for "going native" if they retain the practices of the acquired side.

Successful team leaders address these dilemmas by enlisting political support. Faced with dilemmas in delegation, for example, one parent company manager had his boss review the capabilities of acquired supervisors and sought his counsel on the allocation of responsibilities and duties. This made them jointly responsible for decisions. Another manager faced with dilemmas in innovation commissioned a study group, involving both his direct reports and other functional managers in the parent company, to "test" the effectiveness of acquired company practices. As a result of this test, not only did the acquiree retain key practices, it was also invited to introduce them to managers in other subsidiaries.

To lead a team effectively, leaders carefully and purposefully manage their own transitions. Our observations of several executives who have succeeded at this yield some guidelines for managing one's own transition to team leadership:

1. Spend time with your boss, learning of his or her priorities and expectations and educating him or her about your area of the business.

2. Spend time with your peers, learning what they will or won't need from you and what you will and won't need from them.

3. Spend time with your direct reports, learning who they are and what they do, what challenges them and what does not, how they like to be managed, and what turns them off.

4. Keep track of yourself and your experiences. Make mental notes and written ones about what is working and what is not working. Be conscious of your learning during the transition period. Keep a journal of your experiences—this is an excellent tactic for building in some

"think" time, venting, planning, and learning about managing transitions and yourself.

5. Plan your delegation of responsibilities and keep track of progress and accomplishments. Share the "test" with your direct reports.

6. Continually get feedback about yourself and your work. Set a climate where people are encouraged to tell the truth and can air their differences of opinion. Get them involved as designers and supporters of the new team.

7. Don't expect love. This is a hard time for many people around you as they will be "letting go" of old reporting relationships and favored ways of doing things.

8. Do expect accomplishment and loyalty. Set aggressive goals for your people and hold people to them. Let them know that when decisions are made, you expect them to follow through.

CHAPTER 10

Reculturation

It is frequently the implementation phase which is more significant in determining success or failure than is the validity of the original strategic concept behind a particular merger effort.
    —W. Michael Blumenthal, CEO, Unisys, Speech at the University of Michigan, December 3, 1986[1]

Up to now we've only been swallowed. What's coming up next is digestion.
    —Manager in acquired company about to meet his new division head[2]

Unisys was born in name and in spirit in late 1986 following the final meeting of the Merger Coordination Council and task force heads. Plans for reconfiguring product operations, international and domestic marketing, and all staff functions were anointed and management assignments were completed. The new company was poised to attain the mass and scope needed to survive the computer industry shakeout—coming faster than anyone had expected.

In the case of Graphic Controls and Times Mirror, integration proceeded smoothly after GC came to accept its status as a subsidiary. One executive who had rated the Times Mirror–GC relationship a "3 to 4 out of 10" one year after the sale gave the relationship a "6 to 7" three years hence. The improvement was attributed to GC delivering promised increases in profits and sales. In his view, as GC met its commitments, Times Mirror's confidence in and respect for its management style increased.

This chapter considers the magnitude of changes in the postmerger period and their impact on corporate cultures. It reports on organizational, personnel, and cultural changes in Unisys from 1986 through 1990 and on changes at GC following Clarkson's departure.

MAGNITUDE OF POSTMERGER CHANGE

Taken together, the *degree of integration* between businesses and the *extent of cultural upheaval* on one or both sides determine the magnitude of postmerger change. To this point, we have described integration as ranging from modest levels of financial control to the partial integration of the two companies' operations and functions to the full consolidation of businesses (Chapters 4 and 6). We have also considered different forms of acculturation following a combination (Chapter 7). These two factors yield five different types of postmerger change (see Figure 10.1).

The Best of Both. This is the case of achieving synergy between companies through their partial to full integration. Studies find this "additive" kind of combination to be most successful—and risky.[3] It can also be the bloodiest. Financial and operational synergies are achieved by consolidation. This means crunching functions together and often leads to reductions in force. Line operations may be merged or brought under top level control. The optimal result is cultural integration—the blending of both companies' policies and practices. And, in the ideal case, the combined company culture reflects the best of both.

Preservation. This is the case where two companies operate more or less independently with modest degrees of integration. Strategists Phillippe Haspeslagh and Alison Been-Farquhar call this a "preservative" type because the aim is to maintain an acquired subsidiary's autonomy and identity.[4] This model is typically found in diversified companies that promote cultural pluralism among business units.

Figure 10.1
Magnitude of Post-Merger Change

	Low		High
High	ABSORPTION Acquired Company conforms to acquirer—Cultural assimilation		TRANSFOR-MATION Both companies find new ways of operating—Cultural transformation
Degree of Change in Acquired Company		BEST OF BOTH Additive from both sides—Cultural Integration	
Low	PRESERVA-TION Acquired Co. retains its independence—Cultural autonomy		REVERSE 'MERGER' Unusual case of acquired Co. dictating terms—Cultural assimilation

Degree of Change in Acquirng Company

To succeed, it requires group management to protect the "boundary" of the subsidiary, limiting intrusions by corporate staff and minimizing required integration.

Absorption. This is a combination where the acquired company is absorbed by a parent and assimilated into its culture. The studies of Phillippe Haspeslagh and David Jemison shows that companies who successfully effect such changes generally bring in new management and conform a subsidiary to corporate reporting relationships and regimens.[5]

253

Certainly there are short-run costs to this approach, but the researchers find that companies able to bear these costs and rebuild the business enjoy greater returns than those who fail to bring a troubled subsidiary fully into the fold.

Reverse "Merger." This is the mirror image of the previous type of combination. Here the acquired company dictates the terms of the combination and effects cultural change in the lead company. Ross Perot's challenges to General Motors exemplify an attempt to initiate such cultural change after his company, EDS, was acquired by the automotive giant. More often a reverse merger involves an acquired business unit or division absorbing the operations of a parallel unit in an acquirer.[6]

Transformation. Here *both* companies undergo fundamental change following their merger. Synergies come not simply from reorganizing the businesses, but rather from reinventing the company. This is the trickiest of all the combination types and requires a significant investment and inventive management. Certainly it has become fashionable for CEOs to term their mergers a "transformation." Indeed, the term has been applied to many forms of broad-based organizational change. There are, however, several distinctions between traditional approaches to change versus the transformational type. Traditional models of change, for example, emphasize orderly, incremental, and continuous steps. Transformation, by comparison, is discontinuous: It involves many simultaneous and interactive changes and the selection of "breakthrough" ways of thinking, organizing, and doing business. Whenever companies follow tried-and-true models of integration or simply absorb their partners, there is little in the way of real innovation or breakthrough thinking. Even when companies go through an additive combination, and seemingly draw the best of both, integration often involves compromise or horse trading, and change is positioned as a renewal of existing strengths.

Transformation, by contrast, poses a sharp break from the past. It involves a death and rebirth: Existing practices and routines must be abandoned and new ones discovered and developed (see Figure 10.2).

Figure 10.2
Change Versus Transformation

Change	Transformation
Continuous	Discontinuous
Renewal	Death/Rebirth
Focus on Content	Focus on Context
Path to a Known State	Odyssey to an Unknown World

W. Michael Blumenthal understood that the "old" Sperry and Burroughs would have to die in the creation of Unisys. He knew he would have to win the confidence of people, reshape the structure of the two corporations, and give the combined company a new sense of purpose. This puts the emphasis on context as much as content—not only what is being changed but especially why and how people need to think about it. Initially, Sperry managers in particular were skeptical about Blumenthal's intentions. "There's a touch of the cynic in us," said one, adding, "the proof is in the pudding." Later, a manager commented, "A crisis mode permeates every work day. Forty percent of my day is planned. The other sixty percent just comes up and kicks me in the ass." But as Blumenthal kept up his message of partnership and focused managers on new challenges in the computer industry, a third remarked, "you never saw a group of guys turn around faster. This merger is creating the craziness that makes my job fun."

The end state is unknown in a corporate transformation. In the case of Unisys, no one in either Burroughs or Sperry was sure what structures would be developed or whether or not they would have a job. Blumenthal conceptualized the transformation as follows:

> You have to be able to visualize the process of creating. What I did was to say I've got an immediate problem; I've got a one year problem; I've got a two year problem. I didn't exactly know how to get from here to there, but I visualized a new company.

TRANSFORMATION: UNISYS

The creation of Unisys extended over several months as transition teams reported their findings, executives were appointed through the organization, and businesses were reorganized to unite Burroughs and Sperry people and expertise.

New Top Leadership. The office of the president was an interim step in re-creating the top management of Unisys. Frankly neither Stern nor Kroger were comfortable in a joint command position. Stern claimed that the four-person executive office made the company the "laughingstock of the industry." He angled to be named chief operating officer and Blumenthal's second in command. However, Blumenthal put him off, and, in the end, Stern was unwilling to mold into the collegial style Blumenthal set for his team. Stern left in August, 1987 and later became CEO of Northern Telecom. Kroger, in turn, left in December to later lead a new international computer system company owned by Intel Corporation and Siemens A. G. Into the leadership void Blumenthal elevated seven younger executives to form a Management Board. This enabled him to promote a group of young top executives. And it surrounded him with potential successors from within the corporation.

Cultural Change. Burroughs and Sperry people had distinct philosophies about what made their companies successful. At Burroughs, for example, a high-quality/high-margin product line was the recipe for success. This strong "product" orientation had marked the company from the days of William Burroughs' adding machines. At the time of the merger, Burroughs' entire product lines were carefully planned and coordinated years in advance and shepherded through development through a centralized system (see Figure 10.3).

Figure 10.3
Cultural Transformation at Unisys

BURROUGHS

- OPERATIONS AND FINANCE ORIENTATION
- PRODUCTS ORIENTATION
- BOTTOM-LINE ORIENTATION
- CENTRALIZED CONTROL
- FUNCTIONAL STRUCTURE
- MERITOCRACY EMPHASIS
- NUMBERS ORIENTATION
- AGGRESSIVE STYLE

UNISYS

- CLIENTS AND MARKET ORIENTATION : More proactive to customer base
- SOLUTIONS ORIENTATION : More responsive to customer needs
- RISK TAKING ATTITUDE : Encourage innovative undertakings
- DECENTRALIZED DIRECTION : Autonomous decision making in LOB's
- LINE-OF-BUSINESS-STRUCTURE : Full concentration in a field
- MERITOCRACY EMPHASIS : Reward for performance
- NUMBERS ORIENTATION : Emphasis on financial position
- AGGRESSIVE YET POLISHED STYLE : Effective managerial presentation

SPERRY

- CLIENTS AND MARKET ORIENTATION
- SOLUTIONS ORIENTATION
- RISK TAKING ATTITUDE
- DECENTRALIZED CONTROL
- LINE-OF-BUSINESS STRUCTURE
- OLD BOY'S NETWORK
- PEOPLE ORIENTATION
- POLISHED STYLE

This gave Burroughs a niche in smaller markets, where customers could obtain specialized applications, and in larger markets, like banking, where customers could use "standalone" machinery. And it paid off. Stock rose from a low of $28 per share to over $65 in Blumenthal's tenure as CEO. The "bottom line" counted at Burroughs.

Still, industry critics said Burroughs had a "box" mentality. The company operated through a functional organization with top-down oversight of R&D, product engineering, and manufacturing. The sales force sold all Burroughs' products through geographically organized regions in the United States and abroad. By contrast, Sperry was organized along "lines of business." This way it could develop and market industry-specific products through vertical lines of business (LOBs) to large customers.

Sperry's comeback began when the firm decided to become a "solutions" company in the information system industry. Sperry's strategy was to link its computers with IBM's and other companies', creating integrated computing networks. No longer was its focus exclusively on mainframe hardware. Instead, it offered a line of mini- and personal computers, specialized software, communications technology, and a full portfolio of services.

This strategy, too, had begun to pay off at Sperry. The company did not enjoy an earnings increase comparable to that of Burroughs, but it had made significant inroads into sectors such as the airlines and state and local governments. Sperry was also gaining in customer satisfaction, and its user groups had become enthusiastic supporters of its new solutions strategy.

However, Burroughs people had a different picture of the company. They belittled their counterparts for "giving away the store" in sales and customer service. They found "holes" in Sperry product offerings. Furthermore, they saw Sperry providing inordinate numbers of systems and service personnel to customers leaving the impression that the organization was "fat" and lacking the wherewithal to maximize profitability. Sperry managers countered that their customers were large and complex and that systems and service support were essential to long-term account development.

What would it take to make the new company a success? The chairman's hope was to combine Burroughs' financial acumen and product excellence with Sperry's solutions orientation and marketing savvy. Fine in theory. But could Burroughs bring discipline into product development while retaining Sperry's strength as a systems integrater? On the marketing side, there was much to recommend Sperry's line of business organization. This would give sales personnel a focus—"what they learn from their first customer call in the morning could be helpful in their next one"—noted one Sperry executive. To move to this model, however, would mean changing over Burroughs' field organization. "It can never work," confided one Burroughs executive, "and even if it could, Mike would never go along with the added expense."

New Product Directions. Cost reduction was an imperative in the combined companies' product areas. And Burroughs managers came in like gangbusters. Several small plants were closed and others downsized. Computing systems suffering price/performance problems were deemphasized leading to reductions in Sperry staffing. The sense of domination was compounded when Sperry's senior operations executive resigned and two Burroughs executives were given top posts. On paper these changes seemed reasonable—even Sperry people regarded Burroughs' engineering and manufacturing capability to be superior. But, still, there was a sense of defeat. Then came some dramatic moves: Unisys, though still committed to serving both companies' existing customer bases, announced its intentions to develop open computing architectures for the future. A joint R&D team of former Burroughs and Sperry engineers succeeded in designing a UNIX operating system that would link mainframes, minis, and microcomputers. This development was hailed inside Unisys as a real sign of the "Power of 2."

Remaking Marketing and Sales. Sperry's premerger organization had consisted of seven LOBs. Sales and service personnel were assigned industry specific accounts. Burroughs had a geographic sales organization. Its sales force specialized in product knowledge and would sell to all comers. There had been much debate in Burroughs over the merits of an LOB structure before the merger. Always it was rejected in favor of a strong product orientation from engineering through to field sales and service. Hence there was "incredible pessimism" in the two organizations as to whether a consensus could be reached on one unified marketing approach.

Sales and marketing executives from both sides labored for nine months to evaluate the potential and expense of an LOB structure for Unisys. They were chartered with giving the company a "bold" worldwide strategy and direction. The move to some form of line of business would ensure, in their eyes, "focus, productivity, and value-added expertise." This would also allow precious development funds to be invested in areas offering maximum market penetration and return.

As a first pass, the team came back with recommendations to form three LOBs (in industry, government, and transportation/communications). This would meet cost savings targets and still give the company some focus in its sales efforts. The cost savings appealed to Blumenthal. But, he countered, why pack Sperry's strength in transportation and communications together with Burroughs' expertise in banking? The team came back with an abandoned proposal for four LOBs, more costly, but more likely to yield greater future market share.

Blumenthal reviewed the proposal coldly. He chewed out one manager from government operations for failing to do his homework on cost implications. He chilled another for dissembling on market projections when all he wanted was the truth. But in the hallways during a break, he met with both criticized executives to assure them that there were no hard feelings—and that both would run their organizations. The marketing and sales team came back with more data, more focus, and a clearer and crisper look at the advantages and disadvantages of the four LOB model. Pulling out a cigar, Blumenthal put up four fingers, congratulated them for sensational work and announced, "Ladies and gentlemen, now we can get to work."

Successes in Human Resources. In other key areas of integration, there were also many successes. For example,

Richard Bierly, senior vice president of human resources, was credited by many with "stamping out the 'takeover' mentality." John H. Shelsy, an officer of the Manufacturer's Association of the Delaware Valley, noted several months after the merger: "Somebody's doing something right there. We haven't received a flood of résumés or received panic phone calls." John H. Bourbeau, head of a Michigan outplacement firm, recalled, "If I rate Unisys's outplacement program with others...it would get very high marks."[7]

There were three key facets to integration in Human Resources. First, the department had to reorganize itself, with new jobs, titles, people, and programs. To take one example, a task force was commissioned first to study the history and experiences of the Management and Organization Development groups of both Burroughs and Sperry and then host an off-site retreat to establish a new strategy. The training team decided to scrap the existing models of management education in each company in favor of a "three-tiered" program focused on entry-level managers, managers of managers, and senior executives. Professors from the Business School of the University of Michigan and the Wharton School of the University of Pennsylvania were hired to lead seminars and case studies for trainees—the first time either company had involved leading academicians in their educational programs.

Second, the Human Resource Department had to design new policies for Unisys. There were, for example, distinct advantages to each of the benefit programs of Burroughs and Sperry. To keep the best features of both would, however, add millions to the combined company's benefit package. Mike Losey, a former Sperry HR manager, accordingly formed a team and developed a "flexible" package that would allow people to choose their own set of benefits. The program was no more costly than existing ones and had a very favorable reception. It was aptly named "The Power of Choice." There were differences in job grading and titles between the two companies. "Too many Sperry vice presidents," groused one Burroughs executive, "the place is run like a goddammed bank." "No recognition" for top technical talent, complained a Sperry manager. A new job grading system was developed that made titles "worthsomething" and that established a promotion ladder for technical people who didn't want to move into management.

Finally, HR had responsibility for helping people to overcome their "survivor" status and adapt to change. Managers were given a 32-page guide book called "Managing the Transition" that offered guidance on how to handle people and build work teams. To follow this up, internal organization development specialists led nearly 1,000 employees in focus group discussions and then briefed appropriate managers on the findings. Then, to add to team building within the overall HR department, Unisys had its first worldwide human resource strategy conference where representatives from all locations could come together, review progress and problems, and set a collective strategy for rebuilding the business.

Problems in MIS. In contrast, there were severe problems in integrating of the two companies' management information systems. At premerger Sperry, for example, order entry and distribution functions of the MIS system were "owned" by marketing and sales. In premerger Burroughs, this was under the control of product operations. "Our top priorities were keeping the business running and having an impact on our earnings-per-share targets," recalls a top MIS executive. As a result, the company developed a patchwork solution that would delay shipments and create consternation in field organizations. Recalls the manager,

> We pulled the switch and brought everything to its knees. We put a massive overload on the system. The amount of money we saved by not developing a new system we're going to more than blow on our inability to track our product shipments. It was a classic problem of the two systems being too big to run in parallel. If I had really thought things through, I would have dug my heels in and said add a year to all your plans and let's do it right.

The MIS systems hang-ups reached a point where Joe Tucci, president of U.S. information systems in Unisys, remarked, "We can't get to the next phase of the merger without resolving it." Still, Blumenthal stuck to his guns on the need for speed:

Sure there are always trade-offs; you can't always have speed and accuracy. I'd rather move fast and clean up later, than move slowly and prolong the disruption that accompanies uncertainty. This probably won't be the last time we'll have to face the consequences of such trade-offs.

1987–1988

The success of the merger was evident in the financial results of Unisys in 1987 and 1988. The combined company enjoyed significant increases in its gross profit margins, return on equity, and earnings per share in those two years (see Figure 10.4) and won Wall Street over.[8] To further its "solutions" strategy, Unisys acquired Timeplex, the leader in digital transmission systems, in early 1988. Sometime later the company acquired Convergent Technology to address low end product development. The transformation in Unisys was astonishing to people. During the merger, they were fixated on protecting their product lines. Two years afterward, they were introducing whole new lines of product and service "solutions."

Figure 10.4
Unisys Results—1986-88

	1986	1987	1988
Gross Profit Margin	31%	42%	44%
Return on Equity		13.3	14.3.
Earnings per share	(.54)	2.93	3.27

The four-LOB model was also proving a success, despite logistical hang-ups in order entry and shipments. By the end of 1988, Unisys was a vendor for 9 of the top 10 foreign banks and 23 of the 25 largest U.S. ones. Over 50% of the airlines worldwide were using Unisys systems. And the company was the leading supplier of computing systems to the federal government.

Furthermore, Unisys was having great success in winning people over. The company's 1987 attitude survey found that over 60% of the work force understood why the merger had taken place and two-thirds agreed that people from Burroughs and Sperry had an "equal chance" of getting ahead in Unisys. Plainly, commitments to full communication and meritocracy in job assignments were validated by the great majority of employees. Importantly, 65% expressed loyalty to the combined company. There were signs as well that most were settling in to their new jobs. Three-fourths of those surveyed said that they understood "what was expected of them" in their new jobs and 95% expressed "ownership" over their jobs. (See Figure 10.5.)

Figure 10.5
Unisys—Post-Merger Attitudes

61%	Understand Why the Merger Took Place
65%	Express Loyalty to the New Company
66%	Say There Are Equal Chances to Get Ahead
	(Comparable Ratings from former Burroughs and Sperry employees)
75%	Understand What Is Expected of Them.
95%	Feel "Ownership" over Their New Jobs.

Problems Brewing. At the same time, the combined company faced some new business problems. Inventory levels were creeping up as were levels of staffing. Sales began to slide in mid-1988, and finished goods inventory would mount at Unisys. Staffing levels were increasing to premerger levels in many factories and offices. Paul Stern had always "hawked" these indicators in the "old" Burroughs. To many eyes, the nine-person Management Board was not as attentive, and costs would eventually escalate "out of control."

In addition, the government's investigation of fraud in defense department procurement targeted Unisys. The "Ill Winds" investigation charged former Sperry executives with illegal activity, but the consequence was that Unisys's defense business "went in the toilet." Blumenthal was outraged. He had been assured by Justice Department officials, prior to the merger, that there were "no problems" at Sperry. In fact, Sperry had been under intense investigation at the time. A heavy fine only added to Unisys's problems in the defense business.

Finally, there were signs that the merger had not solved some existing organizational problems in Burroughs and Sperry. The 1987 employee survey found 40% of the work force and half of upper management complaining that different departments "don't work well together." This had been a serious problem in both companies prior to the merger—a result of tall structures and internal rivalries. Organization building had not eliminated the "chimneys," and managers continued to advance their own department's interests, often at the expense of other departments. Some 70% of those surveyed reported that the merger had "no impact" on interdepartmental cooperation. More broadly, only 44% said that a "Unisys way of doing things" was emerging.

Plainly, mergers don't fix existing problems. Blumenthal had been worried from the beginning that middle managers and "bureaucrats" in both companies would resist change and fight the notion of building a whole new company. Employees saw this resistance in the 1987 survey, and, although they reported "things are better than expected," problems in the business and in the management would confront Unisys in 1989 and 1990.[9]

1989–1990

By mid-1989, Unisys, like every computer manufacturer in the industry, was selling fewer mainframes at lower margins. This, coupled with the expense of acquisitions, was creating cash flow problems. Commercial customers were not moving to open UNIX systems, as hoped, and Unisys was not making enough money from its software and services. The company posted a loss in 1989 and inventory levels skyrocketed. A major restructuring and downsizing was undertaken, eliminating 11.5% of the work force.

A New CEO. In early 1990, James Unruh was named CEO. Unruh made improvement in the company's balance sheet his top priority. He was also committed to improving teamwork and interdepartmental cooperation. This improvement, he believed, had to start at the top.

Unruh held an off-site team-building session with his top executives shortly after taking office. To prepare himself, he listed his concerns about the Management Board and desired changes in its modus operandi. Among the problems he noted were the chimney mentality and the tendencies for top executives to view themselves as heads of their particular businesses, rather than leaders of the overall company. He found "turfism" in the group and defensiveness when examining business problems. Finally, he noted that the group "talked" participative management but did not live it as a management team. In turn, he wanted the team to acknowledge their interdependencies, confront problems openly and candidly, and together run the business.

At the team-building meeting, Unruh aired his concerns frankly and led his team through a heated discussion of their strengths and failings. There was a long discussion of trust—whether Unruh entrusted top executives with enough responsibility and whether the team trusted Unruh to lead them. Then the team diagnosed and prioritized the central problems in the business, including inventory turns, the profitability of open systems, and the clear definition of a "Unisys way of computing." Two-person teams of Management Board members were challenged with developing new strategies to address these problems. This would encourage cross-department cooperation in top management. The management group as a whole would assume responsibility for evaluating and implementing recommendations.

Unruh and his team left the meeting charged up and working together better. Managers were given more leeway in managing head count and expenses, and together they agreed to alter their bonus system to reward collective rather than simply individual results. Unruh himself made an important symbolic change to herald his team oriented management style: He had a wall demolished at Unisys' headquarters that had separated the CEO from his people.[10]

New Cultural Messages. Unruh also began to issue messages signifying a "Unisys way of doing things." Five themes were emphasized at the company's 1990 management conference:

1. **Ownership.** Simply put, we want everyone to approach his or her responsibilities as if this were *their* company.

2. **Teamwork.** As a team member, we don't have to directly control all the resources—we leverage them from wherever we find them.

3. **Involvement.** The objective here is to get all our employees involved in the business—it will save time *and* improve results.

4. **Innovation.** We don't recognize or reward the risk taker. I'm told we punish failure. I'm establishing a President's Innovation Award to help. But we all must find ways to encourage innovation...our future depends on it.

5. **Industry knowledge.** We need an organization staffed with people having strong industry understanding upon which to act.

Through 1990, the company sought to bring these messages to life. Product development and marketing were reorganized to formalize matrix relationships between major product divisions and the LOBs. Two executive vice presidents were appointed to head these two sides of the business. Employee involvement was expanded with over 100 projects initiated to push decision making down in the organization. Meanwhile, Unruh spread his new cultural messages through videotapes and many informal meetings with employees in lunchrooms, factories, and offices.

Blumenthal's Departure. W. Michael Blumenthal resigned as chairman of the board in October 1990.[11] He left convinced that the strategy to merge with Sperry had been sound but was troubled by debt and the performance of the Timeplex and Convergent Technology acquisitions. As of this writing, Unisys is still awash in red ink but has raised sufficient cash to meet its debt obligations. There have been many postmortems on the advisability of the merger and some second-guessing over Unisys's decision to keep its defense business. But most analysts agree that neither Burroughs nor Sperry would have survived the market shakeout and many still give the company a "fighting chance."

Blumenthal's goal of competing "head to head" with IBM was not to be realized. Big Blue retains over 70% of the mainframe market and Digital Equipment Corporation has surpassed Unisys to take second place in the overall computer industry. Blumenthal has taken a licking from Stern and even some who remain in the company. Still, he defends his decisions and accomplishments:

> Experts said it couldn't be done—the idea that I could come into this industry knowing nothing about it, with a company that was going sideways if not down, and use that as a platform for building Unisys....If this company starts going sideways again, I would have proved that I could make it more profitable, but I would not have proved everything I wanted.

Plans to build a $20 billion business have been dropped by Unruh who acknowledges that "Unisys is still a company under construction." Perhaps a market analyst described the current situation most succinctly, "It's been a rough period after a glorious start."

CULTURE CHANGE AT GC

How do cultures change after a merger or acquisition? Management scholars focus on the structural changes wrought by a combination and how new rules and regulations, new resource allocations, and, especially, new leadership alter the ways an acquired company operates and does business. In addition, cross-cultural anthropologists contend that "natives" go through a socialization process wherein they learn and are rewarded for new behaviors. Ultimately, of course, this process of "going native" changes their attitudes and the way business is conducted in their culture.

Three years after the acquisition, GC had begun to acculturate to life in a large, parent company. The overt threat to its culture had subsided, top managers had pulled themselves back together, profitability was recouped, and many GC and Times Mirror managers were developing reasonably good working relationships. There were some changes in GC's policies and practices. Yet other policies were unchanged, sometimes contrary to Times Mirror's wishes, and there remained an independent, identifiable, and strong GC culture.

Cultural Preservation. Times Mirror, it seemed to GCers, would tolerate their management style as long as financial results were good. This made high levels of profitability "mandatory." Otherwise, GCers continued to cite family feeling and the participatory style of GC managers as cultural exemplars. The open disclosure of financial data, the reliance on collaborative problem solving, and the continued use of "theater-in-the-round" communication channels all suggest that GC had, in many respects, preserved its values and ways of life.

GC managers also became more open and proactive in their relationship with counterparts at Times Mirror. Still, the parent company continued to be a "phantom over the shoulder" in top-level decision making, and there was the constant threat that its executives would swoop in the event of a downturn. Moreover, while GC's style had been accepted by Times Mirror, it had not been especially encouraged. GCers' occasional efforts to "evangelize the heathens" had proved unavailing.

Elements of Assimilation. At the same time, GC was in other respects being assimilated into Times Mirror and giving up elements of its cultural identity. As feared, the new owner's "technostructure" had worked its way into the subsidiary. GCers became much more financially oriented and were sure to "know their numbers," when queried by parent company staffers. GC's financial people gained new clout because they and top brass at Times Mirror "spoke the same language." Parent company executives were neither versed in GC's product line or markets, nor did they seem to be very much interested in them. Instead, they managed by the "numbers" and GC's financial departments, theretofore a "second class citizen," gained prestige and power. There were also subtle changes in behavior in GC. Some GC managers, for example, began to dress more formally and came to adopt the title of "Mr.," rather than their first name, in dealings with subordinates. A more subtle sign of assimilation was a decision in GC to reorganize into two large divisions. Clarkson and the "old guard" at GC had favored smaller divisions because of the sense of identity it afforded manufacturing people and the opportunities it gave them to influence product development. Times Mirror, and a key power group in GC, by comparison, favored the "economy of size" that would come from consolidation. Although the decision was openly debated and yielded a consensus, the move to two divisions was seen by some in the company as a further sign that GCers were "withering up and becoming businessmen."

REPLACING THE CEO

All of this weighed heavily on CEO Will Clarkson and his team. Many seemed to favor continuing their "strong stand" vis-à-vis value differences with Times Mirror. Others argued that GC should accommodate to "new realities." Some top managers empathized with Clarkson, the standard bearer of the old culture, noting he was in a "pissy dilemma"—trying to remain true to his philosophy and values while struggling to deal with superiors who explicitly devalued them. Others saw him as a "hindrance" to effective integration.

Clarkson was told, four years after the sale, that he would not find any future career opportunities in Times Mirror—"too much of a maverick." Accordingly, he decided to select an executive vice president to oversee operations while he contemplated his career plans. Two candidates emerged from the participative selection process traditionally used by GC. Don Quinlan, an operations man, was by then well known to Times Mirror and was strongly aligned with the financial leadership in GC. The other candidate, Lyman Randall, was closely aligned with Clarkson and had been the point man in several conflicts with the parent company. Top managers in GC were divided as to who was better equipped to lead the company.

GC then undertook what it termed a "participative selection process" where data were gathered on the qualifications of each candidate and a selection team interviewed their peers and superiors. Times Mirror became impatient with the process and introduced outside candidates. In the end, the selection process, with Times Mirror input, resulted in the appointment of the operations manager. Afterward, Clarkson, five and a-half years after the acquisition, with 33 years in GC, left the company. For the first time, someone outside of the Clarkson family would head GC. Quinlan, the new CEO, thereupon began to speak out against excessive participation and other "time-wasting" practices. He also changed the signage in front of headquarters to read "GC—A Times Mirror Company."

Who Keeps the Culture? Clarkson had two views of the potential impact of new leadership on the company's culture:

> On the one hand, I've always believed and acted like the "tone is set at the top." A CEO, by what he says and does, creates and keeps a company's culture alive. I just don't think that (Quinlan) truly believes in participative management. Sure he cares about people and will do a super job of running the business side of GC. But the company will change under his leadership. . . .
> On the other hand, I remind myself that the culture has spread throughout the company and is in the hands of a great many people. They'll practice participative management and they'll really want to develop people.

Clearly the new CEO had a different outlook than his predecessor on managing people and the business. At management meetings and in videotape presentations to employees, he stated that the company had to become "lean and mean" in the face of business challenges. GC people not only heard the words, they saw the changes: Selective staff reductions were undertaken in line with new strategic directions. Top management meetings became crisper and more "businesslike." There were few discussions of company philosophy and group process analysis, a specialty of the old leadership, ceased.

Deculturation. The effects, on some, were demoralizing. "Nobody talks about *community* anymore or seems to care about it," said one top manager, adding that *results* were all that mattered and that how you achieved them was "unimportant." A companywide attitude survey showed that over half the work force thought the company was putting profits ahead of people. Pressure for production increased, and it became acceptable, even fashionable, to talk about "deadwood" in the company.

People began to experience more pressure and more fear on their jobs. Declines in participation and two-way communication led to a significant drop in supervisors' understandings of the goals of the company and in their confidence in senior management. Confidence in the company's future and its leadership dropped 15% from previous surveys.

Quinlan was untroubled by the data and attributed them to the continuing "shakeout" in the company. Emphasis on profits and the attendant pressures felt by people were all part of "tough love." In his view, the U.S. business climate required a stronger emphasis on performance and individual rather than group accountability. He believed that managers still "cared" about people but were holding them to "higher standards."

The new initiatives coming from top management were countercultural. Attacks on participative management and changes in top management behaviors signaled that GC no longer valued cherished traditions which, in the eyes of employees, were integral to the company's success. Moreover, emphasis on a "lean and mean" organization was contrary to the ethos of "family feeling," and efforts to crack down on deadwood counterfeited the time-honored tradition of obtaining "extraordinary results from ordinary people."

GC was undergoing a period of deculturation. Its old ways were being abandoned, but there was no consensus over the desirability or value of new ways being introduced from the top. At a meeting of top management, now five years after the sale, the discussion went round and round, with some praising what was happening in the company and others challenging it, until Randall, sensing the mix in values and the consternation felt by his peers, said that this was like blind men "feeling the elephant." Some were handling the trunk and others grabbing the tail. All were seeing parts of the "truth," but all were blind to the totality of the beast.

FEELING THE ELEPHANT

The turmoil subsided in the room. GC's top managers eased back into their jobs and moved into a reflective period. To help managers understand our survey and interview data, one of us drew an elephant (reproduced in Figure 10.6) to interpret how different groups of people were experiencing the GC culture. The picture reflected competing values among executives of the "new" GC:

- **Profits versus people.** Everyone says (in surveys and interviews) that GC has to earn higher profits. But it also needs to keep people to be "on board." The data say that management has been overemphasizing profits at the expense of its people orientation. Some of you favor this emphasis. Others say it risks losing the commitment of employees.

- **Pressure versus vision.** Everyone we talked to agrees that GC people need to work harder and smarter to succeed in today's environment. Some top managers think this requires a "kick in the butt," while others favor a new vision and direction.

- **Top-down leadership versus participation.** Some GCers say that the new leadership stands on its hind legs and threatens people. Others say that management continues to lead by listening to people and letting them participate in decisions. GC's leadership has sent "mixed messages" to people about the worth of participative management and is itself divided over how to lead the company.

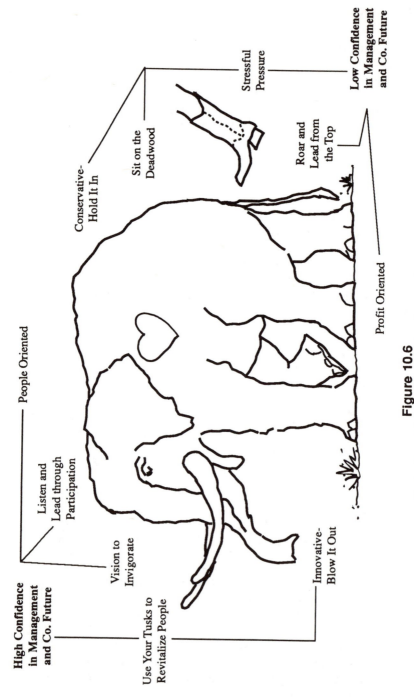

Figure 10.6
Deculturation at Graphic Controls
"Feeling the Elephant"

- **Innovation versus conservatism.** GC doesn't appear to be a leader in organizational development anymore—it is not "high stepping" into the future. Instead, management seems to be "holding things in" (the elephant's rear). People say the company needs new processes, products, and technologies. Can new leadership develop these through people?

- **Sitting on deadwood versus blowing the trumpet.** Some GCers call for sanctions and reprisals against deadwood. Others ask for leadership to revitalize people. Can new leadership motivate and retrain older employees, or must "deadwood" be sacrificed in service to competition and the "bottom line?"

RECULTURATION AT GC

The new CEO and his top team labored over the elephant and its meaning. They then moved into their traditional "self-study" mode to redefine the company culture. Each top manager developed a position paper specifying his or her central values for running the company. Over the course of several months, these views were refined to complete a roster of beliefs and values that top management regarded as integral to the future success of the company and the welfare of its people. Their roster addressed commitments to people, but also to customers, innovation, products, strategy, the profit objectives of the company and job security. A brochure, entitled "Sharing a Vision," was distributed to the work force and signaled what the company would stand for under the guidance of new top management.

However, this was only a part of the effort toward *reculturation* in the company. Bottom-up innovations in work design, profit sharing, and even participative management gained the staunch support of top management. Still, GC's top managers were distressed at continuing declines in ratings of people's confidence in them and troubled that so many did not see their vision in practice. This led top executives to hold an off-site retreat, now seven years after the acquisition, to deliberate about the future of the company.

A Leveraged "Buy Back." Executives were quarrelsome at the retreat and disagreed sharply as to whether the company had "lost its bearings." There was also a sharp division as to whether or not Times Mirror had "hamstrung" management with its demands on profitability. Top management agreed, however, that none of them had that "gleam in the eye" they had shared during Clarkson's reign. They left the meeting resolved to "do something" to get that back again.

Six months later, as Times Mirror began to focus its business and divest some subsidiaries, GC managers proposed that their parent consider their divestiture. After months of negotiations, GC management repurchased the company through a leveraged buy back. Employees thereupon held a party for management at a local pub and dubbed the gathering "A New Beginning—Family Again."

In the first year after the buyout, top managers worked "60 hour weeks" and climbed a steep learning curve comparable, in the words of one, to "baptism by fire." GC's top management also became "a closer knit group, mutually supportive of each other" as they not only shared a mutual financial obligation, but began, once again, to share deep personal feelings among themselves.

Today there is more of an "urgency" in top-management meetings than in Clarkson's time. The agenda is covered expeditiously and decisions made on the spot. When an issue cannot be readily resolved, members of the group most often defer to Quinlan—the "boss." There is likewise less overall tolerance for "deadwood." It is feared that those who are not doing their fair share "may be jeopardizing the whole organization."

Along with added worries, however, there is enjoyment of autonomy regained. Quinlan says he has more time to devote to running the business since he no longer puts in hours managing the relationship with Times Mirror. A return to a single annual review meeting has simplified greatly the "burden" of detailed financial reporting.

The most recent GC survey (ten years after the sale) showed signs that people were regaining their good feelings about the company culture. The majority of GC people see the company once again putting an equal emphasis on people and profits. Longer-term employees, those who worked for GC prior to the

Figure 10.7
Data on Reculturation at Graphic Controls
"Family Again"

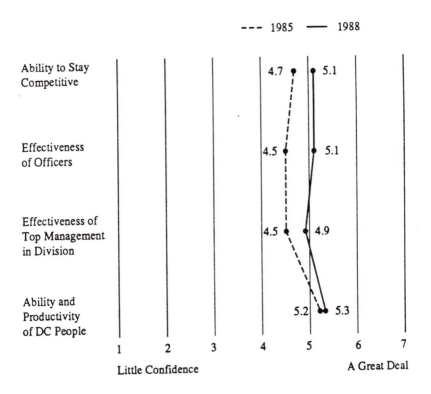

acquisition, reported the sharpest increase in their trust of management and the company's commitment to people.

Certainly GC's culture today is different from its pre-acquisition days. The managerial philosophy and style is less participative—particularly at the top. However there is a marked increase in the number of people who contribute to decisions through their work teams, on task forces, and in cross-divisional committees compared with years past. The leadership style of the division heads is viewed as quite participative, and division management groups have gained the confidence of a greater proportion of GC employees.

Clarkson was right. The tone is set at the top. Quinlan has been characterized as a "workaholic," and people in GC say that they have a heavier work load and more pressure on their jobs than ever before. Not all of his direct reports are satisfied with the chances they have to participate in decisions, and some have, in a fashion, become "conformists." However, Clarkson was also right that it would be the managers, and supervisors, and everyday working people in GC who would keep the "old" culture alive. The reculturation of GC is most clearly seen in the regained confidence of the work force. (See Figure 10.7.)

Clarkson is missed in GC. To keep his spirit alive a training room was built in his honor and a plaque honoring Will Clarkson described him as GC's "organizational architect." Quinlan and his team have finally regained people's confidence, and the business, newly independent, has won people over. All of this is part of reculturation. The "old" must die and the "new" must take shape.

Employees say that the company again "steers its own course." They also note that management is more available, celebrates with them at retirement parties and new employee introductions, and is more apt to join in on events sponsored by the reinvigorated employee social club. Becoming "family again" has meant something special to those in GC. Top management distributed stock throughout the company after the buyout and instituted a companywide profit-sharing system that has paid out handsomely. This makes everyone a little more "profit oriented" but not necessarily at the expense of people, as confirmed by the most recent employee survey which shows people are every bit as important as profits.

PART FIVE
SPECIAL TOPICS

CHAPTER 11

Tracking the Combination

Division manager: "Things seem to be settling down now. These things take time but we're on the right track."
—Group vice president's comments on current status of acquisition[1]

Division employees: "No one wants to make the first mistake. . . . Management is not visible. . . . Salespeople are not prospecting. . . . Nobody will make decisions. . . . Lack of real communication—just 'corporate-speak'. . . . This thing is going 'off the rails'. . . ."
—Feedback from employees in group vice president's division[2]

Mergers and acquisitions have the potential to affect employee morale and productivity, work processes and quality control, group and intergroup relationships, customer service and satisfaction, community standing and reputation, and practically every other aspect of an organization. Even so, relatively few executives formally assess how the combination is going or solicit systematic feedback from managers and employees.

Of course, most managers profess to have some awareness of what is going well and what is not. But when they consult exclusively with their peers and direct reports what they hear is often censored and self-serving. This gives them a distorted picture of progress and false assurance that problems will pass so long as they stay the present course. Months later, the picture is clearer: Transition trauma hits the bottom line, and executives have no recourse but to move into damage control.

This chapter reviews the components of a formal program to track the progress of a combination: what to look for, how to do it, and who should be involved. The recommendations are to begin tracking as soon as possible and to continue it as long as it is needed and proves worthwhile.

WHY TRACK CHANGE?

The purpose of tracking is to assess how the combination is progressing: Do people understand why change is occurring and support it? What are early impressions of the combined company? How is implementation going and what is needed to improve things? How are people coping with stress? Are signs of commitment emerging? And how is management perceived and evaluated? It is also important to monitor the impact of change in concrete terms: progress versus integration schedules, rates of turnover and grievances, changes in quality and productivity, and sales and profit margins of course.

Many executives downplay the relevance of a formal tracking system because "my people alert me to problems" or because "I have an open door policy." What we hear instead from managers and employees sounds like this: "Management doesn't want to hear this, but . . . "; "I wouldn't tell my boss this, but to be perfectly frank with you . . ."; and "Senior management is shielded. They have no idea what is really going on down here . . ."

This is not an indictment of executives' receptivity or of their sensitivity to the human side of change. Even in companies having a good communication climate, a merger upsets normal methods of intelligence gathering and two-way information exchange. Executives are busy with planning and oversight. Managers are busy, too, and wary of loose talk. People at all levels become more cautious in who they talk to and what they say. Trust has yet to develop between employees and new leaders. And there is always the risk that somebody will "shoot the messenger."

Psychological factors also interfere with effective and straightforward communication: Stress impairs perception and judgment. "Wishful hearing" abounds. Even among the best listeners, there can be "information overload." And, from the ranks, receptive executives get an abundance of "bad news." Staying alert to all of the ways combinations are affecting their operations, customers, employees, and reputations taxes executives' cognitive capacities. As a result, important information is often overlooked or misinterpreted.

Benefits of Formal Tracking

A formal program to track the combination offers several benefits:

1. Determines if the transition is proceeding according to plan or veering off course. A formal tracking program provides decision makers with feedback on how the combination is affecting people and the business. In one merger case, interviews revealed that unclear work charters, timetables, and financial targets were preventing task forces from coming to decisions about the design of merging units. The CEO was, according to interviewees, observing the merger from "10,000 feet." When briefed on the problems, however, he met with each task force to clarify their situation. In another case, cost savings in an acquisition were compromised by the hiring of ex-employees as consultants. By not monitoring placement activities, management did not get a handle on the problem until it hit profit-and-loss statements.

2. Identifies "hot spots" before they flare out of control. In one manufacturer, the secrecy of preacquisition negotiations created an air of distrust between employees and management. An attitude survey, conducted a few months following the firm's sale, showed morale eroding among production workers. Attributing this to "postmerger stress," management initially pooh-poohed the data. However, when follow-up interviews showed that employees felt neglected by management and were agitating for union representation, senior management moved swiftly to open communication channels and respond to aggrieved employees.

3. Ensures a good flow of upward communication. Bad news seldom rises to the top of an organization. An effective tracking program gives employees the chance to communicate to upper management and provides a mechanism for top echelons to hear from those closest to the action. Often managers are dismayed to learn of the discrepancy between actions and words. In one case, for example, management of two merging sales forces ballyhooed the benefits of each company cross-selling the other's products. Salespeople were eager but had outdated sales literature, no demos, and no idea what to charge customers or when deliveries could be made. Busy with all the "paperwork" involved in processing employee transfers, setting up office space, and servicing existing orders, sales managers pushed these complaints aside. Once senior marketing management learned of these problems through focus group interviews, however, they said "screw the bureaucracy" and sales aids soon flowed to the branches.

4. Highlights needs for midcourse corrections. Tracking lets executives assess the impact of change and make important midcourse corrections. An East Coast publishing firm had hoped to, within one year, consolidate the operations of two fiercely competitive midwestern firms recently acquired. Tracking showed that "bad blood" between the two acquirees could not be overcome without a "bloodletting." Needing managerial talent from both companies, the responsible parent company executive decided to keep the two subsidiaries separate for a time. Revised plans called for gradual integration over a three-year period.

5. Demonstrates interest in the human side of change. A tracking program also has tremendous symbolic value: It is a tangible reminder to employees that their leaders care about them and their opinions. Asking people how the combination has affected them, their coworkers, and their ability to perform demonstrates that management is interested in the human side of change.

6. **Involves more people in the combination process.** A tracking program is a cost-efficient way to involve large numbers of people in the combination process. Entire work forces or select samples can participate in surveys and interviews. Employees can meet with managers in focus groups or "skip-level" meetings. Human resource specialists can gain a "big picture" understanding of the combination through systematic monitoring. All of this allows more people to participate in and influence postmerger change.

7. **Sends a message about the new company culture.** How a combination is managed starts to define the new company culture. A formal tracking program signals the importance of two-way communication and conveys management's genuine interest in people's problems and perspectives. By comparison, the absence of any formal feedback channels can imply that management doesn't give a damn about what people think or feel.

WHAT TO LOOK FOR

Combination tracking should address a number of key questions about how things are going and people's reactions:

- Is the combination meeting financial and operational goals?
- Are schedules on target, and are changes being effectively implemented?
- Do employees understand and support the need for change?
- What is the effect on people's well-being and esprit de corps?
- Are managers at all levels taking steps to minimize negative reactions and build positive feelings?
- Are productivity or work quality being affected?
- Do people understand their new roles and what is expected of them?

A tracking program can also hone in on management's needs during the transition:

- Do managers have enough training to facilitate the combination?

- Do managers have sufficient information to give their people a clear picture of where, when, why, and how change will be occurring?

- Are managers being given the resources and support needed to reorganize their departments and rebuild capability?

- Are new policies, procedures, and systems helping managers to do their jobs?

As Change Is Announced. A tracking program should be focused on key issues during specific phases of the combination. Soon after a combination or reorganization is announced, for example, it is helpful to assess people's initial reactions. An employee survey right after a high-tech acquisition showed that acquired employees did not understand fully the reasons behind the sale. This led parent company management to host employee meetings in the subsidiary to explain their rationale. Later there were rumors of massive reductions in force. This led management to communicate clearly the magnitude and scope of proposed layoffs. Finally, there was concern over the viability of a merged product line. Alerted to this, marketing people sponsored product demonstrations in company lunchrooms to ease employees' concerns.

As Implementation Occurs. As planning gives way to implementation, tracking programs should focus on the following:

- Are new job assignments and reporting relationships clear?

- Do people understand new policies and procedures?

- Do they have the equipment and resources they need?

- Do they know how to get the information they need?

- Do employees believe that they will benefit from success?

- Do they know and believe in the goals of their work group, functional area, and the combined company?

This information gives leaders a quick fix on "little problems" (e.g., people not knowing what to say when answering the telephone or which forms to use) and "big issues" (e.g., perceived inequities in salary schedules and perks between departments).

Postmerger Issues. Twelve to 18 months following a merger—after things quiet down and people grow accustomed to new regimens—is a good time to systematically take a company's pulse. A comprehensive assessment reveals how the company has emerged from the combination and how ready it is to achieve future goals. In the case of two companies in the entertainment industry, for example, a postmerger survey showed people to be uncertain about the combined company's culture. Key managers from merged units formed a task force to clarify "new" values and translate them into new practices. Executives can also use such data to shape their long-range organizational planning.

HOW TO TRACK PROGRESS

A variety of methods can be used to collect data about a combination. Certainly there are distinct advantages to, for example, interviews versus employee surveys (depth versus breadth of opinion) or to focus groups versus informal conversations (more structure versus spontaneity). Good tracking programs rely on multiple methods of data gathering, including the following:

Attitude Surveys. Employee attitude surveys are excellent sources of information, whether conducted early (to assess expectations), during (to evaluate how change is being handled), or after a combination (to determine levels of satisfaction or discontent).

An entire work force can be surveyed, or, alternatively, particular groups can be targeted, or a cross-section of the organization sampled. For a survey effort to be successful, employee participation should be voluntary (people cannot be forced into sharing their true thoughts) and anonymity should be ensured. This means keeping individual surveys strictly confidential.

Survey efforts can be handled in-house or conducted by outside vendors. Expertise needed includes the ability to write reliable questions, draw representative samples, compute statistical results, analyze and interpret trends, distinguish between critical and general findings, and feed the results back to executives and employees. The decision to go in-house versus outside should be based on both ability *and* credibility: Surveyor's trustworthiness may affect employees' candor in answering questions and expressing opinions.

Interviews. Confidential interviews allow employees to expand on their opinions, offer detailed explanations, and provide examples. Interviews should be relatively unstructured when general information is desired or guided by a set of questions when specific data are needed. Again, outside consultants offer expertise, dispassion, and credibility. However, when executives personally conduct interviews, they send a message of genuine interest and gain a better feel for the data. Another benefit of executive interviews: They allow senior managers to put aside everyday issues and think broadly about the transition.

Interviews take time—usually at least an hour to conduct and an equal amount of time to analyze and consolidate results. Thus, care needs to be taken to select interviewees who truly represent the sentiments of the broader work force. When collecting companywide data, it is useful to sample a mix of employees who are both supporters and critics, who come from all levels, and who represent various departments, divisions, and locations. It also helps that interviewees be reasonably articulate and forthright—people who will speak up whether they are in favor or critical of the combination.

Requisite interviewing skills include the ability to elicit information, ask follow-up questions, and probe deeper without threatening the interviewee. Especially if coming from the buying company side, the interviewer must be sensitive to the impressions being left through professionalism, friendliness, sensitivity, and body language. And, as with a survey, interviewers need to assuage concerns about confidentiality.

Focus Groups. These are interviews conducted with groups of employees. They save time by getting anywhere from two to ten people to respond to questions about the combination. They also let participants build upon the responses of one another. But, especially in a climate of low trust, they may cause people to clam up. The facilitator must be skilled to elicit true feelings and, as well, to prevent focus groups from degenerating into "bitch sessions."

Another method of group data gathering is a "skip-level" meeting. Here employees can meet with managers two or more levels senior to them to air opinions and gain a broader understanding of the merger. One company we worked with had small groups of employees meet to generate opinions and questions and then elected a spokesperson to present them to senior management. This protected the anonymity of individual employees while ensuring that top management heard uncensored information.

Observations and Informal Conversation. Managers can also assess their situations through observation and informal conversations with supervisors and employees. One manager we worked with monitored who spoke up at combined team meetings and how long they talked to gauge his progress in building camaraderie. When he found several "wanting" and "wrung out" employees speaking up, he adjudged the group was making progress. Another manager tracked car departures from the parking lot to assess postmerger commitment. When he found the parking lot still emptying at 5:00 six months after the acquisition, his fears about problems with recommitment were reinforced.

Management by walking around, conversations in hallways and lunchrooms, and after-work "bull sessions" all provide occasions for data gathering about a combination. We recommend, too, that managers keep an eye out for merger-related graffiti, cartoons, underground memoranda, and such. They provide a good indicator of true sentiment and are often worth a few laughs (see Figure 11.1).

Records. Many corporate reports and records contain combination-relevant data. Records of turnover, absenteeism, grievances, and the like are good indicators of merger morale. Tracking customer orders, productivity levels, quality control, waste, and such before, during, and after a combination can be useful in evaluating progress and spotting problems.

Figure 11.1
Cartoon in Employee Paper Depicting Merger Stress

Customer Surveys. Interviewing customers or sending them questionnaires provides a company with an important perspective on how the combination is going. Specific problems or questions can be examined in a systematic manner. This also tells customers that they have not been forgotten amid all the hustle and bustle of change.

Exit Interviews. Interviews conducted with people leaving during or soon after a combination can be used to find out what, if any, aspects of the transition influenced decisions to seek employment elsewhere. If a repetitive pattern is found, action can be taken to address the causes of turnover.

CASE EXAMPLES

Most organizations have built-in methods for combination tracking. Existing personnel, production, and sales records can easily be adapted for purposes of tracking a merger across relevant time periods. Companies that conduct regular employee surveys can adapt the content and timing to tap into postmerger sentiment. So, too, there are data gathering specialists who can be chartered with monitoring responsibilities. For example, human resource specialists can apply their skills to individual and group interviews. Market researchers can evaluate customer reactions. And program planners can devise scheduling-and-monitoring systems to track the implementation of change.

There are advantages, however, to using outside expertise. A tracking program is only as good as the information it generates. Outsiders may be seen as neutral "third parties" to employees and thus serve as better conduits of their true feelings. Furthermore, their expertise can speed up problem identification and aid in the interpretation of findings.

In addition, outsider experts are not apt to be caught up in merger stress. Many firms have internal specialists well versed in data gathering techniques. However, these specialists are often wracked by worries and have other responsibilities during a combination. It helps when outsiders, who are more or less immune to changes, guide internal monitoring efforts.

Finally, in many organizations, an outsider is needed to confront senior managers who are themselves the source of merger problems.

The best approach is to use both internal and external experts to track a combination. Outside experts bring know-how and dispassion while internal professionals are familiar with their company's culture and people. In the merger of

Burroughs and Sperry, involving 110,000 people, there was no way that the two of us, as external consultants, could track the full impact of the combination. Accordingly, training sessions were held with company human resource and organization development staff members to prepare them for monitoring. These professionals, through interviews and focus groups, involved nearly 1,000 employees in discussions of the impact of the merger on local operations.

Top-Level Tracking at Unisys

Systematic top-level tracking played a useful role in the formation of Unisys. The day after he made the bid to acquire Sperry, Blumenthal asked us to conduct our own "sensing" of the merger. We were to operate as impartial eyes and ears and, then, preserving individual confidentiality, provide the CEO and his team with feedback on the impact of their actions.

Right after the announcement, Burroughs and Sperry senior managers were interviewed. These were the opinion leaders to whom people looked for guidance. Hence it was important to determine whether or not pledges of partnership and meritocracy were deemed credible. When the contours of integration became clear, data collection focused on staff groups in the two companies' headquarters who would face widespread reductions in force. During combination planning, task force leaders and members were contacted to assess progress of their groups. Later, as senior-level positions were announced and functional structures started to flesh out, time was spent with line executives to assess how the organization-building process was proceeding.

We sent Blumenthal periodic summaries of our findings and met with him to discuss the implications for action. In these sessions, he tested the reliability of our samples and validity of our conclusions. He wondered, for example, to what extent interviewees were "using" us to paint a biased or self-serving picture and if the trends could be related to the bottom line. Often we were the bearers of bad news. Needless to say, Blumenthal was a skeptical and sometimes defensive consumer of interpretive information.

Still, many of the issues raised in tracking reports led to swift action. Early on, for example, interviews found that Blumenthal's courting of Sperry people was creating a backlash of resentment in Burroughs. The CEO made it a point, thereafter, to meet more often with Burroughs' executives and to have more visibility in the company's Detroit headquarters. Blumenthal was briefed on the clash of cultures between the two companies. Though never fully accepting our observations about these differences, he nonetheless addressed himself to desired values and accepted the mantle as "keeper" of the new culture. The need to coordinate task force studies was raised again and again. Blumenthal thereupon assigned executives as liaisons to task forces to ensure that the groups were not at cross-purposes.

Blumenthal also used us as a sounding board and reality check regarding communications, the reactions of executives, the pace of change, and his own assessments of progress. We discussed and argued regularly over the merits of cost cutting, signs of favoritism in management appointments, the respective roles of Stern and Kroger, and the need to get middle managers more fully involved in transition training. The point is not to overstate our role. Rather it is to emphasize that top level tracking has special value to CEOs who make use of it.

Employee Attitudes at Graphic Controls

At the other end of the spectrum, it was data collected from hourly and clerical employees that helped top management at Graphic Controls to recalibrate their reactions to the acquisition by Times Mirror. In the first year after the acquisition, employee surveys showed that 60% of the work force found management to be "uptight" about the acquisition, and as many said the company was becoming more interested in making profits than interested in people. Furthermore, there was a perception that problems were being caused as much by GC management's reactions to the acquisition than by Times Mirror. These survey data dovetailed with interviews that said that management was obsessed with new owners and was fixated on protecting the company by putting more emphasis on profitability. (See Figure 11.2.)

Figure 11.2
Post-Acquisition Employee Survey
Graphic Controls

Attitudes about Acquisition...		
	Yes	*No*
Satisfied with the way top management has handled the acquisition?	51%	13%
Been kept informed about acquisition-related changes?	52	26
Has the acquisition had a significant impact on the company?	61	10
Has the acquisition had a significant impact on your supervisor?	45	12
Has the acquisition had a significant impact on you and your work?	34	8
Attitudes about Its Consequences...		
	Top Management	*All Employees*
...Management seems more "uptight"	100%	62%
...Management seems *less* interested in people's welfare and well-being	0	43
...People in the company have *less* trust in one another.	0	38

The survey data were, in turn, fed back to employee groups throughout the company for analysis and action planning. After plenty of discussion, it was agreed that top managers would be more accessible to people and would no longer purposely "shield" them from changes required by Times Mirror. Instead, everyone would work together to accommodate new realities and pitch in to achieve cost savings. GC formed several quality circles in plant facilities thereafter and developed a gain sharing plan to reward cost reductions.

Surveys showed a "rebound" in morale three years after the sale. Then came the departure of Clarkson, the appointment of a new CEO, and a period of reculturation culminating in the "buy back" of the company. What is important to note is that systematic data collection and managerial self-study helped to guide this transformation of the company.

A Merger Monitoring Group

Soon after another aquisition, executives reviewed several approaches to tracking the combination. One option was to have human resources representatives track change. This would, however, take time away from their counseling and, frankly, HR was perceived as biased by several senior managers. "They always cry wolf," one confided. Another option was to have a team of professional consultants do the tracking. This would be costly. Furthermore, it was suspected that the consultants too would be biased. "You always see yourself as St. George," one remarked, "but we're the ones who have to fight the dragon." Then a third option came to the fore.

Why not create a cross-company team to monitor the impact of the combination on people and functions? A merger monitoring committee was commissioned, led by a team of external consultants and staffed by employees, 20 in number, from nearly all functions in both companies. Members were prepared for tracking through a seminar on merger dynamics and training in interviewing and fact-finding.

The committee met monthly for six months following the sale. Between meetings, members would interview people in their work area and host informal "conversation hours." Several members teamed up to correct for possible biases and ensure broad exposure. The monitoring group's first report included a 6-page executive summary, detailed summaries by major functions, and 150 pages of back-up documentation. Subsequent reports addressed three fundamental questions: What's going right? What's going wrong? Issues and recommended actions.

It wasn't easy for monitoring committee members to work together. In a sense, the committee was a microcosm of the organization. Several members were emotionally overwrought in the early stages of the combination and brought their anger into committee meetings. In this respect, the committee functioned as a support group. It also had its share of paranoiacs and game players who created conflicts and left the committee divided on some of its interpretations and recommendations. Furthermore, some executives concluded that the committee was full of "crepe hangers" and "alarmists" and dismissed the findings and the committee concept out of hand.

What this monitoring process did show, however, was that 20 or so people from both companies could serve as credible voices for the "masses" in each organization and issue practical and timely recommendations on how to improve the combination—with respect to business decisions and the handling of people. The committee disbanded six months after merger, having lost a third of its membership through voluntary severance, but satisfied that it had represented the work force and gained top management's ear. Committee members left with a small gift: a calendar of "Murphy's laws."

CHAPTER 12

International M&A

Japanese acquirer: "They were like a frog in a small pond. They couldn't see the wider ocean, which is what we show them."

American Acquiree: "They're all very profit conscious, more interested in the plant and what it produces than how it affects the community."

—Two views of Japanese acquisition of an American company, *The Wall Street Journal,* July 30, 1990[1]

The dark side of Europe's restructuring is the unavoidable human cost. Says Gary Hamel, a professor at the London Business School and consultant to many multinationals: "Making acquisitions is the easy part. The fundamental management challenge for European companies is to learn how to integrate these national operations into an effective whole."

—"Merger Mania Is Sweeping Europe," *Business Week,* December 19, 1988[2]

The motivations behind the 1989 merger of Canada's Molson Breweries and Carling O'Keefe, the Canadian brewing operation of Australia's Elders IXL conglomerate, included factors common in today's merger wave: globalization, the fight for market share, and increased competitiveness, all stimulated by government deregulation. A GATT (General Agreement on Trade and Tariffs) ruling opened up Canada to European imports and the Canada-U.S. Free Trade Agreement threatened an influx of cheaper, more efficiently produced American beer across the border. Canadian sales were flat as aging baby boomers turned to wine as their preferred drink. The merger of Molson and Carling breweries would cut costs and improve capacity by consolidating breweries.[3]

Certainly there were stresses and strains in this merger. Noted a union representative: "When you take two plants and make them one, no matter how you do it, nobody's going to like it." There were also conflicts between the action-oriented, profit-driven orientation of Carling and the professional but slower-moving style of Molson. What gave this deal some twists, however, were its international aspects.

First, Canadian law requires that beer be brewed in the province in which it is sold. This dictated the integration strategy, forcing the closure of some efficient plants and the continuance of less efficient ones. Second, a multilateral committee of labor, management, and government officials devised a "Merger Adjustment Program" providing redundant employees from both sides with separation allowances, pension payouts, and continuing benefits. The use of such committees is commonplace in Canada. Finally, there were cross-national aspects to the clash of cultures here. Molson viewed Carling's Australian owners as "cowboys" who would "loot" Canadian workers and customers. On the other side, Elders' senior management regarded Molson as being insular and lethargic, not unlike O'Keefe in its pre-Elder days.

This chapter considers the aspects of merger management unique to international and multinational deals. It looks, briefly, at the trends in international M&A and then examines the human and organizational problems posed in international deal making, integration, and postmerger management. The clash of international cultures is given detailed attention.

INTERNATIONAL DEALS: SCALE AND SCOPE

International mergers, including the combination of non-U.S.-based companies, U.S. buys in foreign markets, and foreign acquisitions of U.S. firms increased exponentially in the 1980s and are expected to continue at pace in the 1990s. Europe, for example, is seeing megamergers led by corporate raiders like Sir James Goldsmith, who bid $21 billion to take over and break up BAT Industries PLC, another British firm, and the Compagnie de Suez, a $72 billion French conglomerate with holdings in banking, insurance, and minerals. There has also been a dramatic increase in strategic deals where companies combine to capitalize on the freeing of the European market in 1992. The high-tech merger of Siemens and Nixdorf, French food giant BSN's acquisition of RJR Nabisco's European cookie unit, and advertiser TBWA's purchases of small agencies throughout the continent are all examples.

A spell of merger mania is also gripping Japan. Deregulation in banking, for example, has led to the merger of many *shinkin* banks and credit cooperatives and the combination of small suppliers. The Japanese have also been bullish in the international marketplace. Japanese firms accounted for one-fourth of the foreign acquisitions in Europe in 1990 and have added significantly to their presence in London's financial markets, the hub of European M&A activity. Bridgestone's $2.6 billion purchase of Firestone Tire & Rubber Co. and Sony's acquisition of RCA Records and Columbia Pictures are notable but atypical of Japanese buys in the U.S. Most of their acquisitions center on small ($5 to 20 million) companies in services, food, auto parts, and medical equipment.

Overall, foreign purchases of American companies today account for some 15% of U.S. takeover activity.[4] But buying in America poses distinct problems for both acquirers and acquired companies. Six of the seven largest U.S. tire companies have been taken over by foreign companies since 1986. The results? Bridgestone's efforts to introduce new technology into Firestone have actually caused productivity to drop. And Continental, a German giant, has had problems with General Tire's unions—most recently a long strike over pay and benefits in General's biggest plant in the United States.[5]

In turn, U.S. acquisitions of foreign companies continue to grow and have had a larger than average purchase price when compared with other types of acquisitions the past few years. Here, too, there can be special problems. One U.S. acquirer, for example, devised a general agreement on layoffs and severance arrangements prior to a European purchase but then had to adapt the agreement, at great cost, to national codes and labor laws in ten of the countries in which it now had plants or sales offices. In another case, prior promises on employment and job security given by the target company to local communities forced a U.S. acquirer to "rethink" its strategy of plant closures rather than breed ill will or get involved in threatened lawsuits.

Cross-continental mergers have an impact on global competition, levels of profitability, employment rates, and so on. Our concern is with the human, organizational, and cross-cultural nuances of international M&A. With this emphasis, it is also important to consider the merger of the overseas arms of combining U.S. companies whose integration strategies and people management practices are influenced by multinational dynamics.

MOLSON–CARLING O'KEEFE

Carling O'Keefe was Canada's third largest brewer at the time of its acquisition in 1987 by Elders, which also brews Foster's beer.[6] Over the next 20 months, under the leadership of Australian Ted Kunkel, the company developed many of the attributes of a typical Elders' operation—high risk taking, aggressive, and bottom-line oriented. Molson, number 2 in Canada, had a proud heritage as North America's oldest brewing company, founded in 1786. Its parent company also owned the Montreal Canadians hockey club and had close ties with the Canadian government.

John Carroll had led Molson as president and CEO since 1986. His leadership embodied a company culture that placed a high emphasis on quality and thoroughness. As one executive described the company, "We have high professional standards. Maybe we were hierarchical, with somewhat formal, slow communication and decision-making procedures, but we were changing all that." In April 1988, Elders proposed merging the Molson–Carling O'Keefe brewing operations, with both companies sharing equal ownership. The synergies made sense. A merger proposal called for the rationalization of 16 plants to 9. This would leave one plant in each Canadian province and increase utilization to 90%. After extensive negotiations, financial terms were set, and the parties agreed to a 50/50 ownership deal.

Following the sale, Kunkel became the executive chairman and CEO of Molson Breweries worldwide, and Carroll was named president and CEO of Molson Breweries in Canada. Ten additional senior executives were announced to lead Canadian operations, seven from Molson and three from Carling O'Keefe. Thus the CEO from one merger partner would work with a majority of senior executives coming from the other side.

While awaiting government approval for the merger, a first meeting of the two management groups was held in March 1989. A Molson manager had vivid impressions of the session:

> The two groups faced each other across the table. You could almost hear their thoughts! All of the Molson people thought that Carling was just short-term profit driven—that they didn't care to invest in growth. And the Carling people thought that Molson was pretty slow moving; and they thought they could run our business better. This was a rocky beginning to team building—a real clash of cultures.

The friction was exacerbated by delays in approval from Canada's Competition Bureau. Meanwhile, salespeople were still pitted against one another in the marketplace and prohibited from cooperating in a joint attack against Labatt's, their chief competitor.

Once the merger was approved, integration was stalled by disagreements over the new organization structure. Molson managers resisted proposals to "Elderize" the merged company through the centralization of staff functions and decentralization of line units. In turn, Carling people said those in Molson "refuse to listen to anything but their way of doing things."

The breakthrough came when a proposal was offered to "regionalize" line operations. This would blend the two companies' structures and philosophies and result in a new way of operating the business. A detailed "organizational blueprint" was then issued offering managers guidance on staffing and team building.

Still, after several months, there were few signs of any reculturation in the combined company. Molson managers continually emphasized their customary precision and professionalism. And Molson employees suspected that Elders would "bleed" the company rather than build the Canadian brewing operation for the future. This, too, took on a nationalistic dimension. As on manager asked: "Why should I throw myself into building this company when all the money is going to be sucked out and sent to Australia?"

Despite the rocky start to the Molson–Carling O'Keefe merger, Kunkel, Carroll, and other senior executives orchestrated a careful and, ultimately, successful merger management process. Several senior executives were taken off of their regular duties to guide the integration process, top managers took to the road to sell employees on the benefits, managers at all levels went through merger sensitization and organization-building seminars, and a special communications effort was launched that far exceeded the companies' past experiences.

It should be noted, of course, that the actual combining of Molson and Carling O'Keefe took place within Canada. Ironically, cultural differences between English- and French-speaking Canadians proved more troublesome than between Canadian and Australian top management. Still, the case gives a flavor to some of the key dynamics to international M&A. There was intense haggling over the price and terms of the merger. Some of this had to do with the contours of the deal. But, as one executive commented during the deal making, "We're hanging tough because don't want those 'cowboys' to run away with the Molson heritage."

Integration was hung up by regulatory red tape and then by the companies' competing models of doing business. Some of the tension concerned differences in structure and style. But these also reflected business norms emphasizing buttoned-down professionalism in Canadian business and a more gung ho attitude in Australia. Finally, there continued to be discontent in the Molson work force over foreign ownership, compounded by plant closures and layoffs. These general merger dynamics can be found in domestic deals in the United States. But they have distinct nuances in international M&A activity.

INTERNATIONAL
BUYING AND SELLING

Simply answering standard questions as to the financial, strategic, and organizational profiles of foreign companies puts an expensive burden on U.S. companies buying abroad, particularly on smaller buyers and those lacking experience in the host country. A Euromoney publication recommends that buyers consult stock exchange–related information, relevant surveys, guides, and periodicals, computer data banks, and regulatory filings, as well as industry experts, trade associations, government agencies, suppliers, and customers.[7] It notes, however, that the expense of this research, when coupled with the risk of failure, leads many firms to abandon their international plans.

Beyond this, U.S. buyers also have to understand how foreign laws, accounting standards, trade practices, labor agreements, and such may impinge on the deal. Finally, there is a need to consider geopolitical factors and market dynamics. The merger between Ford and Volkswagen in Argentina and Brazil, for example, was affected by war, political instability, volatile economic swings, labor unrest, and bad weather.

Scanning Europe: Understanding Human Resources. With the European Community harmonizing laws and regulatory processes in anticipation of 1992, a major U.S.-based defense contractor saw the need and opportunity to establish a stronger manufacturing presence in Europe through acquisitions. In order to guide its scanning of candidates, senior management assigned the company's human resources function with the responsibility of reviewing employment practices and conditions in each of the EC member countries.

A matrix was prepared comparing, across the countries, such issues as the employment of U.S. executives; unionization and collective bargaining practices; the ability to control salary, wages, and benefits; taxation rates, work hours, health and safety regulations, as well as laws and customs pertaining to notification of layoffs, termination arrangements, and labor reviews in the event of an acquisition or takeover.

A numerical rating was assigned for each country in each HR area. The ratings could range from 1 (very negative from an acquirer's perspective) to 5 (average by European standards but more restrictive than in the U.S.) to 9 (attractive and unrestricted). Scores for the U.S. were included as a comparison point for executives. This enabled them to apply their existing frame of reference to a review of acquisition candidates throughout Europe.

Leadership. Foreign mergers and acquisitions entail a higher degree of risk than otherwise. Investments abroad also are more difficult to monitor. This is why some buyers name their own executives to run foreign subsidiaries. As an example, Elders insisted that their man Kunkel be named CEO of the combined Molson operations. That way he could keep a close watch on costs and provide a direct and trustworthy link to Australia on Molson's operations. Still, Kunkel had had some years of experience heading Carling in Canada so was less of an "outsider."

Who should manage an acquisition in another country far away from the buyer's headquarters? Companies have different philosophies, but in answering this question buyers need to consider fully the impact of foreign leadership on the acquiree's relationships with workers, customers, vendors, and governments. When buyers deem it essential to appoint their own management, selection criteria should include overseas experience, facility with the native language, and a proven capacity to manage a multicultural work force. The leadership question should be addressed and settled when the two sides negotiate their deal.

Autonomy Versus Control. Companies based in different countries may also have differing philosophies about how much autonomy to grant acquired foreign subsidiaries. German owners, for example, often export their own executives to head technical functions in their overseas acquisitions. A study of British acquisitions in the United States, by comparison, finds British buyers far less inclined to exercise hands-on management.[8] Interestingly, the study found that this left some acquired American managers with too much autonomy, resulting in inadequate feedback on performance. The upshot: It is important to establish broad parameters of autonomy versus control during the preacquisition phase.

There are, of course, myriad other factors to consider when making a deal to buy (or sell) across countries. The joining of foreign subsidiaries of two merging U.S. companies, for example, was complicated when the parent companies' purchase-and-sale agreement contained provisions on employee severance that contravened various national laws. In another case, the merger of two foreign companies was hung up when negotiators could not agree on the correct translation of several technical provisions in their deal. Suffice it to say, as the British study concludes, that only by experiencing several false starts and learning from their mistakes are international acquirers able to understand more fully the most appropriate way of handling an acquisition.

MULTINATIONAL MERGING

All of the merger stresses and strains we've described are cross cultural. Reactions to the high tech combination of Siemens and Nixdorf, for example, parallel those in Burroughs and Sperry. Siemens' managers, poised to run over the target company, instead joined with their counterparts in over 100 merger planning committees. Nixdorf employees were both hopeful and sad about the deal. "Siemens is good, it's stable," noted one, while another, when queried about losing independence, traced a tear track down his cheek.[9]

So, too, prescriptions for managing merger stress are more or less universal. The study of British mergers found that "clear vision" and "honourable rhetoric" were two key factors in success. The research noted that in two-thirds of the successful cases, a top manager in the buying company, usually the CEO, "communicated essential information to all levels in the acquired business *directly* and *personally*, through in-plant meetings, area conferences, or social occasions." Testimonies from acquired employees emphasized such points as "They did what they said they would" and "They stuck to their word."

There are, however, differences in laws and customs which can influence merger stress. In many European countries, for example, national laws and labor agreements protect employee job security and delineate provisions for layoffs and plant closures. Only in rare instances do these provisos guarantee people their jobs in the event of a merger. But they do establish standards for notification and a security net for employees not found in the United States.

At the same time, they complicate work force planning and employee assistance for acquirers. Unisys, for example, had to develop separate severance plans for each country in which Burroughs or Sperry did business and had to negotiate with several different unions in Europe. In the case of its Japanese subsidiaries, moreover, country management controlled all personnel matters to ensure respect for Japanese laws and customs.

Integration Planning: HP and Apollo—Europe. Forming and operating a multinational integration team adds complexity to the merger process and generates even more conflict than usual. The integration of Hewlett Packard and Apollo in Europe, for example, involved manufacturing facilities, sales offices, distribution channels, and service centers in 16 countries. These facilities were incorporated as companies in each nation. To complicate matters further, the integration of these various "entities" would be influenced by U.S. and European corporate headquarters, by marketing and sales management, by worldwide manufacturing, and so on.

Five interrelated committees were needed to plan, oversee, and implement HP and Apollo's European integration:

1. *European Merger Management Team.* This group was charged with leading the European integration and coordinating efforts *across* countries. It was chaired by HP's European Workstation managers and was staffed by both HP and Apollo managers.

2. *Country merger project managers.* This group contained one key manager from each European country. His or her job was to plan and monitor integration *within* each country. Members of this group reported into the European Merger Management Team.

3. *Functional merger managers.* This group was responsible for coordinating functional integration *across* Europe. Its members represented sales, marketing, support, communications, sales compensation, and so on. It also had responsibility for coordinating sales policies *between* Europe and the United States and the Pacific.

4. *Finance and administration managers.* This group had the job of integrating administrative structures and systems, financial reporting and taxation, as well as management information systems *across* Europe. It, too, had to coordinate this with the effort in the United States.

5. *Workstation business managers.* These were the country presidents, regional managers, and functional heads who had to run the two businesses and manage sales integration in *each* country as well as the integration of manufacturing and distribution throughout Europe (see Figure 12.1).

This integration effort generated unimaginable numbers of briefing books, teleconferences, faxes, and memoranda, not to mention air and train travel, face-to-face meetings, and conferences. Early on there were power struggles between country business managers and project managers as to who was really "calling the shots." Then there were flare-ups between relatively autonomous Apollo country business managers and the much more centralized HP European headquarters. Finally, there were battles between the U.S. and Europe over sales charters and organization.

In the end, HP Europe absorbed Apollo, leading to the resignation of most Apollo country business managers. HP Europe did, however, gain its own independent Workstation sales force—the model favored by Apollo. And many Apollo sales representatives have prospered in their new environs.

Figure 12.1
Merger Committees:
HP and Apollo—Europe

	European Merger Management Team Leadership and oversight for integration across Europe	
Country Merger Project Managers Plan integration across countries; coordinate with HP worldwide		**Workstation Business Managers** Run the business within countries; manage the actual integration
Finance & Admin. Merger Managers F&A integration within countries; coordinate with HP worldwide		**Function Merger Managers** Sales, marketing, support integration; coordinate with HP worldwide

POSTMERGER MANAGEMENT

There can also be more than the usual complexity in implementing change in multi national mergers. Again, in the HP and Apollo case, problems with overcapacity necessitated work redistribution throughout the European manufacturing organization. Manufacturing managers in Germany, France, and Scotland fought for their charters and enlisted the aid of local and national governments to lobby for their cause. After much to-ing and fro-ing, the closure of Apollo's plant in Scotland was described as a "sad affair." Fortunately, HP provided generous severance and outplacement services for employees, nearly all of whom have found employment in their local area.

The merger between Philadelphia-based SmithKline Beckman and Beecham, headquartered in London, is another case where transnational integration has produced special problems.[10] At the start, SmithKline Beecham's chairman hoped that "mixing" people, "working on management development," and creating a new incentive system, "closer to the norm of American (rather than British) companies," would stimulate smoother integration and improved performance. Instead, the combined company has been preoccupied with cost cutting and the centralization of controls—a massive undertaking between two corporate headquarters on different continents. Meanwhile, there is speculation that the combined company's R&D pipeline is running dry and that the competition, including newly merged Bristol Myers Squibb, is positioned to take advantage.

Of course, implementing change can be just as problematic for foreign companies who buy U.S. firms. Japanese acquirers have shown a marked preference for introducing change slowly, focusing on technological and process improvements. Still, this can cause upheaval and discontent as suggested by the case of New Hampshire Ball Bearings, a company acquired by a Japanese competitor, Mineaba Co.

Eschewing their sensitivity to American customs, the new owners removed stools and desks from the plant to eliminate idle talk and unscheduled breaks. Japanese product managers began to walk the factory floor and timers were installed to determine whether or not equipment is operating below capacity. "The company used to be a family, where you felt good about working hard and where they cared about you," recalled one employee, "Now, they want us to work like animals."[11]

"A Japanese flag flies above the plant alongside the stars-and-stripes," reports *The Wall Street Journal*, and employees at the plant in Peterborough, New Hampshire, the village immortalized in Thornton Wilder's *Our Town*, a play about small-town New England life, say "we don't know what 'ours' means anymore." Japanese managers counter that the company's "old style" may have been comfortable but "eons behind major competitors in Sweden and Japan." Indeed productivity is up 45% at the plant since the acquisition though many of the plant's original 625 workers have been laid off. And Japanese managers don't mingle with towns-folks and are seldom seen outside of the plant.

No postacquisition turnaround is easy and few are pleas-ant for the people involved. Still, there are nuances to this case, including the Japanese managers' relentless emphasis on efficiency and the American's preference for folksiness, that have compounded problems and produced bitterness. These emanate from the broader clash of national cultures.

CULTURE CLASH IN INTERNATIONAL MERGERS

In international combinations, differences in national cultures often figure into cross-company conflicts. At the root of many such conflicts are value differences based in national cultures. As Robert Bellah's studies affirm, individual auton-omy, self-determination, and upward mobility are dominant values in the United States.[12] In Europe, by contrast, a long-standing class system, fewer opportunities for self-advance-ment, and more fatalism about the future influence people's aspirations and work behavior. In turn, a primary emphasis on group affiliation and a deep respect for hierarchy define many Asian cultures.

Values differences are generally expressed in different *behavioral norms* in countries. The English tend to be deliberate and cautious in their decision making. This is frustrating to American buyers and sellers, who may view this as a sign of inattention and inaction. The Japanese put an emphasis on long-term relationships and social rituals. Some Amer-icans misunderstand this as a sign of mistrust and downplay the importance of ceremony in trust building.

Violating *protocol* and *customs* can also set off bad feel-ings between combining managements. The French have em-braced the American notion of a power breakfast, but the Germans and South Americans do not like to mix business with the morning meal. Americans are more apt to engage in backslapping, joke telling, and informal wordplay than more standoffish and formal Europeans who take offense at presumptions of friendship. Nodding one's head in Greece means an emphatic no. The "OK" sign used in the United States—index finger to thumb—is an obscene gesture in Brazil and Peru. And while Americans are quick to use first names to break down interpersonal barriers, businesspeople in other countries expect to be addressed by their professional or academic titles.

Making a Deal: Cross-cultural Issues. In his guide to overseas acquisitions, R. Duane Hall notes that "In many world areas, people are examined more closely than the proposition, for it is believed that [even] if the proposition is sensible, its chances for success rest upon the reliability and competence of the people involved."[13] This can be an elusive concept for Americans because of their experience and faith in making business decisions based on facts and figures. Experienced acquirers generally respect the customs and practices of doing business in a host country when courting foreign sellers. Several, for example, arm their executives with specially prepared guidebooks on making overseas acquisitions. Still, it is commonplace for even experienced buyers to shake their heads at the slow pace and emphasis on relationship building that attends overseas deals.

Foreign buyers can also be put off by the customs and complexities of buying in the United States. When Kiel AG (pseudonym for a Swiss multinational) approached Edwards Engineering (a pseudonym for a midsize Georgia firm) early contacts were promising. Over the course of negotiations, however, the Swiss, accustomed to shrewd and laborious bargaining, were wary of the Georgians' open manner and willingness to make off-the-cuff compromises. But then a team of lawyers, representing the engineering firm, weighed in with reams of documents and legalese. The Swiss firm, according to business brokers on the scene, saw this as "some sort of power play." The lawyers, in turn, unable to pin the Swiss down on details, advised U.S. managers that they could be in a "trap." The deal fell apart—a case of cross-cultural misunderstanding.[14]

Managing Across Cultures. The general rules for minimizing a culture clash apply to international merger management: Expect cultural differences, educate both sides about each other's culture, and develop an understanding of and respect for differences. Differences between national cultures may disrupt international integration or be a source of creativity and innovation. Different cultural groups contribute unique perspectives and offer new ideas that have the potential to result in more knowledge and innovative changes. Certainly the Japanese have learned a great deal from their international joint ventures and U.S.-based acquisitions, the ball bearing case aside. But learning to work together across cultures is not an easy matter.

For example, even if top executives are well coached in cross-cultural values and norms, middle managers and employees, who will deal with foreign counterparts, can upset cross-company relationships by their insensitivity. It makes sense, therefore, to ensure that everyone involved with a foreign partner is briefed on different national values and how business gets done in a host country. Leaders, in turn, need to alert employees to stereotypes and how they can be self-limiting and hinder dialogue. It helps when employees understand the conceptual and perceptual variations of people from other cultures. This can help them work more effectively with foreign coworkers as well as consumers.

Working with Japanese Owners. Many of the merger management methods described in this book are relevant to international combinations, but require some adaptation. For example, when a Canadian firm was purchased by a Japanese conglomerate, managers who attended merger sensitization seminars were briefed on Japanese business norms and acquisition practices. Company newsletters and videos featured stories on Japanese culture and interviews with scholars who described the ancient and modern history of Japan.

In another case, managers in Union Bank in California were taken aback by the "inscrutable" attitude of their new owners, the Bank of Tokyo. For years, Union Bank executives had prospered under the hands-off approach of British owners, Standard Charter Bank. After the sale to Bank of Tokyo, local management sought clarification of their new owner's business objectives and expectations for the integration. However, the Japanese, wanting to learn from the Californians, withheld any input. This confounded the Union Bankers who felt outside of the decision-making process and could only "guess" at what the Japanese wanted. This was a culture clash between the U.S. cards-on-the-table-style of decision-making and more circuitous Japanese consensus style. Cultural differences were clarified when top executives from the two sides discussed their distinct decision making models and clarified their intentions. This led to a deeper discussion of integration objectives and a closer look at the desired working relationship between the companies. In particular, the "act and then think" approach of Union Bank was given close scrutiny and finally understood by the Japanese who agreed to establish a priority channel for approving major Union Bank investments.

GLOBAL M&A

The formation of global corporations represents a dramatic evolution from the U.S. multinational of the 1960s. These giants treated foreign operations as distant appendages for producing or selling products designed and engineered "back home." The chain of command and national loyalties of multinational companies were clear. Today, the United States no longer dominates the world economy or holds a monopoly on M&A. Although legally headquartered in Paris, New York, or Tokyo, global enterprises are being run as "stateless" corporations.

There are global companies that are *unicultural* in the sense that they operate from a strong, centralized core and expect subsidiaries to conform to parent company structures, policies, practices, and customs. Increasingly, however, there is an emphasis on *multiculturalism* in companies. This means ways of operating and doing business are adapted to local circumstances—whether local means a wholly owned subsidiary, a joint venture, or a foreign plant or work force.

Many experts project an increase in global mergers and acquisitions, with all of the attendant gains and losses in profitability, market share, plant utilization, employment, and the like. We believe that culturally sensitive merger management in deal making, integration, and postmerger organization building will increase the likelihood of gains and lessen the chances of losses. Just as important, however, is that this approach to merger management promises to en-

hance global understanding and deepen cross-cultural respect. This will yield longer-term benefits to employers and
employees that extend well beyond the transaction itself.
Moreover, the benefits may apply not only to business but
also to the welfare of the world.

Postscript

Winning Hearts and Minds

Men differ about whether mergers are examples of the triumphs or of the failings of the free market system and the profit motive.
—Peter O. Steiner, *Mergers.*[1]

Announcer: *Hey, if the recent grocery store merger mania has you wondering which aisle the peanut butter is on, check out Hughes Markets. It's one that hasn't changed hands. Or anything else, for that matter. Hughes still has the same low prices, the same high quality, and the same friendly service they've always had. . . . So come to your nearby Hughes, where the only buyout you have to deal with is getting double your savings on coupons.*
—Supermarket advertisement in Southern California [2]

Mergers, acquisitions, and downsizings have left their mark on working Americans' psyches and confirmed for many their ingrained suspicions about the real motives of top business executives. The words of one GE employee whose plant was closed are an all-too-familiar refrain: "I'm the third generation in my family to work at this plant. My grandfather said it, my father said it, and today I'm saying it, 'You just can't trust General Electric.'" Middle managers and workers alike question what's behind all the changes they experience and who will gain what by them. Confidence and faith in the leaders of big business is at an all-time low. Furthermore, nearly three-fourths of the American work force don't trust what their own top management tells them and as many think that their companies will take advantage of them given a chance.

Political economist Robert Reich, of Harvard's John F. Kennedy School of Government, finds widespread disillusionment with "paper entrepreneurism" in American industry.[3] He notes that junk bond deals, asset stripping, and other Wall Street financing tactics have "enforced short-term thinking, discouraged genuine innovation, and consumed the careers of some of our most talented citizens. It also has transformed many American companies into fearful and demoralized places characterized by cynical indifference and opportunism."

Corporate combinations and related restructurings have changed the fundamental *psychological contract* between employer and employee.[4] This implicit deal once committed both sides to a mutually beneficial relationship, with employees supplying hard work and loyalty and their company offering steady employment and advancement. To maintain their part of the contract, many managers sacrificed a full family life, moved across the country and back again, and took job assignments that fitted the company's needs rather than their own. Their rewards were security and self-esteem as well as the pay and perks of management positions.

As the rules of the corporate game have changed, however, so also has the psychological work contract. It is being rewritten with managers and employees ever more conscious of looking out for themselves. Terry Elledge has seen reorganization from both sides. Six years ago the Pacific Financial Company cut its work force by about one-third—quite a shock for a firm that had not laid off anybody in more than 100 years. Elledge helped orchestrate the shake-up, but when the company cut back further, Elledge decided to leave. Now a management consultant, Elledge sees the current psychological work contract this way:

> It used to be "You have something I need and I have something you need." Now both employers and employees have become more protective, distant, and skeptical. And to validate these feelings, both sides have come to

believe that "people are taking advantage of me." Individuals these days are more likely to walk out for something better, while companies are more inclined to fire people.

The changing psychological contract clearly places more responsibility on individuals to assess and design their own careers. Paul Hirsch urges members of today's corporate work force to become "free-agent managers" and operate like professional baseball players: "Free agents make it a point to always know their alternatives, to have a clear idea of where they could jump if unexpected roadblocks arise in the present job. They work hard at their present jobs but never take them for granted. They direct much of their energy toward shaping and securing their futures."[5] Blumenthal and other top executives we have worked with find this to be too cynical and self-serving. What do they have to offer?

BUILDING THROUGH M&A

It is fair to say that America needs more innovativeness, less deadwood, the motivating juice of a little competition, and fundamental changes in our industrial order and economy. But breakup raids and paper transactions seldom further a company's strategy or add to its productive capability and competitive prowess. Hence our attention has been given to boards of directors, CEOs, and managers who make strategic deals and seek to build a new business with their partners. They are in it for the long run and regard their mergers and acquisitions as essential to industry competitiveness and, in some instances, survival.

W. Michael Blumenthal chafed at the label "raider." Many of his friends urged him against a takeover attempt of Sperry—it would put him in league with "arbs" and rob him of his good reputation. But Blumenthal believed it essential to join with Sperry to survive the computer industry shakeout. In the same way, the other CEOs and executives we have worked with believe what they're doing is in the best interests of not only stockholders, but also of managers and employees, customers and suppliers, and, in the long run, the communities in which they do business.

This can be a rationalization for ruthless acts. It can also be used as subterfuge. But productive builders who believe in what they are doing can convince people of their good intentions and win them over with meritorious deeds. This means managing mergers more effectively—with the right purpose, a fair price, a good partner, and fortunate timing—if only they follow a good process for putting the companies together. This also means, crucially, managing people the right way.

LEADERSHIP FROM THE TOP: THEORY AND PRACTICE

What does it take to lead a corporate transformation where 1 plus 1 is greater than 2? What does it take to preserve an acquiree's autonomy and sense of purpose? Throughout this book, we've studied Blumenthal and Clarkson in action. Behind their leadership is a set of beliefs and values about *organizations*, *people*, and *processes* that guided their efforts to build Unisys and save Graphic Controls, respectively. In important respects, their beliefs and values contrast with conventional models of top managers as tough-minded, rational analysts who lead through top-down, centralized control. Our work with Blumenthal and Clarkson convinces us that top executives need an alternative way of looking at themselves and their work to succeed at M&A. This can be represented through key assumptions and values (see Figure 13.1).

Assumptions About Organizations. To begin, some high-level executives treat organizations as though they are composed of discrete "parts" that can be analyzed and managed one by one, then in aggregate, to build to a "whole." Much of the literature on management strategy and strategy implementation rests on this mechanical assumption. It is also advanced in business school training and executive seminars. This reductionist mind-set implies that there is an *objective* reality "out there" amenable to detailed analysis and malleable by micromanagement.

By contrast, Blumenthal and Clarkson subscribed to a more organic view of organizations. Blumenthal, for instance, described companies as "social structures with a continuing

COMPETING MANAGEMENT THEORIES		IMPLICATIONS FOR PRACTICE	
Conventional Management Perspective	Alternative Management Perspective	Managing a Merger of Equals *Blumenthal*	Retaining Cultural Identity *Clarkson*
Assumptions about an organization			
Mechanical	Organic	Company has life and soul	Company reflects value system
Parts of a machine	Whole > sum of parts	Envision a new company based upon partnership	Affirm what is important and maintain independence
Strategy directs behavior	Culture directs behavior		
Values about people at work			
Rational and calculative	Emotional and expressive	Deal with fears	Cope with grief
Individual self-interest	Collective norms and values	Sensitivity and meritocracy	Mourning and recommitment
Rewards shape behavior	Relationships shape behavior	Rally to a flag	Regain purpose
Process orientation			
Logical and controlled	Intuitive and orchestrated	Joint-company participation	Acquired company self-study
Objective	Subjective	Facts *and* insights	Facts *and* feelings
Minimize the human factor	Maximize the human factor	Briefing books and ceremonies	Flip charts and poetry

Figure 13.1
Merger Management in Theory and Practice

life and soul of their own." He saw himself as building a new company culture and recognized that people's *subjective* reactions to the combination would determine its validity as much as any specific decisions or pronouncements. Accordingly, he followed the high-minded principles of partnership and meritocracy in merging Burroughs and Sperry and appealed to people's sense of fairness and faith in the future. "People want a sense of belonging. They want a flag under which to fly. They want to be loyal to their organization." Armed with these convictions, Blumenthal was leading what philosophers call the "social construction" of reality in turning the two combining companies into Unisys.

Clarkson, in a similar vein, saw organizations as "value systems" whose character and effectiveness would hinge on people's participation in the business and "sense of mission." Hence he and his team focused on retaining long-standing company values in the combination with Times Mirror. A self-described architect, he regarded GC as a "laboratory for innovation." Defending his efforts to retain GC's independence, he noted, "GC could have been an absolute gem for (Times Mirror) to observe, watch, foster, and then use, where appropriate, to teach other parts of their two billion dollar business. . . . Let's experiment and learn." Unfortunately, Times Mirror executives had a different view of this. Clarkson recalled, "The innovative mission of the enterprise was not only devalued, but often the subject of disdain."

These two merger managers sought to *humanize* management strategy by bringing people back into the equation. Blumenthal used vision to embolden his people to create the new. Communication was one of his strong suits so he went on the stump to defend the takeover and rally support. "Think of a CEO who is brilliant in every other way but who is very bad at communicating and likes to sit in his office and figure out how to make another buck or is already working on the next deal," he noted, "that won't win people over." He also designed and led a complex transition structure to bring new organizational architecture into being.

Clarkson and his team banded together, likening themselves to King Arthur and his knights, to retain GC's values and learn to work with Times Mirror. Over time, they also learned to work more effectively with their counterparts in the parent company.

Values About People. Machinelike assumptions about organizations can translate into a view of people as calculating and self-interested, only out for themselves. These values are dominant in political models of merger behavior where it is presumed that individual functions and managers aim to maximize their power and resources often at the expense of others.

This political orientation was antithetical to Clarkson who was deeply committed to human development and to "authenticity." "Maybe I should have been a chameleon, or just kept my mouth shut," he observed. "I'm sure I was a lousy company head for quite a while," he recalled. "I remember one person saying as I was walking through the parking lot, with my head down, 'You look like hell today, aren't you having any fun?'"

Clarkson and his team held their grieving meeting to vent their anger, expunge their anguish, and come to collective resolve on a new course of action. Still, GC managers found themselves often powerless in the face of Times Mirror's prerogatives. But, again, after much soul searching, GCers came to see how they were acting like "ungrateful little brothers." This helped them to redefine the relationship—respecting requirements for change without "losing our integrity or sense of purpose."

Blumenthal was more instrumental in his dealings with people. Certainly he was willing to use "money and persuasion" to hold on to key executives. But he recognized that, as the leader of the merger, he would need more "sensitivity to human fears and foibles—and a fairly good dose of sympathy." He told us, "When you said to me the first time, 'people really get scared in this situation, they're anxious,' I said to myself, 'I have to be tolerant toward that and I have to try to assuage it and channel it constructively.' " He also spoke about people's desires to "have something to believe in larger than their own self-interest." Acting on these values, he policed the political aspects of the combination and counseled executives through the trying integration period.

Both leaders recognized that managing human emotion and expressiveness was integral to their work. Clarkson, by training and tradition, delved deeply into his own emotional life and worked with his colleagues to define for themselves a state of equilibria and acceptance. Blumenthal, less introspective and more matter of fact, nonetheless acknowledged that building trust and good relationships were key to success in his merger. He noted, "I worked very hard to bring that about."

Process Orientation. Subscribers to a mechanistic view of people and organizations often show a preference for detached and dispassionate analysis, depend on objective measurement and documentation, and base their decisions on rigorous and rationally derived conclusions. Much of what is known as management science proceeds in this fashion. This is presumed to minimize, if not eliminate, human factors that might result in bias or other types of error.

The psychological view we have been examining acknowledges the predominance of human factors in the merger process and instead proposes that merger managers *work with* these psychological factors rather than attempt to *suppress* them. Both Blumenthal and Clarkson themselves experienced the full gamut of merger syndrome symptoms and talked openly to colleagues about them. They also trusted their executives' counsel and relied on their own "gut feelings" in handling merger stresses and strains.

GCers' analysis of their situation was certainly value laden. Yet this kind of self-scrutiny helped to clarify how the company's relationship with Times Mirror was personified in Clarkson's unhappy experience. Only when he was confronted with the consequences—more intrusiveness by Times Mirror and the loss of employee confidence—could he "let go" of his personal feelings and adapt to the "new realities." This was consistent with his emphasis on acting based on facts *and* feelings.

The problem-solving process in Unisys was, by appearances, dominated by objectivity and logical analysis. Yet the recommendations that came from this study mixed facts with insight. To an extent, this was a result of Blumenthal's willingness to give executives free rein in designing the new organization, so long as cost projections were met. More than this, it was a by-product of another unwritten principle: "When in doubt, do it now." This encouraged executives to take risks and recommend something bold and new.

The participative process used to build Unisys depended on executives' abilities to act on good faith and work together with their counterparts. It was simply impossible to plan all contingencies. Blumenthal orchestrated the process through meticulous briefing books and periodic reviews. But symbols and ceremonies, ranging from the red hats at an early gathering of the clan to a culture-building ceremony at the creation of Unisys, affirmed the undertaking and enabled managers to "write a new script" for the preordained conquest.

In turn, deep respect for human intelligence and long standing traditions of self-assessment were kept alive at GC throughout the combination period. A verse of a poem, "The Miserable, Wretched, Sorry Saga of Rubber Margins," written by a GC manager gives a flavor to GCers' intelligence and to the fraternity of leaders in the company:

And "shit" I said in wisdom wise
I kinda like and respect these guys
And to admit the truth entire
We needed our feet held to the fire.

Glad to know you, glad you came
Thanks for guidance and wisdom
And much pleasure with the pain
But Holy Christ, please never again.

This emphasis on soul-searching and resolve to be something more than "businessmen" helped those at GC to regain perspective in dealing with Times Mirror. Furthermore, they stimulated intensive self-study over deculturation in the company and gave impetus to its "buy back" ten years after the sale.

That Clarkson and Blumenthal could support and validate people through the merger process, and could lead through participation and by example, rather than by fiat and detachment, is testimony to the effectiveness of humanizing the merger process. Blumenthal said it simply: "It's not only what you do, it's how you do it."

To be sure, Blumenthal and Clarkson were, at times, tough-minded, decisive, and product oriented, the conventional requirements of merger managers. But they were also tenderhearted, tentative, impassioned, and deeply committed to principle—in proportion and as they appreciated the need.

REALISM IN THE RANKS

There is still the risk of incurring cynical fallout when companies signal that merging is just a "numbers game" and that they don't really care about people. Meeting with Blumenthal well after layoffs and plant closings, we pressed him on how he would justify these costs of his merger to his young son, 20 years hence. He countered,

> I hope he's studying economics and understands that in a market economy adjustment to changing circumstances is the best guarantee of a rising standard of living. And that the failure to adjust is the best guarantee of a decline. . . . If you're a leader, you have to make decisions that are in the best interest of the organization. You have to have respect and understanding and consideration for the way in which it affects individuals, but you cannot shield them from the decisions that have to be made. If you do, you are presiding over the decline of the organization and in the end you hurt everybody.

Certainly Blumenthal's legacy in Unisys is mixed. One former Sperry manager, for example, reported: "His name incites an angered frenzy in everyone who had been impacted by the merger." He added, "No one will ever wish to duplicate the tragedies of the merger—the layoffs, broken careers, divorces, and suicides." Some survivors in Unisys acknowledge that the combination gave the firm a fighting chance in the industry. Others believe that the combination foredoomed both companies. "It was Bumenthal's lack of in-depth knowledge of the industry, linked with his ego, self-confidence, and compulsion for action that led [to the merger]," argued one critic. He believes that Sperry would have been able to succeed on its own. Others contend that Burroughs would have succeeded and Sperry would have failed.

Yet, another former Sperry executive praised Blumenthal as a merger manager: "Although many executives would argue that Blumenthal tended to 'micromanage,' I repeatedly saw situations where his intervention was appropriate, ethical, and balanced. He challenged aggressively but listened for competence, insight, perspective, and advocacy." His conclusion: "A case could be made that the only problem with the Sperry and Burroughs merger was that there were not enough Blumenthals to go around!"

It is plain enough that people in Unisys are still struggling through their protracted postmerger period. Their pain is real, as it is in the other companies described in this book. So are the moments of joy and satisfaction. The larger message is that companies can lessen the harm of mergers through credible communications about what change has to take place and careful and caring management of the human and organizational process. But some of the onus is on working people to take heed of changing economic conditions and to form new psychological contracts at work. The best companies, in turn, give people more options for developing their careers and put more emphasis on retraining and redeployment, and, where necessary, on the successful outplacement and well-being of displaced employees. And the best employees take advantage of those services.

The management and recommitment of survivors is high on the roster of postmerger corporate challenges. People need to believe that sacrifice will lead to a better future. This means that combined companies need to cultivate realism among employees about future possibilities all the time training and preparing them for developments that might involve job change and even job loss. When companies work with their people, in partnership, to manage merger-related change, a measure of family feeling is evoked. Firms that operate like families cope with hard times as well as the good times.

In the cases described here, the examples of Blumenthal and Clarkson, of Mike Pickett of Merisel and Samuel Tibbetts of Unihealth America, and other top managers are complemented by that of middle managers like Rhea Serpan, at AT&T, Katy Stone at Alpha Computer, and merger planners like Alex Mandell of CSX/SeaLand. Implementing meaningful change depends on the skill and good intentions of such managers and on the willingness of employees to commit themselves to an uncertain course.

Many working people today recognize that the only constant is change. Hence they are learning personal skills in self-and-career management and appropriate techniques for coping with an uncertain and ambiguous working world. Time and again we hear that people in the ranks want to be involved in change. This requires top managers to reach out to them, middle managers to actively involve them, and employees themselves to take the initiative.

Certainly Human Resource departments are important to making the merger process work. HR people can help executives factor in human, organizational, and cultural considerations in precombination planning. They are needed to support executives making online integration decisions and to offer care, counsel, and an ear to troubled employees. HR's role in handling layoffs and healing survivors is crucial in the postcombination period. It is important, then, to get human resource teams up to speed on merger dynamics and organized in the event of a deal to deliver needed services. It is crucial, too, for human resource executives to model the right process when managing their own teams.

We hope that the work of human resource executives like Mike Losey and Dick Bierly of Unisys, and Pete Peterson of Hewlett-Packard, provides an example to others.

CHARTING A BETTER COURSE

This book has considered what companies and their leaders do (and can do) to improve their success in mergers and acquisitions. Sure success depends on sensible strategies and financial know-how. But it also depends on people-minded management of the transition process, from top to bottom, and on winning people's hearts and minds over to a new way of doing business. The "map" of merger challenges in Chapter 1 highlights how difficult it is to travel from the "Sea of Uncertainty" to the "Beacon of Light." We close with a summary of recommendations for charting a better course:

Precombination Prescriptions

1. **The successful search requires the buyer to develop a coherent and agreed-to strategy, set clear combination objectives, and gain a good understanding of the seller's organizational makeup and culture.** Buying company managers and staff have to be on the same wavelength and leaders need to ensure that target management is handled with respect.

2. **Good deals don't necessarily lead to good combinations.** Both buyer and seller need to be prepared strategically and psychologically to join and top management has to define and enforce guidelines for the combination.

Managing the Merger

3. **Uncertainty, anxiety, and stress are to be expected in a combination.** Full and frank communication, formal and face to face, along with care and counseling, are needed to help people cope with the upset. Managers, human resource professionals, and communication specialists have to be at their best—when conditions are such that they are usually at their worst.

4. **To truly integrate, managers from both sides need to be assembled into fact finding and transition management teams.** Their charge is to exchange knowledge, develop rapport, and plan for integration. Top executives need to orchestrate the work of transition teams and coordinate planning. Conflicts can't be ducked. Differences have to be faced and worked through.

5. **Mergers and acquisitions threaten traditional ways of doing business and the beliefs and values of organization members.** Managers need to compare the benefits of integration in light of cultural differences between the two companies and build the new on a common cultural framework.

Managing the Aftermath

6. Winners in a combination need to be crowned gratefully, losers let go of graciously, and survivors need to be handled gracefully. Integration mistakes can be reversed. Mistakes in handling people live on.

7. The basic building blocks of a combined company are its work teams. Managers need to sign people up, unit by unit, and mold them into a team. This requires helping people "let go" of the past and getting them excited about the future.

8. Organization building complements team building. While middle managers build their teams, top executives have to ensure that strategies are being advanced and combination goals realized. This means managing upwards, downward, and sideways. Once new teams and structures are in place they need to be anchored in a new company philosophy and culture. Otherwise, the new will crumble and people will lose faith.

Taking the Journey

9. Track the combination, involve people, and listen to them. Expect bad news. Also expect managers to respond to it with energy and innovation. Don't shoot the messengers.

Finally, it is important to remember that along with all the trials there can be triumphs. Mergers and acquisitions bring opportunities and growth. We find that most people want to believe that their merger makes good business sense. And some see it as a stimulus for needed change in their organizations. In Graphic Controls, the transition from independence to subsidiary status to a buy back was painful, but the company has become more profit minded and still retained its family feeling.

For most who travel the arduous M&A route simply getting through the course builds confidence that the perils facing modern-day organizations can be managed. When a combination is well led and well managed, moreover, it can be a rallying point for building a new organization. In any case, mergers and acquisitions *are* career events for managers and employees. Many say that they are the most exciting, intense, and exhilarating times of their work careers. Alternatively, they can be filled with dread, despair, even death. How they are perceived depends on whether or not executives can chart a better course and lead their people through trials and on to triumph.

10. **M&A is here to stay. Learn from the experience—good and bad.**

One of our interviewees commented, "Although many may be tempted to believe that 'merger mania' is behind us, ever increasing competition linked with the globalization for trade will, in fact, only serve to accelerate and reinforce the need for merger management competence at the highest levels of management." Still, he wondered whether the mixed experiences of Unisys would cause people to downplay the value of the case. He gets the final word on the subject:

> Ultimately, the degreee of difficulty associated with the Sperry/Burroughs merger, plus the transition the whole computer industry had to work through, simply proved to be too much. Bad timing. In a way it was unfortunate that all the 'piloting' was wasted on a plane that encountered massive turbulence. Still, as with the history of flight, many early pioneers failed. But others learned from them, discarded techniques that did not work, and adopted and improved those that did.

APPENDIXES

APPENDIX A
Assessing Strategic Fit

The synergies and benefits that come from a combination are to some extent unique to every situation. Professor Gordon Walters has surveyed top executives, investment bankers, and merger brokers to identify the criteria they use in assessing the strategic fit of combination candidates. He breaks these criteria into four sets:

Productivity: Are there benefits to

1. Using one company's personnel, skills, or technologies in the operations of the other company?

2. Using one company's expertise in marketing, production, quality control, research, or other areas in the other company?

3. Expanding capacity or reducing underutilization?

4. Creating economies of scale?

5. Improving efficiencies or reducing risk in supply of specific resources, goods, and services between companies?

6. Providing a system of reporting that will produce faster and more informed management decisions?

Distribution/Marketing: Are there benefits to

7. Improving competitiveness through gains in market share and position?
8. Creating economies in distribution capacity?
9. Penetrating new markets?
10. Reducing risks and costs of diversifying?
11. Broadening the customer base?

Entrepreneurial: Are there benefits to

12. Reducing risks and costs of opening new markets?
13. Gaining executive wisdom in new markets?
14. Transfering technology and professional expertise?
15. Promoting visibility with investors, bankers, and customers?
16. Fulfilling ambitions of executives?

Financial: Are there benefits to

17. Reducing overhead costs because of redundancies, economies of scale?
18. Reducing capital costs, supplier services, banking relationships?
19. Improving cost profile because of divestitures, plant closings, consolidations, or relocations?
20. Other financial synergies?

APPENDIX B
Factors Influencing Organizational Fit

Organizational shape: Size—how big are two companies? ratio of line/staff? Formal organizational structures—tall or flat? centralized or decentralized? Design of businesses: functional, product/market groups, or holding company? Relationships among functions/divisions—interdependent or not? matrix?

Systems: Budgeting and control—compatible methods, time periods, criteria? Planning and targeting—how formal, detailed, rigorous, aggressive? Role of top management—oversight or direct management? MIS—architectures, coverage, degree of sophistication? Policies and procedures—how extensive, formal or informal? Communications—downward, upward, lateral?

Operations: Opportunities for rationalization? Manufacturing and service organization: stand alone or connected? Quality control and productivity—measurement? management philosophy? Physical assets—equipment and buildings? Supply and distribution arrangements? Inventory management? Geographic spread—national/international considerations?

Marketing: Opportunities for integration/cross-selling? Sales and marketing organization structure—layers and responsibilities? Product identity and reputation? Customer base and perceptions—how developed, assessed, and evaluated? Role in product development? Relationships with operations, suppliers, distributors?

Home office: Finance and administration organizational structure? Role in planning, budgeting, and control? MIS organizational structure? Computing hardware, software, voice and data communications? Human resources organizational structure? Perception of human resources function in company?

Leadership and management: Management philosophy and practices—well defined? broadly reinforced? Leadership style—top down, participative, laissez-faire? Top team harmony? Depth of management talent—by function? Relationships between superiors and subordinates—formal or informal? Decision making styles—consultation? delegation?

Human Resources: Demographics of the employee population? Skill base—education and sophistication? Reward systems—compatible compensation, incentives, commissions, fringe benefits? Titles and levels of authority—same job grades? Performance appraisal systems—formal? meaningful? Morale and spirit—how maintained and measured? Strength of employee identity with corporate goals? Employment market—how mobile? Training programs—for whom? what type? Human resources development and succession planning? Employee relations and union status—anticipated problems?

Orientation toward change: Rate of innovation and technological change—R&D and process improvements? Creativity of products and marketing approach? History of change and change management in the company?

APPENDIX C
Comparing Organizational
and Cultural Characteristics

It is important to assess both organizational fit and cultural compatibility in a merger or acquisition. There is a difference between surface organizational characteristics (who and what) versus deeper cultural rhythms and beliefs (how and why). Examples:

Measurement and Control Systems

Organizational	*Cultural*
What measurement and control systems are in place? (e.g., what type? computerized or not? key statistics? frequency of reporting and reviews?)	How are measures and controls used by management? (e.g., financial comparisons versus budget, goals, or trends? in-depth analysis? for planning or control or both?)
How is information communicated between staff to line management? (e.g., format? frequency? in which direction does it flow?)	How is information used by line and staff management? (e.g., power games? problem solving? paperwork exercise? for action or to pya?)

Leadership and Management

Organizational	*Cultural*
How would you describe the organization's structure? (e.g., tall or flat? centralized or decentralized? ratio of line to staff?)	How do various groups in the area work together? (e.g., cooperative or competitive? turf conscious? each goes its own way?)
How would you describe the decision making structure? (e.g., chain of command? delegation of authority and responsibility?)	How does top management operate and make decisions? (e.g., teamwork or group of individuals? planning or seat of the pants? conformity or more entrepreneurial?)
How long has the top team been together?	How do people get ahead in the company?

APPENDIX D
What to Say in a Merger or Acquisition

Upon announcement, let employees clearly and factually know

The reasons behind the combination

Specifics of the agreement

What the company and its people will gain or lose

How the company will proceed with integration and change

General facts about the merger partners—size, products, history, key executives, and locations; send out newsclippings

How business should be conducted during the transition period

Immediate implications for job security

What to say to customers or clients

Changes in policy or procedures

If known, information also can be communicated carefully regarding

Changes in company name or logo

Changes in organizational structure and management positions

Whether or not there will be any reductions-in-force; plant closings, or divestitures

Changes in product lines and marketing strategy

Areas of integration or reorganization

Changes in compensation and benefits

Even if plans are not finalized, people can still be told

Who will be making the decisions

When decisions are expected (not promised) to be made

How both sides will be involved in making the decisions.

The criteria to be used in decision making (e.g., reducing administrative costs, minimizing effects on customer service, achieving better utilization of production facilities, etc.).

As integration decisions are made, communicate information regarding...

Changes in organizational mission and strategy

Changes in organizational structure and systems

Changes in management and reporting relationships

Changes in job titles and job descriptions

New career paths and opportunities

Changes in procedures, policies, forms, and systems

Staff reductions and reassignments

Layoffs and provisions for job loss (e.g., severance pay, outplacement, hiring freeze, and so forth)

The rationale for all of the above

APPENDIX E
Ways to Communicate

Announcement letter. As the combination is announced to the media, shareholders, and other outside groups, deliver a letter to all employees outlining the rationale underlying the change, descriptions of the companies or departments involved, and any immediately known details on plans for integration. Indicate when an employee meeting—including a question-and-answer session—will be scheduled. The letter should be signed by the CEOs of both companies.

Meetings with the full work force. As soon as possible after the merger is announced, assemble the work force in large group meetings to introduce them to new key management and explain in depth why the combination is occurring. Let people know who will be making transition-related decisions and when decisions can be expected.

Managers' meetings. Inform key managers on both sides on the strategic implications of change, senior management's vision and measures of success, and what process will be used to manage the transition. These managers are the opinion leaders, watched and listened to by others.

Follow-up meetings with work groups. Have managers and supervisors meet with their reports to reiterate points made in the large group meeting and clarify what is known to date about how changes will affect their work groups. Managers need to be armed with information to charge up their reports who are outside of the decision-making loop. Work with internal human resources and communications specialists to prepare "Q&A" packets for managers which anticipate questions frequently asked by employees and provide suggested answers.

Road shows/videotapes. Visits to both sides' key field locations—manufacturing plants, research facilities, and sales offices—help bridge the (often wide) communications gap with headquarters. Trips to key customers are reminders that their needs are not being forgotten during the transition and provide reassurance that service or product quality will not slip. For sites which cannot be visited in person, provide videotapes of all announcements and special events. Employees today want to see as well as read the news.

Newsletters. In regular company newsletters, place articles reporting developments about progress, as well as on personal stress management in the midst of a major organizational change. Employees are kept "in the know" best by a special newsletter, say a weekly "Integration Update." This publication shows how the rationale and goals of the change are being translated into action. It also introduces new management and familiarizes employees with the products and services of the other company or unit. The intent of a special transition newsletter is to signal that this change is special and keep people abreast of plans and developments.

800 numbers. Some firms use toll-free "800" "rumor control hotlines" to anonymously solicit employee questions and concerns. Rumors—and official company responses—can be published in a weekly "tip sheet" distributed to the full work force.

REFERENCES

Introduction

1. J. W. Hunt, S. Lees, J. J. Grumbar, and P. D. Vivian, *Acquisitions—The Human Factor* (London: Egon Zhender International/London Business School, 1970).

2. Author's interview.

3. The Federal Trade Commission found that the earnings of firms merged in the 1960's were less than the sum of the earnings of the two firms separately in 3 out of 4 cases (FTC Bureau of Economics, *Economic Report on Corporate Mergers*, 1969, pp. 260–261). Another study of this period concluded that the profitability of the combined firms as a percentage of sales dropped in 34 out of 59 cases. See S. E. Boyle and P. W. Jaynes, "Conglomerate Merger Performance," *Economic Report to the Federal Trade Commission* (Washington, D.C.: U.S. Government Printing Office, 1972).

On the financial success rate of mergers in the 1970s and 1980s, see M. Lubatkin, "Mergers and the Performance of the Acquiring Firm," *Academy of Management Review*, 8, 1983, pp. 218–225, and "Merger Strategies and Stockholder Value," *Strategic Management Journal*, 8, 1987, pp. 39–53; on the impact on market share, see D. C. Mueller, "Mergers and Market Share," *Review of Economics and Statistics*, 67, 1985, 259–257; on the performance of acquiring companies, see A. Michel and I. Shaked, "Evaluating Merger Performance," *California Management Review*, 27 (3), 1985, pp. 109–118. McKinsey & Co.'s study of 58 acquisitions in this period found that in 34 cases, the financial return failed to exceed the cost of capital expended and that the purchasing company lagged its competition in the stock market (cited in "Do Mergers Really Work?" *Business Week*, June 3, 1985, pp. 88–100).

How about the savings that come through divestitures and downsizing following a combination? Economist Michael Fifth concludes that any gains in profitability are generally offset by debt and losses ("The Profitability of Takeovers and Mergers," The Economic Journal, June 1979, p. 316); goodwill charges can also cripple a company's earnings (R. Metz, "Share Prices Don't Always Improve with Mergers, Study Finds," Boston Globe, May 28, 1985, p. 42). Another study found that while profits can rise up to 40% after a massive restructuring, they decline markedly over the next several years. See G. Meeks, Disappointing Marriage: A Study of Gains from Merger (London: University of Cambridge, Department of Applied Economics, Cambridge University Press, 1970).

Summing up this research, lawyer and former FTC official Kenneth Davidson ("Looking at the Strategic Impact of Mergers," *Journal of Business Strategy*, 2, 1981, p. 17) writes: "Economists generally concur that mergers have not helped a firm's profitability....Some firms become more profitable and some processes are made more efficient, but these gains are balanced by transactions that create inefficiencies and losses. According to this view, neither the acquiring firm nor society is benefitted overall."

4. W. T. Carleton, R. S. Harris, and J. F. Stewart, *An Empirical Study of Merger Motives*, Bureau of Competition, Federal Trade Commision and Office of Economic Research, Small Business Administration, December, 1980.

5. Quoted in Hunt et al., *Acquisitions—The Human Factor*.

6. Cited by J. L. Lawrence, "Some Play the Merger Game Just for Action," *Los Angeles Times*, October 6, 1985.

7. Statistics on divestitures cited in M. Lefkoe, "Why So Many Mergers Fail," *Fortune*, July 20, 1987.

8. R. B. Davis, "Compatibility in Corporate Marriages," *Harvard Business Review*, 46 (4), 1968, pp. 86–93

9. B. Burrough and J. Heylar, *Barbarians at the Gate* (New York: Harper & Row, 1990).

10. B. Uttal, "Corporate Performance: A Surprisingly Sexy Computer Marriage," *Fortune*, November, 24, 1986, pp. 46–52.

11. From "A New Strain of Merger Mania," *Business Week*, March 21, 1988, p. 122

12. D. B. Jemison, "Value Creation and Acquisition Integration: The Role of Strategic Capability Transfer," in M. Liebcap, ed., *Corporate Restructuring Through Mergers, Acquisitions, and Leveraged Buyouts* (Greenwich, Ct: JAI Press, 1987).

13. On human resource management in a merger, see P. Pritchett, *Making Mergers Work: A Guide to Managing Mergers and Acquisitions* (Homewood, IL: Dow Jones-Irwin, 1987); also C. C. Hunter and T. J. Rouse, "The Human Toll of Merger Mania: An OD Response," in C. N. Jackson, ed., *Targeting Change: Organizational Development* (Alexandria, VA: American Society of Training and Development, 1985).

14. On the dynamics of different types of combinations, see P. Shrivastava, "Postmerger Integration, *Journal of Business Strategy*, 6, 1985, pp. 65–76; for a useful typology of types, see A. F. Buono and J. L. Bowditch, *The Human Side of Mergers and Acquisitions* (San Francisco: Jossey-Bass, 1989).

15. J. R. Cooke, Speech to the *Business Week* Planning 100 Seminar, November 11, 1983, and F. D. Wallace, "Some Principles of Acquisitions," in W. Alberts, ed., *The Corporate Merger* (Chicago: University of Chicago Press, 1966).

16. *The Wall Street Journal* study reported by Herve de Carmoy, "Translinks 1992," M&A Monthly, April 1990, p. 4.

17. *Business Week*/Harris Executive Poll, in "The End of Corporate Loyalty?" *Business Week*, August 4, 1986, p. 49, and P. Hirsch, *Pack Your Own Parachute* (Reading, MA: Addison-Wesley, 1987).

18. On cynicism, see D. L. Kanter and P. H. Mirvis, *The Cynical Americans* (San Francisco: Jossey-Bass, 1989).

Chapter 1

1. J.W. Hunt, S. Lees, J.J. Grumbor, and P.D. Vivian, *Acquisitions—The Human Factor.*

2. I. Barmash, *Welcome to Our Conglomerate — You're Fired* (New York: Delacorte Press, 1971).

3. Lamalie Associates, Inc., study cited by L. Reibstein, "After the Takeover: More Managers Run, or Are Pushed Out the Door," *The Wall Street Journal,* November 15, 1985, p. 33.

4. H. Levinson, "A Psychologist Diagnoses Merger Failures." *Harvard Business Review,* 48 (2), 1970, pp. 139–147.

5. Blumenthal quoted in B. Uttal, "A Suprisingly Sexy Computer Marriage."

6. For skepticism about the Burroughs/Sperry combination; see *Fortune,* June 9, 1986; *Business Week,* June 23, 1986, p. 128; and Wertheim & Co., Inc., "The Burroughs/Sperry Combination," June 9, 1986.

7. On sources of precombination problems, see D. B. Jemison and S. B. Sitkin, "Acquisitions: The Process Can Be a Problem," *Harvard Business Review,* 64 (2), 1986, pp. 107–116.

8. On the merger syndrome, see M. L. Marks and P. H. Mirvis, "Merger Syndrome: Stress and Uncertainty," *Mergers and Acquisitions,* 20 (2), 1985, pp. 5–55, and "Merger Syndrome: Management by Crises," *Mergers and Acquisitions,* 20 (3), 1985, pp. 70-76.

9. I. L. Janis, *Victims of Groupthink* (New York: Houghton Mifflin, 1972).

10. On common cultural differences, see W. F. Forbes, *Human Problems of Mergers and Acquisitions* (New York: Standard Research Consultants Opinion Survey, 1978).

11. Research on psychological preparation by I. L. Janis, *Psychological Stress* (New York: John Wiley, 1958).

12. D. A. Nadler, *Beyond the Magic Leader* (New York: Delta Consulting Group, 1986).

13. The strategic-management perspective argues that although mergers and acquisitions have the potential to create value, management has to combine the businesses in a strategically sound way; see M. E. Porter, "From Competitive Advantage to Corporate Strategy," *Harvard Business Review*, May–June 1987, pp. 43–59, and D. M. Schweiger and J. P. Walsh, "Mergers and Acquisitions: A Strategic Human Resource View," in K. M. Rowland and G. R. Ferris, eds., *Research in Personnel and Human Resource Management*, 8, 1990.

14. On some of the political aspects of combinations, see J. A. Yunker, *Integrating Acquisitions: Making Corporate Marriages Work* (New York: Praeger, 1983), and G. A. Walter, "The Political Perspective on Managing Change in Mergers and Acquisitions," Paper presented to Academy of Management, San Francisco, 1990.

Chapter 2

1. Quotes from N. Machiavelli, *The Prince* (New York: E.P. Dutton, 1974).

2. M. Sinetar, "Mergers, Morale, and Productivity," *Personnel Journal*, 60, 1981, pp. 863–867.

3. S. Brill, "Two Tough Lawyers in the Tender-Offer Game," *New York*, June 21, 1976, p. 54.

4. On time lost due to obsessing over a merger, see B. J. Wishard, "Merger—The Human Dimension," *Magazine of Bank Administration*, June 1985, pp. 74–79.

5. On reasons behind postmerger drift, see M. L. Marks, "Merging Human Resources: A Review of Current Research," *Mergers and Acquisitions*, 17 (2), 1985, pp. 38–44.

6. Statistics compiled from W. T. Grimm and Merrill Lynch (*Mergerstat Review*), ADP/MLR Publishing Co. (M&A Data Base) and *Mergers & Acquisitions*. New terminology cited in "The New Urge to Merge," *Newsweek*, July 27, 1981, pp. 50–58.

7. Asher Edelman story: C. Ansberry, "For these MBAs, Class Became Exercise in Corporate Espionage," *The Wall Street Journal*, March 22, 1988.

8. Statistics on international M&A from Merrill Lynch, *Mergerstat Review, 1989.*

9. On merger history, see R. P. Nelson, *Merger Movements in American Industry, 1895–1956.* (Princeton, NJ: Princeton University Press, 1959), and D. Gussow, *The New Merger Game* (New York: Amacom, 1978).

10. K. M. Davidson, *Megamergers: Corporate America's Billion Dollar Takeovers* (Cambridge, MA: Ballinger, 1985), p. 127.

11. Perrin Long from Lipper Analytic Services cited in "A New Strain of Merger Mania," *Business Week*, March 21, 1988.

12. D. L. Commons, "The Tender Trap: The Sneak Attack in Corporate Warfare," *New Management*, 2 (4), Spring, 1985, pp. 7–15.

13. Heinz CEO Anthony O'Reilly and MAC Group Frederick Sturdivant cited in "A New Strain of Merger Mania," *Business Week*, March 21, 1988.

14. W. T. Grimm & Co. studies of divestitures cited in "Do Mergers Really Work?" *Business Week*, June 3, 1985, pp. 88–100.

15. P. Drucker, "Taming the Corporate Takeovers," *The Wall Street Journal*, October 30, 1984.

16. Employment Management Association study reported in *The EMA Journal*, Winter 1988, p. 26.

17. American Management Association, *Tying the Corporate Knot—An AMA Research Report on the Effects of Mergers and Acquisitions* (New York: AMA Briefings and Surveys, 1989).

18. For an analysis of the meaning behind M&A terminology, see P. M. Hirsch and J. A. Y. Andrews, "Ambushes, Shootouts, and Knights of the Roundtable: The Language of Corporate Takeovers," in R. Pondy and others, eds., *Organizational Symbolism* (Greenwich, CT: JAI Press, 1983).

19. J. Rentsch "Expectations for Mergers and Acquisitions," Paper presented at Academy of Management Meetings, Chicago, IL, 1986.

20. Discussion of Allied-Signal and Bendix from J. E. McCann and R. Gilkey, *Joining Forces* (Englewood Cliffs, NJ: Prentice-Hall, 1988).

21. P. H. Mirvis, "The Future: Change and Renewal," *Marathon World—One Hundred Years on the Frontier* (Findlay, Ohio: Marathon Oil Co., 1988).

22. General Signal story in B. Uttal, "Knighthood is still in Flower at General Signal," *Fortune*, October 6, 1980, pp. 58–64.

23. Pet, Versatec, and other companies cited in M. Magnet, "Acquiring Without Smothering," *Fortune*, November 12, 1984, pp. 22–30 and "Help! My Company Has Just Been Taken Over," *Fortune*, July 9, 1984, pp. 44–51.

24. CIGNA study by authors.

25. T. Perry, "Merging Successfully: Sending the 'Right' Signals," *Sloan Management Review*, 1986, pp. 47–57.

26. R. H. Hayes and G. H. Hoag, "Post Acquisition Retention of Top Management," *Mergers & Acquisitions*, 9, 1984, pp. 8–18.

27. Robert Half International (New York: RHI, September 9, 1989).

28. "Confessions of a Raider: An Interview with Carl Icahn," *Newsweek*, October 20, 1986, pp. 51–55.

29. Murphy interview from M. L. Marks and P. H. Mirvis, "The Merger Syndrome," *Psychology Today*, October 1986, pp. 36–42.

Chapter 3

1. Quotes from M. A. Carre, and P. M. Bouvard, "The Courtship and Honeymoon of Successful Mergers," *European Business*, 25, 1970, pp. 36–43.

2. W. I. Boucher, *The Process of Conglomerate Merger, prepared for the Bureau of Competition, Federal Trade Commision, June 1980.*

3. P. Hirsch, "Happy Endings to Mergers," *Across the Board*, February 1988, p. 21.

4. Recommended sources on merger and acquisition strategy are M. S. Salter and W. A. Weinhold, *Diversification Through Acquisition: Strategies for Creating Economic Value* (New York: Free Press, 1979); A. Rappaport, "Strategic Analysis for More Profitable Acquisitions," *Harvard Business Review*, 19, 1979, pp. 91–102; and M. Keenan and L. White, eds., *Mergers and Acquisitions* (Lexington, MA: D.C. Heath, 1982).

5. See P. C. Haspeslagh and D. B. Jemison, "Acquisitions—Myths and Reality," *Sloan Management Review*, Winter 1987, pp. 53–58, and I. M. Duhaine and C. R. Schwenk, "Conjecture on Cognitive Simplification in Acquisition and Divestment Decision Making," *Academy of Management Review*, 10, 1985, pp. 287–295.

6. D. B. Jemison and S. B. Sitkin, "Acquisitions: The Process Can Be a Problem."

7. American Management Association, *Tying the Corporate Knot.*

8. J. Kitching, "Why do Mergers Miscarry?" *Harvard Business Review*, 45 (6), 1967, pp. 84–101.

9. A. F. Buono and J. L. Bowditch, *The Human Side of Mergers and Acquisitions.*

10. R. B. Davis, "Compatibility in Corporate Marriages."

11. One study of 50 chief executive officers involved in M&A showed that most gave scant attention to human resource factors in their assessments of the fit between companies (R. J. Boland, "Merger Planning: How Much Weight Do Personnel Factors Carry?" *Personnel*, March–April 1970, pp. 8–13.)

12. D. Robino and K. P. DeMeuse, "Corporate Mergers and Acquisitions: Their Impact on HRM," *Personnel Administrator*, 30 (11), 1985, pp. 33–44.

13. J. W. Hunt, S. Lees, J. J. Grumbar, and P. D. Vivian, *Acquisitions—The Human Factor.*

14. For guides to planning for the "human element" in mergers, see R. C. Shirley, "The Human Side of Merger Planning," *Long Range Planning* 10 (1), 1977, pp. 35–39; A. J. Imberman, "The Human Element of Mergers," *Management*

Review, 1985, pp. 35–37; and A. O. Manzini and J. D. Gridley, "Human Resource Planning for Mergers and Acquisitions: Preparing for the 'People Issues' That Can Prevent Merger Synergies," *Human Resource Planning*, 9, 1986, pp. 51–57.

15. On the the value of having companies compare their cultures, see A. Blumberg and W. Weiner, "One from Two: Facilitating an Organizational Merger," *Journal of Applied Behavioral Science*, 7 (1), 1971, pp. 87–102, and A. K. Korman, A. H. Rosenbloom, and R. J. Walsh, "Increasing the People-Organization Fit in Mergers and Acquisitions," *Personnel*, 55, 1978, pp. 54–61.

16. H. Levinson, *The Great Jackass Fallacy* (Boston: Division of Research, Graduate School of Business Administration, Harvard University, 1973).

17. Peat, Marwick & Mitchell study cited by H. S. Adler, "The Honeymoon Is Key to Corporate Marriages," *Management Focus*, November–December, 1981, pp. 38–41.

18. On generalist's role, see D. B. Jemison and S. B. Sitkin, "Corporate Acquisitions: A Process Perspective," *Academy of Management Review*, 11, 1985, pp. 145–163.

19. W. R. Rockwell, "How to Acquire a Company," *Harvard Business Review*, September–October 1968, p. 123.

20. P. Drucker, "Five Rules of Successful Acquisitions," *The Wall Street Journal*, October 15, 1981.

21. From *Seattle Post-Intelligence*, August 22, 1990.

22. L. Tuller, *Getting Out* (Blue Ridge Summit, PA: Liberty Hall Press, 1990).

23. R. H. Hayes and G. H. Hoag, "Post Acquisition Retention of Top Management."

Chapter 4

1. R. A. Howell, "Plan to Integrate Your Acquisitions," *Harvard Business Review*, 48, 1970, pp. 66–76.

2. S. Brill, "Two Tough Lawyers in the Tender-Offer Game," *New York*, June 21, 1976, p. 54.

3. Yankee Financial Group, Inc., "Burroughs-Sperry Merger," June 21, 1986.

4. Kroger quote found in case study prepared by Professor Tod Jick, "Unisys" (Cambridge, MA: Graduate School of Business Adminstration, Harvard University, 1988).

5. On types of synergy, see S. Chatterjee, "Types of Synergy and Economic Value," *Strategic Management Journal*, 7, 1986, pp. 119–140.

6. On levels of integration, see R. A. Howell, "Plan to Integrate Your Acquisitions" and D. A. Nadler, *Organizational Dynamics of Acquisitions* (New York: Delta Consulting Group, 1987).

7. D. T. Bastein and A. W. Van de Ven, *Managerial and Organizational Dynamics of Mergers and Acquisitions* (Minneapolis/St. Paul: Strategic Management Research Center, University of Minnesota, 1986).

8. M. T. Shanley, *Reconciling the Rock and the Hard Place: Management Control Versus Human Resource Accommodation in Acquisition Integration* (Chicago: Graduate School of Business, University of Chicago, 1988).

9. A. K. Chakrabarti, and W. E. Sounder, "Acquisitions: Do They Really Work Out?" *Interfaces*, 14 (4), 1984, pp. 41–47.

10. H. Levinson, *The Great Jackass Fallacy*.

11. A. Maslow, *Motivation and Personality* (New York: Harper, 1954).

12. Consumer Services Group International, *Organization Integration in Citicorp* (New York: CSGI, 1986).

13. J. Handy, "How to Face Being Taken Over," *Harvard Business Review*, 47 (6), 1969, pp. 109–111.

14. E. Kubler-Ross, *On Death and Dying* (New York: Macmillan, 1969).

15. "How to Survive Your Company's Merger," *Business Week*, September 17, 1979, pp. 146–148.

16. P. Pritchett, *After the Merger: Managing the Shockwaves* (Homewood, IL: Dow Jones-Irwin, 1985).

17. Simulations also offer an interesting way to study merger reactions; see J. H. Astrachan, *Mergers, Acquisitions, and Employee Anxiety* (New York: Praeger, 1990).

18. S. Freud, *Mourning and Melancholia* (London: Hogarth Press, 1974).

Chapter 5

1. A. B. Fisher, "The Downside of Downsizing," *Fortune*, May 23, 1988, p. 42.

2. Bendix manager in J. E. McCann and R. Gilkey, *Joining Forces*.

3. American Management Association, *Tying the Corporate Knot*.

4. On studies of the impact of an announced sale, see T. W. Costello, J. F. Kubis, and C. L. Shaffer, "An Analysis of Attitudes toward a Planned Merger," *Administrative Science Quarterly*, 8, 1963, pp. 235–249; T. Jick, *Process and Impacts of a Merger* (Ithaca, NY: Cornell University Press, 1979); and A. F. Buono, J. L. Bowditch, and J. W. Lewis, "When Cultures Collide: The Anatomy of a Merger," *Human Relations*, 38, 1985, pp. 477–500.

5. R. S. Lazarus and S. Folkman, *Stress, Appraisal, and Coping* (New York: Springer, 1985).

6. W. I. Boucher, *The Process of Conglomerate Merger*, Bureau of Competition, Federal Trade Commision, June 1980.

7. D. M. Schweiger and A. S. DeNisi, "The Effects of a Realistic Merger Preview on Employees: A Longitudinal Field Experiment," Paper presented at the Academy of Management National Meeting, New Orleans, 1987.

8. For research on the value of communications, see D. T. Bastien, "Common Patterns of Behavior and Communication in Corporate Mergers and Acquisitions," *Human Resource Management*, 26 (1), 1987, pp. 17–33, and N. K. Napier, G. Simmons, and K. Stratton, "Communication During a Merger: The Experience of Two Banks," *Human Resource Planning*, 12 (2), 1989, pp. 105–122.

9. D. M. Schweiger and Y. Weber, "Strategies for Managing Human Resources during Mergers and Acquisitions: An Empirical Investigation," *Human Resource Planning*, 12 (2), 1989, pp. 69–86.

10. On Delta's strategy, see R. M. Kanter and T. K. Seggerman, "Managing Mergers, Acquisitions, and Divestitures, *Management Digest*, Special Advertising Supplement, 1987, pp. S14–S18.

11. "Stress from Merger of Breweries Suspected in Deaths," *Vancouver Sun*, March 16, 1990.

12. P. Pritchett, *After the Merger: Managing the Shockwaves* (Homewood, IL: Dow Jones-Irwin, 1985).

13. On postmerger priorities of human resource and line management, see C. C. Hunter, "What is the Role of HRD in a Merger?" *Training and Development Journal*, 40 (4), 1986, pp. 18–23; M. L. Marks and J. G. Cutcliffe, "Making Mergers Work," *Training and Development Journal*, 42 (4), 1988, pp. 30–36; and D. M. Schweiger, J. M. Ivancevich, and F. R. Power, "Executive Actions for Managing Human Resources Before and After Acquisition," *Academy of Management Executive*, 1, 1987, pp. 127–138.

Chapter 6

1. "Organization Integration in Citicorp."

2. D. B. Jemison, "Process Constraints on Strategic Capability Transfer During Acquisition Integration," Graduate School of Business, Stanford University, November, 1986.

3. On limits of experience and other problems in integration planning, see P. C. Haspeslagh and D. B. Jemison, "Acquisitions—Myths and Reality."

4. On the stages of crises in a merger, see J. Gill and I. Foulder, "Managing a Merger: The Acquisition and Its Aftermath," *Personnel Management*, 10, 1978, pp. 14–17.

5. D. B. Jemison, "Process Constraints on Strategic Capability Transfer During Acquisition Integration."

6. On styles of integrating, see G. E. Ledford, Jr., C. Siehl, M. R. McGrath, and J. R. Miller, *Managing Mergers and Acquisitions* (Los Angeles: Center for Effective Organizations, University of Southern California, 1985).

7. Discussion of Allied/Bendix from J. E. McCann and R. Gilkey, *Joining Forces*; for another model, see D. Ulrich, T.

Cody, F. LaFasto, and T. Rucci, "Human Resources at Baxter Healthcare Corporation Merger: A Strategic Partner Role," *Human Resource Planning*, 12 (2), 1989, pp. 87–103.

8. R. R. Blake and J. S. Mouton, "The Urge to Merge—Tying the Knot Successfully," *Training and Development Journal*, January 1983, pp. 41–42, and "How to Achieve Integration on the Human Side of the Merger," *Organizational Dynamics*, 13, 1985, pp. 41–56.

9. J.W. Hunt, S. Lees, J.J. Grumbar, and P.D. Vivian, *Acquisitions—The Human Factor*, Egon Zhender International (London: London Business School, 1970).

10. F. W. Searby, "Control Postmerger Change," *Harvard Business Review*, 47 (5), 1969, pp. 4–12, 154–155.

Chapter 7

1. Author's interview.

2. Quote from middle manager.

3. E. H. Schien, *Organizational Culture and Leadership* (San Francisco: Jossey-Bass, 1985).

4. A. Pettigrew, "On Studying Organizational Culture," *Administrative Science Quarterly*, 22, 1970, pp. 570–581.

5. See A. S. Sales and P. H. Mirvis, "When Cultures Collide: Issues in Acquisitions," in J. R. Kimberly and R. B. Quinn, eds., *Managing Organizational Transitions* (Homewood, IL: Richard D. Irwin, 1984).

6. Avery/Dennison study by authors.

7. A. C. Nielsen/Dun & Bradstreet study by authors.

8. See A. Q. Nomani and J. Valente, "Stronger as a Loner, USAir Loses Its Magic after 2 Acquisitions," *The Wall Street Journal*, August 18, 1990.

9. J. W. Berry, "Acculturation as Varieties of Adaptation," in A. M. Padilla, ed., *Acculturation* (Boulder, CO: Westview Press, 1980), provides the basic research underlying several studies of acculturation following a merger. See A. Nahavandi and A. R. Malekzadeh, "Acculturation in Mergers and Acquisitions," *Academy of Management Review*, 13, 1988, pp. 79–90.

10. For one typology of levels of cultural change, see American Bankers Association and Ernst & Whinney, *Implementing Mergers and Acquisitions in the Financial Services Industry* (Washington, D. C.: American Bankers Association, 1985).

11. G. E. Ledford, Jr., C. Siehl, M. R. McGrath, and J. R. Miller, "Managing Mergers and Acquisitions."

12. A. F. Buono, J. L. Bowditch, and J. W. Lewis, "The Cultural Dynamics of Transformation: The Case of a Bank Merger," in R. H. Kilmann, T. J. Covin, and Associates, eds., *Corporate Transformation* (San Francisco: Jossey-Bass, 1988).

13. From L. P. Cohen, "Failed Marriages: Raytheon Is Among the Companies Regretting High-Tech Mergers," *The Wall Street Journal*, September 10, 1984, pp. 1,18.

14. See R. J. Boland, "Merger Planning: How Much Weight Do Personnel Factors Carry?" and D. Robino and K. P. DeMeuse, "Corporate Mergers and Acquisitions: Their Impact on HRM."

15. *Making Mergers Work in the Financial Services Industry* (Cambridge, MA: Management Analysis Center, 1984); S. Davis, *Managing Corporate Culture* (Cambridge, MA: Ballinger, 1984).

Chapter 8

1. From A. F. Buono and J. Bowditch, *The Human Side of Mergers and Acquisitions.*

2. From the authors.

3. For studies comparing the impact of different levels of integration, see A. F. DeNoble, "An Analysis of the Association Between an Acquiring Firm's Corporate and Business Level Strategies and Its Resulting Postmerger Managerial Decisions," Paper presented to the Academy of Management, Boston, 1984, and M. T. Shanley, "Reconciling the Rock and the Hard Place: Management Control Versus Human Resource Accommodation in Acquisition Integration."

4. R. Bell, *Surviving the 10 Ordeals of the Takeover* (New York: Amacom, 1988).

5. "Confessions of a Raider: An Interview with Carl Icahn."

6. CIGNA study by authors. Quote from Cox in *Insurance Advocate*, May 22, 1982; from stockholder in Letters to the Editor, *Hartford Courant*, August 2, 1982.

7. On making appointments at the front end, see C. M Leighton and G. R. Tod, "After the Acquisition: Continuing Challenge," *Harvard Business Review*, 47 (2), 1969, pp. 90–102, and R. H. Hayes, "The Human Side of Acquisitions," *Management Review*, November 1972, 41–46.

8. Stern quotes from P. G. Stern and T. Schachtman, *Straight to the Top* (New York: Warner Books, 1990).

9. Belous quote and commentary from A. B. Fisher, "The Downside of Downsizing."

10. See J. Brockner, J. Davy, and C. Carter, "Layoffs, Self-esteem, and Survivor Guilt: Motivational, Affective, and Attitudinal Consequences," *Organizational Behavior and Human Decision Processes*, 36, 1985, pp. 229–244.

11. Tenneco, Allied Bank, and Esmark stories reported by R. Willis, "What's Happening to America's Middle Managers?" *Management Review*, January 1987, pp. 24–33.

12. American Management Association, "Responsible Reductions in Force"—An AMA Research Report on Downsizing and Outplacement (New York: AMA Briefings and Surveys, 1988).

13. From "What's Happening to America's Middle Managers?"

14. R. Tomasko, *Downsizing* (New York: Amacom, 1987); see also L. Hirschorn and Associates, *Cutting Back* (San Francisco: Jossey-Bass, 1983).

15. D. M. Schweiger and Y. Weber, "Strategies for Managing Human Resources During Mergers and Acquisitions: An Empirical Investigation."

16. See J. B. Copeland, "Revenge of the Fired," *Newsweek*, February 16, 1987, pp. 46–47.

17. American Management Association, "Responsible Reductions in Force"—An AMA Research Report on Downsizing and Outplacement.

18. On survivors' reactions, see D. M. Noer, "The Effects of Involuntary Layoffs on Those Who Remain in the Organizations." Presentation to the Academy of Management, Anaheim, California, August 1988.

19. H. Levinson, "Easing the Pain of Personal Loss," *Harvard Business Review*, 50, 1972, pp. 80–88.

20. S. G. Harris and R. I. Sutton, "The Functions of Parting Ceremonies in Dying Organizations," *Academy of Management Journal*, 29, 1986, pp. 5–30.

21. Schweiger and Weber, "Strategies for Managing Human Resources During Mergers and Acquisitions."

22. W. Bridges, "Managing Organizational Transitions," *Organizational Dynamics*, 15 (1), 1986, 24–33; for basic research, see J. Bowlby, *Attachment and Loss: Attachment* and *Attachment and Loss: Separation* (New York, Basic Books, 1969 and 1973).

Chapter 9

1. I. L. Mangham, "Facilitating Interorganizational Dialogue in a Merger Situation," *Interpersonal Development*, 4, 1973/74, pp. 133–147

2. From the author's studies.

3. J. J. Gabarro, *The Dynamics of Taking Charge* (Boston: Harvard Business School Press, 1987).

4. B. Tuckman, "Developmental Sequences in Small Groups," *Psychological Bulletin*, 63, 1965, pp. 284–399.

5. R. Harrison, "Role Negotiation: A Tough-minded Approach to Team Development," in W. W. Burke and H. A. Hornstein, eds., *The Social Technology of Organizational Development* (La Jolla, CA: University Associates, 1972).

6. D. Graves, "Individual Reactions to a Merger of Two Small Firms of Brokers in the Reinsurance Industry: A Total Population Survey," *Journal of Management Studies*, 18, 1981, pp. 89–113.

7. J. Gabarro, "When a New Manager Takes Charge," *Harvard Business Review*, May–June 1985, p. 119.

Chapter 10

1. W. Michael Blumenthal. Speech at the University of Michigan, December 3, 1986.

2. From the authors.

3. Additive combinations are described in D. T. Bastein and A. W. Van de Ven, "Managerial and Organizational Dynamics of Mergers and Acquisitions"; for one study on the success rate of such combinations, see H. K. Baker, T. O. Miller, and B. J. Ramsperger, "An Inside Look at Corporate Mergers and Acquisitions," *MSU Business Topics*, Winter 1981, pp. 49–57

4. Preservative combinations are described in P. Haspeslagh and D.B. Jemison, *Managing Acquisitions: Creating Value Through Corporate Renewal* (New York: Free Press, 1991).

5. For absorptive combinations, see P. Haspeslagh and D.B. Jemison, *Managing Acquisitions: Creating Value Through Corporate Renewal* (New York: Free Press, 1991).

6. On Ross Perot, see T. Mason, R. Mitchell, and W. J. Hampton, "Ross Perot's Crusade," *Business Week*, October 6, 1986, pp. 60–65.

7. Shelsy and Bourbeau are quoted in S. Vittolino, "The Making of Unisys," *Human Resource Executive*, September 1987, 1, pp. 14–16.

8. See "So Far, Married Life Seems to Agree with Unisys," *Business Week*, October 3, 1987, pp. 123–124.

9. See P. B. Carroll, "Unisys Chief Is Facing Hard Job as Company and Industry Falter," *The Wall Street Journal*, March 31, 1989, pp. A1 and A4.

10. "Can James Unruh Recharge Unisys?" *Business Week*, July 30, 1990, pp. 72–73.

11. J. Markoff, "Unisys's Creator Stepping Down," *The New York Times*, January 26, 1990, pp. D1 and D6.

Chapter 11

1. From the authors.
2. From the authors.

Chapter 12

1. From R. Suskind, "Peterborough, N.H., site of *Our Town*, Still Resists Change," *The Wall Street Journal*, July 30, 1990.

2. From *Business Week*, December 19, 1988.

3. Some background on Molson and Carling is from business case prepared by C. Beatty and P. Lawton, "Merger Management at Molson," Queen's University, Toronto, 1990. Union official quoted in *Vancouver Sun*, March 16, 1990.

4. Foreign takeover statistics by W. T. Grimm, cited in *The Wall Street Journal*, March 8, 1989.

5. Mergers in tire industry, see "Why Tiremakers Are Still Spinning Their Wheels," *Business Week*, February 26, 1990, pp. 62–63.

6. C. Beatty, "Merger Management at Molson (A)," Case prepared for the University of Western Ontario School of Business Administration, 1990.

7. P. Earl and F. G. Fisher III., *International Mergers and Acquisitions* (London: Euromoney Publications, 1986).

8. J.W. Hunt, S. Lees, J.J. Grumbar, and P.D. Vivian, *Acquisitions—The Human Factor*. Egon Zhender International (London: London Business School, 1970).

9. "Nixdorf Prepares for Siemens Merger," *The Wall Street Journal*, August 23, 1990.

10. "The Beecham-SmithKline Merger Striving to Become a Global No. 2," *The New York Times*, April 16, 1989, and "SmithKline Beecham's Synergy Sputters," *The Wall Street Journal*, March 14, 1990.

11. From R. Suskind, "Peterborough, N.H., Site of *Our Town*, Still Resists Change."

12. R. N. Bellah, R. Madsen, W. M. Sullivan, A. Swindler, and S. M. Tipton, *Habits of the Heart* (Berkeley: University of California Press, 1985).

13. R. D. Hall, *Overseas Acquisitions and Mergers* (New York: Praeger, 1986).

14. Kiel AG dealings are described by R. M. Bryan and P. C. Buck, "When Customs Collide: The Pitfalls of International Acquisitions," *Financial Management*, May–June, 1989, pp. 43–46.

Post Script

1. From P. O. Steiner, *Mergers* (Ann Arbor: University of Michigan Press, 1975).

2. From Los Angeles–area television.

3. R. Reich, *The Next American Frontier* (New York: Penguin, 1973), pp. 166, 171.

4. On changing psychological contract, see M. L. Marks, "The Disappearing Company Man," *Psychology Today*, September 1988, pp. 34–39; and T. R. Horton and P. C. Reid, *Beyond the Trust Gap* (Homewood, IL: Richard D. Irwin, 1990).

5. P. Hirsch, *Pack Your Own Parachute.*

INDEX

A

Absorption combinations, 255–56
Acculturation, levels of, 185–87
Acquired companies' mindset, 104–9
  defensive retreat, 105
  fatalism, 105–6
  psychology of being bought, 106–7
  shock, 105
Acquiree:
  grieving session, 110–11
  preparing, 107–9
    mismatched expectations, 107–8
    raids/rescues, 108–9
    simulations/training, 109
Acquirers, emotional set of, 5–7
Acquisition search, 62, 68–69
Adaptation to change, stages of, 223
Additive combinations, 254
Adoption, as combination script,
  45–46
Age:
  and postcombination status, 205
  and postmerger morale, 225–26
Aggression, 116
Allied-Signal/Bendix corporations
  merger, 44–45, 154–55
  cultural blending, 186
Allis-Chalmers, 39
Alpha Electronics:
  manager preparation, 216
  Multi Plex acquisition, 21-22,
    148–49, 211–14, 243–49
  team building:
    through the ranks, 247–49
    top down, 243–47

American business, merger activity
  in, 33–36
American Management Association:
  acquirers, study of, 70–71
  acquisition upheaval, study of, 115
  mergers and acquisitions course,
    109
  reduction in force study, 214–15
  retraining program study, 218
Andrews, John, 41
Announcement letter, 340
Anxieties, of today's executives, 52
Apple-to-apple comparisons, 161–62
Assimilation, cultural, 185–86
AT&T:
  merger training program, 103–4
  NCR takeover, 43
  team building training, 232–35
Attack and defend, as sign of
    merger syndrome, 18, 20
Attitude surveys, combination
    tracking, 289–90
Audit, of organizational fit, 72

B

"Backup" style of behavior, of
    employees, 12
Bank of Tokyo, Union Bank
    (California) purchase, 314–15
Bastien, David, 94
Beecham Group, SmithKline
    Beckman purchase, 35, 311
Been-Farquhar, Alison, 254
Bell, Dr. Robert, 204

Bellah, Robert, 312
Belous, Richard, 209
Berwind company, 62
Bid, preparing, 63–64
Bierly, Richard, 263, 328
Blacklow, Julie, 82
Blake, Robert, 155-56
Blending, cultural, 186
Blumenthal, Barbara, 49–50
Blumenthal, W. Michael, 5–10, 20,
    23, 30–31, 37–38, 48–50, 86,
    88, 89, 93, 109, 121–24, 147,
    150–52, 150–55, 155–59, 166,
    170, 190–94, 206–9, 253,
    257–65, 267, 269–70, 294–95,
    319–28
Boesky, Ivan, 8
Bourbeau, John H., 263
Bowditch, James, 70, 186
Bridgestone Tires, purchase of
    Firestone Tire & Rubber
    Company, 301
Bridges, William, 223
Bullitt, Dorothy, 82
Buono, Anthony, 70, 186
Burroughs, purchase of Sperry,
    5–10, 20, 48–50, 85–89, 121–24,
    147, 190–94
  Merger Coordination Council, 192
    creation of, 49, 124, 151–53
    final meeting of, 194–95, 253
    first meeting of, 157
    merger principles, 88–89
Bushell, Jay, 205
Business case, making, 87–88
Buyer's mindset, 99–101
Buying a company, politics of, 64–67
  fragmented picture, 65–66
  Hewlett-Packard, Apollo
    Computer acquisition, 66–70,
    77–78
  inadequate screening, 65
  mixed motives, 64–65
  psychology of, 100–101

C

Candidates, sizing up, 62–63
Capital Cities, ABC takeover, 39, 43
Carroll, John, 302, 304
Cash deals, 39
Cellar-Kefauver amendment, Clayton
    Antitrust Act, 34, 35

Center for Effective Organizations,
    University of Southern
    California, 186
Central placement centers,
    establishment of, 212
CEOs:
  departure of, 47–48
  and interest in acquisition, 84
  ten commandments of merger
    leadership, 126–29
  See also Leadership
Chemical Bank:
  and synergy definition, 93–94
  Texas Commerce acquisition,
    93–94
Cho, Yohan, 45–46
Citicorp:
  merger manuals, 102
  and mismatched expectations,
    107–8
Clarkson, William M. E., 2–7,
    4–5, 15–16, 23–24, 31, 38,
    50–51, 92, 105, 111, 197–98,
    272–75, 278, 319–27
Clash of cultures, 20, 171–98
  corporate culture, concept of,
    172–73
  cultural resistance, 195–98
  culture-building ceremonies,
    194–95
  Graphic Controls, 173–77
  in international mergers, 312–15
  managing, 179–85
    creating cultural awareness,
      179–80
    cross-cultural understanding,
      180–84
  as sign of merger syndrome, 17,
    19
  stages of, 177–79
    managing differences, 177–78
    perceiving differences, 177
    putdowns, 178–79
    stereotyping, 178
Clayton Antitrust Act, Cellar-
    Kefauver amendment, 34, 35
Clifford, Steve, 82
Closing a deal, 79–84
  caution before, 81–82
  consequences to acquisition
    parties, examining, 79–80
  follow-through, 80–82
  selling side, 82–84

Combinations:
    absorption combinations, 255–56
    additive combinations, 254
    coping with tasks of, 30
    management of, and postmerger
        morale, 224
    preservative combinations, 254–55
    tracking, 284–85
    vertical combinations, 34
Combination scripts, 29–30, 44–48,
        90
    adoption, 45–46
    conquest, 46
    marriage, 44–45
    occupation, 47–48
    writing a new script, 48–51
Combination tracking, 283–98
    attitude surveys, 289–90
    case examples, 293–98
        Graphic Controls, 295–97
        merger monitoring group,
            297–98
        Unisys, 294–95
    customer surveys, 292
    exit interviews, 293
    focus groups, 290–91
    formal tracking, benefits of,
        285–87
    interviews, 290
    observations/informal
        conversations, 291
    purpose of, 284–85
    records, 291
    tracking, purpose of, 284–85
    what to look for, 287–89
Commercial banks, and deal
        making, 38–39
Commons, Dorman L., 38
Communication, 135–37
    announcement letter, 340
    of developments, 167–69
    800 numbers, 136, 341
    follow-up meetings with work
        groups, 340
    maintaining regular flow of, 136
    of managers, 136–37
    managers' meetings, 340
    meetings with full work force,
        340
    methods of, 136, 340–41
    newsletters, 136, 182, 341
    road shows/videotapes, 182,
        340–41

Conflicts:
    conflict resolution, 165–66
    types of, 164–65
Conglomerate mergers, 34–36
Connecticut General, merger with
        INA, 46, 205
Conquest, as combination script, 46
Consolidation, psychology of,
        100–101
Constricted communication, as sign
        of merger syndrome, 17
Consultants, 65, 155–56
Corporate courtship, 63
Corporate raiders, 36
Counseling, and merger-related
        stress, 133
Coupling, 94
Cox, John, 205
Crisis management, 18, 146–44
    and decision making, 18
    as sign of merger syndrome, 17,
        18–20
Cronyism, 154, 192, 216
Cross-company synergy, 59–60
Cross-cultural understanding, 180–84
    cross-fertilization, promoting,
        182–84
    mutual respect, 184–85
    Time/Warner, clarifying cultures
        at, 81–82
CSX/SeaLand merger, 44, 187–88
Cultural awareness, creating, 179–80
Cultural blending, 186
Cultural compatibility, 76–78
    Hewlett Packard/Apollo
        Computer, 77–78
    testing, 78
Cultural perspective, 29–30
    and clash of cultures, 29
Cultural resistance, 195–98
    regrouping, 197–98
Culture building, 23
Culture-building ceremonies, 194–95
Culture clash, *See* Clash of cultures
Customer surveys, and combination
        tracking, 292
Customs, violating, 312–13

D

Davidson, Kenneth, 35
Davis, Richard, 71

Deal-making steps, 61–64
  bid, preparing, 63–64
  candidates, sizing up, 62–63
  M&A criteria, setting, 61
  negotiating/closing the deal, 64
  partner, searching for, 61–62
  strategy formulation, 61
Decision making, and crisis
  management, 18
Decisions by coercion/horse trading/
  default, as sign of merger
  syndrome, 18
Delta Airlines:
  Western Airlines acquisition,
    139–41
  and postmerger mind-sets, 228
DeMeuse, Kenneth, 72
Dilemmas in delegation, 250
Dilemmas in innovation, 250–51
DirectoriesAmerica, 130
Divestitures, 39–40, 41
  survivors of, 221–23
Dominance/submission scenarios,
  42–43
Downsizing, 21, 40–41, 210–11
  cutback criteria, clarifying, 215–16
  defining principles behind
    reductions in force, 215
  lessons on managing, 214–18
  management, preparing, 216
  managing the politics, 216
  retraining/redeployment, 218
  telling the truth, 216–18
  voluntary separation programs,
    214–15
Drucker, Peter, 40, 81
Dun & Bradstreet, A.C. Nielsen
  merger, 177–78

E

Eberstadt, R. Jr., 30
Education level, and postmerger
  morale, 225–26
Egon Zehnder International, 72, 160
800 numbers, 136, 341
Electronic mail system, and merger
  "dialogue," 136
Elledge, Terry, 318–19
Employees, and merger madness, 12
Employment options, and
  postmerger morale, 225

Engagement:
  new rules of, 36–40
  cash deals, 39
  defensive restructuring/
    leveraged buyouts, 40
  divestitures, 39–40
  faster pace, 38
  hostile dealings, 37–38
  industries in play, 39
  more players, 38–39
  old rules, 37
Erburu, Robert, 3
Esmark, Inc., Norton Simon, Inc.,
  acquisition, 211
Executives on trial, 157–58
Exit interviews, and combination
  tracking, 293

F

Federal Trade Commission, 121
Fight/flight reactions, 116
Fisher, Anne, 209
5-5-4 packages, 214
Focus groups, and combination
  tracking, 290–91
Follow-through, 80–81
Follow-up meetings with work
  groups, 340
Ford Motor Company, 39
Formal tracking, benefits of, 285–87
Formal transition structure,
  designing, 152–56
"Fragmentation" of analyses,
  buyer's side, 65, 80
Franklin, Ned, 243–46
Full integration, 94
Functional task forces, 154–55

G

Gabarro, John, 231, 250
Gender, and postmerger morale,
  225–26
Geneen, Harold, 35
General Electric:
  RCA acquisition, 39, 53, 158
  remaking of, 187
  Utah International takeover, 35
General Motors, acquisition of Ross
  Perrot's EDS, 92, 256
General Signal, and adoption
  scenario, 45–46

Girod, Curt, 155, 159
Global M&A, 315–16
Goldsmith, Sir James, 40, 301
Gould, Inc., 186–87
Graham, Elmer, 45
Graphic Controls Corporation (GC),
   2–5, 15–16, 24, 38, 50–51,
   65–66, 91–92, 104–6, 109–11,
   119, 147–48, 179, 195–98,
   224–26, 253–54, 270–80,
   320–26, 330
   CEO, replacement of, 272–75
   clash of cultures, 173–77
      business-related behaviors,
         174–75
      interpersonal behaviors, 175
      philosophy, 176
      values, 175–76
   combination tracking, 295–97
   culture change at, 270–72
      assimilation elements, 271–72
      cultural preservation, 273
      deculturation, 274–75
      elephant illustration, 275–77
   employee attitudes at, 295–97
   new CEO, 272–75
   post-acquisition employee survey,
      295–96
   reculturation at, 277–80
   retaining identity of, 3–5
   rewriting acquisition story of,
      50–51
Graves, Desmond, 241
Greenmail, 36
Ground rules, 241
Groupthink, 18
Grow Group, 72
Guidelines, providing, 157

H

Hall, R. Duane, 313
Handy, John, 105
Harrison, Roger, 240
Haspeslagh, Philippe, 64, 254, 255
Hayes, Robert, 47–48, 84, 205
Hennessy, Edward, 44–45
Hessler, Kurt, 8
Hewlett-Packard:
   Apollo Computer acquisition,
      66–70, 77–78, 96, 131, 154,
      180, 309–10

cultural compatibility, 77–78
   and organizational fit, 73–76
substantive conflicts, 164
symbolic conflicts, 164–65
"Managing the Transition"
   booklet, 264
"open kimono" phase, 162–63
and postmerger mind-sets, 228
Hirsch, Paul, 41, 58, 319
Hoag, Gerald, 47–48, 84
Home office, and organizational fit,
   335
Hostile takeovers, 37–38
Human resources:
   involvement of, 72–73
   and organizational fit, 336
   people problems, 71

I

IBM, stakes in Rolm, MCI, and
   Intel, 92
Icahn, Carl, 51–52, 204
IC Industries, Pet Inc. purchase,
   46
Identity, 131
   Burroughs/Sperry merger, 88
   Graphic Controls Corporation
      (GC), 3–5
Illusion of control, as sign of merger
   syndrome, 17
Implementation plans, 166–69
Informal exchanges, 138–39
Integration:
   approaches to, 148–51
   cultural, 185
   degree of, 94–97, 188–90
      full integration, 94–96
      partial integration, 96
   domination, 148–39
   formal transition structure,
      designing, 152–56
   managing, 145–70
      crisis management, 146–44
      orchestrating the process, 158–59
      pacing of, 188–90
      participation, 149–51
         benefits of, 150–51
      transition task force, assigning
         responsibilities to, 156–58
   See also Organizational fit
Integration stew, recipe for, 217

International mergers and
    acquisitions, 299–316
buyers/sellers, 305–7
    autonomy vs. control, 306–7
    leadership, 306
    understanding human
        resources, 305–6
    culture clash in, 312–15
    making the deal, 313
    managing, 313–14
    working with Japanese owners,
        314–15
    Molson-Carling O'Keefe merger,
        302–5
    multinational merging, 307–9
    integration planning, 308–9
    postmerger management, 310–12
    scale/scope of deals, 300–302
Interviews, and combination
    tracking, 290
Interview training, use of, 212
Investment banks, and deal making,
    38–39
Involvement, achieving, 138–39
    informal exchanges, 138–39
    merger raps, 140–41
    transition task forces, 138

J

Jemison, David, 55, 149, 255
John Deere, 39
Johnson, Bob, 130

K

Kay, Bill, 69–70
King Broadcasting, sale of, 81–83,
    109–10
Kitching, John, 70
Klockner-Humboldt-Deutz, 39
Knowledge building, 160–64
    apple-to-apple comparisons,
        161–62
    new methods, 163–64
    "open kimono" phase, 162–63
Kohlberg Kravis Roberts, RJR
    Nabisco takeover, 35, 301
Kroger, Joe, 8, 86, 88, 89, 124, 154,
    191, 195, 207, 258, 295
Kubler-Ross, Elisabeth, 106, 218
Kunkel, Ted, 302–4, 306

L

Labor lawyers, and collective
    bargaining agreements, 73
Law firms, and deal making, 38–39
Lawsuits, of laid-off employees, 216
Lawton, Peter, 12
Layoffs, See Downsizing
Leadership, 121–31, 320–26
    critical success factors, 125–29
    human purpose/direction, creating
        sense of, 121–23
    leadership team, assembling,
        123–24
    and organizational fit, 335–36
    organizations, assumptions about,
        320–23
    organization vs. cultural
        characteristics, 337
    postmerger realism, 326–28
    process orientation, 324–26
    ten commandments of, 126–29
    values about people, 323–24
    winning people over, 129–31,
        317–31
Learman, Jeannette, 49
Ledford, Gerald, 186
Leighton, Charles, 205
Level and department, and
    postmerger morale, 225
Leverage buyouts, 40
Levinson, Harry, 79, 100–101, 218
Line management, role of, 141–43
    minimizing postmerger drift,
        141–42
    retaining key talent, 142
    visiting/being visible, 142
Lorenzo, Frank, 47
Losey, Mike, 164, 263
Love and war, merger images of, 42
Lutheran Health Society (LHS),
    HealthWest merger, 97–98

M

McDonnell-Douglas merger, 171–72
Magic leader, 23
Management:
    appointments, 205–9
        at Unisys, 206–9
    legal requirements in layoffs,
        training in, 216
    and merger-related stress, 12
    and organizational fit, 335–36

organization vs. cultural characteristics, 337
preparing for downsizing, 216
and team building, 235–43
  ego massaging, 238–39
  ground rules, 240
  laying it on the line, 239
  managing diversity, 243
  modeling new behaviors, 242
  performance management, 243
  reporting relationships, 240
  re-recruitment of employees, 238
  role negotiation, 240
  team formation, 235–38
  team organization, 239–41
See also Crisis management
Management Analysis Center, levels of integration study, 188–90
Managers' meetings, 136, 340
"Managing the Transition" booklet, 264
Mandell, Alex, 187–88, 328
Map, mergers, 12–13
Mapping mergers, 12–13
Marietta, Martin, 44
Marketing, and organizational fit, 335
Marriage, as combination script, 44–45
Maslow, Abraham, 101
Massey-Fergusson, 39
Measurement and control systems, organization vs. cultural characteristics, 337
Mellon Bank, acquisition with Girard Bank, 47
Mercer, Robert, 40
Merger bulletins, 136
Merger management, 25–28
  cultural perspective, 27–28
  political perspective, 26
  psychological perspective, 26–27
  strategic-management perspective, 25
Merger mania, 31–33
Merger of equals, 46, 70–71
Merger raps, 140–41
Merger-related stress, 1–2, 4, 10–12, 116–21
  Coping with, 19–20
  exacerbating factors, 118–21
  managing, 132–35
    counseling, 133
    realistic previews, 134–35
    self-assessment, 132–33

    sensitization seminars, 134
    wellness programs, 133–34
  reasons for, 117–18
Mergers and acquisitions:
  in American business, 33
  anxiety produced by, 1–2
  building through, 319–20
  contested terrain, 29–54
  criteria, setting, 61
  human costs of, 51–54
  international, 299–316
  managing the aftermath, 3330
  managing the merger, 329
  merger waves, 33–36
  postcombination prescription, 330
  precombination prescriptions, 329
  of publicly traded companies (table), 31
  scripts, *See* Combination scripts
  strategy formulation, 61
  success in, 1–26
  what to say in, 338–39
Merger stress, 11–13
  and "backup" style of behavior, 12
Merger syndrome, 16–20, 116
  signs of, 17–18
Merger waves, 33–36
  first, 33–34
  fourth, 35–36
  second, 34
  third, 34–35
Merisel Computer Products, 125–26
Meritocracy, 88, 206, 266
Middle managers, and merger madness, 12
"Mirror image" strategy, 179
Mobil Oil, Montgomery Ward takeover, 35
Molson Breweries-Carling O'Keefe merger, 134, 139–40, 153–54, 299–300, 302–7
Moore, Brian, 154
Motivations to sell, 83–84
Mount Sinai Hospital, Samaritan Hospital merger, 71
Murphy, Samuel W. Jr., 53
Mutual respect, 184–85
Myers, Ken, 133

N

Nadler, David, 23
Navistar International, 39

Negotiating the deal, 64
"Neutral zone," as transition stage,
    223
New beginning, as transition stage,
    223
New Hampshire Ball Bearings,
    311–12
Newsletters, 136, 182, 341
Novations Group, 181

O

Observations, and combination
    tracking, 291
One-on-one talks, between
    managers and team members,
    230
"Open kimono" phase, 162–63
Operational synergies, 92
Operations, and organizational fit,
    335
O'Reilly, Anthony J. F., 39
Organizational fit, 70–76, 333–36
    assessing, 333–34
        distribution/marketing criteria,
            334
        entrepreneurial criteria, 334
        financial criteria, 334
        productivity criteria, 333
    auditing, 72–73
        human resource involvement,
            72–73
    dimensions, 70–73
        human resources, 71
        management control systems, 71
        size/shape, 70–71
    factoring in, 187–88
    factors influencing, 335–36
    "misfits," 73–76
    See also Integration
Organizational involvement, and
    postmerger morale, 224
Orientation toward change, and
    organizational fit, 336
Outplacement services, use of, 212

P

"Packaged" integration plans, 146
Partial integration, 96
Partnership, and Burroughs/Sperry
    merger, 88

"Perfect world" model of behavior,
    25
Performance, decrease in, 30
Performance management, 243
Perry, Lee, 47
Personal agency, loss of, 219
Peterson, Pete, 328
Pettigrew, Andrew, 172
Pickens, T. Boone, 53
Pickett, Mike, 125–26, 327
Platt, Lew, 180
Pluralism, cultural, 185–87
Political perspective, mergers, 28
Post-acquisition employee survey,
    Graphic Controls Corporation
    (GC), 295–96
Postcombination problems, 22–25
Postcombination status, 202–5
    self-assessment, 202–3
    winners/losers/survivors, 203–5
        age, 205
        power politics, 204–5
        strategic factors, 203–4
Postmerger change, magnitude of,
    254–58
    absorption combinations, 255–56
    additive combinations, 254
    preservative combinations, 254–55
    reverse "merger," 256
    transformations, 256–58
Postmerger drift, minimizing, 141–42
Postmerger mind-sets, 228–30
Postmerger morale, factors affecting,
    224–26
Potential synergies, 92–93
Powell, David, 155
Power-based conflicts, 164
Power parameters, 42–43
Precombination processes, 15–18
    organizing to buy or sell, 59–84
    strategic/psychological preparation,
        85–111
Preoccupation, as sign of merger
    syndrome, 17
Preservative combinations, 254–55
Prime Computer, redeployment
    strategy at, 212–13
Pritchett, Price, 108–9, 141
Protocol, violating, 312–13
Psychological enlistment, of team
    members, 235–41
Psychological preparation, 100–101
    AT&T training, 103–4
    Citicorp merger manuals, 102

Psychological safety, 101–2
Psychological perspective, mergers, 26–27
Putdowns, 178–79

Q

Quinlan, Don, 272–75, 278

R

Randall, Lyman, 273–74
RAPE (Retire Aged Personnel Early), CIGNA, 205
"Rational actor" model of behavior, 25
Realistic previews, 134–35
Records, and combination tracking, 291
Recrimination, 216
Reculturation, 253–81
  postmerger change, magnitude of, 254–58
Reductions in force, *See* Downsizing
Reduction task force, Alpha Electronics, 212
Regrouping, 197–98
Reich, Robert, 318
Relationship building, 164–66
  conflicts, types of, 164–65
  problem solving/conflict resolution, 165–66
  transition team building, 165
Relocated employees:
  assistance for, 220–21
  welcoming, 222
Remaking, as form of acculturation, 187
Rentsch, Joan, 42–43
Reporting relationships, 240
Restructuring, 40–41
Resume development services, use of, 212
Retention bonuses, 209–10
Retraining program study, 218
Reverse "merger," 256
Road shows/videotapes, 182, 340–41
Robino, David, 72
Rockwell, Willard, 81
Roderick, David, 43, 45, 179–80
Role negotiation, 240
Rules of engagement, 36–40
Rumor mills, 16

S

Sales, Dr. Amy, 173
Schein, Edgar, 172
Schneider, Chuck, 3, 196
Schweiger, David, 135, 138
Screening phase, 62, 68–69, 79
  inadequate screen, 65
SCREW (Survey of Capabilities of Retired Early Workers), CIGNA, 205
Search/selection:
  screening, 68–69
  strategic fit, establishing, 69–70
  strategy setting, 68
Self-assessment, 132–33, 202–3
Self-interest, as sign of merger syndrome, 16
Sensitization seminars, 134
Sensory input, loss of, 219
Serby, Frederick Wright, 169–70
Serpan, Rhea, 232–33, 235, 327–38
Severance packages, 214–15
Shanley, Mark, 96–97
Shelsy, John, 263
Sibling rivalry, buyer's side, 142
Siehl, Karen, 185–86
Siemens/Nixdorf combination, 301, 307
Sitkin, Sim, 65
Social support, and postmerger morale, 225
Sony Corporation, RCA Records/ Columbia Pictures acquisition, 301
Southern California Edison, San Diego Gas and Electric proposed merger, 97–98
"Sperry/Burroughs Partnership, The," (pamphlet), 9
"Spoilers," 230
Staff support, 155
Stereotyping, 178
Stern, Paul, 124, 191–93, 206, 207, 258, 266, 270, 294
Stone, Katy, 21–22, 247–49, 328
Strategic-management perspective, 25
Strategic preparation, 89–97
  integration, degree of, 94–97
  merger vs. acquisition, 90–92
    making intentions clear, 91–92
  synergy, source of, 92–94
Strategy formulation, 61

Stress reactions, as sign of merger
     syndrome, 17
Sturdivant, Frederick, 39–40
Substantive conflicts, 164
Superior vs. inferior, as sign of
     merger syndrome, 18, 19
Support, loss of, 219
Survivors, 218–19
   of divestitures, 221–23
   helping cope, 219–22
   parting ceremonies, 220
   relocated employees, assistance
        for, 220–21
Symbolic conflicts, 164–65
Systems, and organizational fit, 335

T

Takeovers, 35
   hostile, 37–38
Takeover targets, sense of fatalism
     of, 105–6
Team building:
   AT&T training for, 232–35
   challenges of, 231–32
   and internal conflict, 239–40
   tasks, 235–43
       psychological enlistment, 235–39
       role development, 239–411
       trusts/confidence, 241–43
   through the ranks, 247–49
       articulating a philosophy, 247–48
       reaching out, 248–49
   top down, 243–47
       new functional structures,
            245–46
       new leadership, 244–45
       new managers/supervisors,
            246–47
       new tone, 247
Tenneco, 39, 210–11
Tenure, and postmerger morale,
     225–26
Texaco, Imperial Oil of Canada
     merger, 181
3-3-1 programs, 214
Tibbitts, Samuel, 98–99, 327
Times Mirror, acquisition of Graphic
     controls, 2–5, 15–16, 38,
     50–51, 65–66, 91–92, 104–6,
     109, 173–76, 179, 195–98,
     224–26, 253–54, 271–80, 295–96

Time/Warner, clarifying cultures at,
     181–82
Tisch, Laurence, 39
Tod, Robert, 205
Tomasko, Robert, 215
Top leadership, *See* Leadership
Top managers, and merger
     madness, 12
Top talent, retaining, 209–10
Tracking, *See* Combination tracking
Transformations, 256–58
   Unisys, 258–70
   vs. change, 257
Transition:
   managing your own, 250–52
       dilemmas in delegation, 250
       dilemmas in innovation, 250–51
   speed of, 169–70
Transition management tasks,
     159–69
   implementation plans, 166–69
   knowledge building, 160–64
   relationship building, 164–66
Transition teams, 138, 154–55
   assigning responsibilities to,
        156–58
   building, 165
Tucci, Joe, 264
Tuller, Lawrence, 83–84
Turnarounds, 97
Turner, Ted, 39
Turnover, 30, 71

U

Unihealth America, 97–99
Unisys (United Information
     Systems), 257–70, 320–26, 330
   combination tracking, 294–95
   Convergent Technology
        acquisition, 265
   culture, creating, 190–94
   culture-building ceremonies,
        194–95
   financial results:
       1987-88, 265–67
       1989-90, 267–70
   management appointments, 206–9
       "player draft," 207–9
       selection criteria, 206–7
   new CEO, 268
   "Power of Choice" program, 263

reductions in force, principles
  behind, 215
Timeplex acquisition, 265
tracking, 294–95
transformation, 258–70
  cultural change, 258–61
  human resources successes,
    262–64
  MIS problems, 264–65
  new product directions, 261
  new top leadership, 258
  remaking marketing/sales,
    261–62
Unruh, James, 193, 206, 268–69, 270
USAir, "mirror image" strategy,
  enforcement of, 178–79
USX/Marathon merger, 43, 179–80,
  186
  marriage script, 45

Vertical combinations, 34
Videotapes, 182, 340–41
Voluntary separation programs,
  214–15

W

Weger, Yaakov, 138
Welch, Jack, 187
Wellness programs, 133–34
We vs. they, as sign of merger
  syndrome, 17, 19
White knights, 4, 35, 43
Win vs. lose, as sign of merger
  syndrome, 18
Work force, meetings with, 136, 340
Workman, David, 133

V

"Valuing diversity" program, 243
Van de Ven, Andrew, 94

X

Xerox Corporation, Versatec
  purchase, 46